‹❦ DEDICATION ❧›

This book is lovingly dedicated...

...with sorrow to the many members of my family who perished during the relentless suffering and nightmare of the Holocaust. Within these pages their memories continue to live.

...with deep gratitude to those who, with the help of God, supported me during those horrifying years. They were the bridge between the lost and the living.

...with pride, to my beloved children, Hershel, Yossi, Mati, and to my grandchildren and great-grandchildren who have indeed created "a world after this."

Contents

ACKNOWLEDGMENTS

My greatest debt of gratitude is to my children, Hershel Lieber, Yossi Lieber, Mati Jacobovits, and to my son in-law's brother, Mayer Jacobovits. With their encouragement and collaboration as one team, we worked over a three-year period to prepare this book for publication. I sincerely thank Goldy Berger for her encouragement over the years to write my story, and my brother Ben Leser for his support and help in remembering many details. I am deeply appreciative to Alida Brill who was able to find my voice and project my feelings. She gently took me through the difficult and indescribable memories of the six years told in this book.

There is no way I can ever express or repay the debt of gratitude that I owe to Hashem. His Hand was always visible to Mechel and me in the darkest of times. It is my hope and prayer that the generations who rose from the ashes of the Holocaust continue to walk in the path of our ancestors in practice and in faith.

My thanks also go to the publisher, Yaakov Peterseil, the production director, Daniella Barak, and my editor, Dvora Kiel, for their professional expertise in preparing the manuscript for publication.

PREFACE

The Second World War is known by a variety of terms. Often it is referred to only as WWII. In Russia today it continues to be called, as it was during the Soviet period, the Great Patriotic War. After the attack on Pearl Harbor by the Japanese, World War II also involved the Pacific region. However, for Jews from Europe, and indeed for Jews throughout the world, the period is known primarily as the Holocaust.

Holocaust is a word derived from Greek, which means quite literally "completely burnt" but which has its origins in the concept of a burnt offering or sacrifice to a higher being. Therefore in more recent times many Jews have preferred to call it the *Shoah*, which is the Hebrew word for calamity or catastrophe. In Yiddish the word is *churben*, destruction (pronounced: **khur**-ben, based on the Hebrew *chur-**ban***). In English, when capitalized the word Holocaust refers specifically to the mass genocide of Jews and others perpetrated by the Nazis during and preceding World War II.

Hitler and his forces eventually would term their murderous actions "The Final Solution of the Jewish Question." Their goal was to eliminate all Jews in continental Europe and to move beyond that into the British Isles. Indeed, we now know they had prepared a list of prominent English Jews they intended to have arrested first. The Allied victory came not a minute too soon.

Approximately six million Jews were killed during the period of the Shoah. But it is impossible to arrive at a reliable number for those who died shortly after liberation from the suffering they endured during the war

1

years. When one adds the non-Jews who were also killed, it is estimated that the Reich extinguished between ten and eleven million lives. The others murdered included: Christians – both Protestants and Roman Catholics – lay and clergy who worked against Hitler; non-Jews who hid Jews; male homosexuals; the Roma people, or "gypsies"; the mentally ill; the disabled; political dissidents of all kinds; intellectuals, communists, Slavic ethnics, Freemasons, political activists, Jehovah's Witnesses, and members of the underground resistance movements throughout Europe.

The elimination of Jewish life in Europe was carefully planned, efficiently orchestrated, and devastatingly successful. Its demonic architect, Adolf Hitler, had assistance from other brilliant devils and demons such as Adolf Eichmann. The period began on January 30, 1933 with Hitler's rise to power and ended on May 8, 1945. It is in reality a very short period of time in which to have murdered so many people.

Persecution of Jews was not a new concept. Many of Hitler's devices and strategies were in fact borrowed from earlier times, such as the wearing of Jewish armbands with the Star of David imprinted on them, which dates back to the time of the Inquisition and even before. In Venice, Italy, Jews were required to wear yellow hats when leaving the ghetto. The "Spanish" Inquisition, which was carried out in Catholic countries in Europe and the Americas, began in 1478 and did not end until 1834. The main motivation of the Inquisition appeared, on the surface, to be the conversion of Jews. However, the inquisitors engaged in widespread torture, imprisonment, death by hanging, and the infamous auto da fé spectacles particularly popular in Portugal. These featured the burning of Jews at the stake and were held in the public square after a "religious ceremony" of sorts. During this period, Jews were on the run throughout the Iberian Peninsula; many settled in Holland, which was a relatively tolerant country. Others fled to precolonial North America, particularly Charleston, South Carolina; Newport, Rhode Island; and New York (New Amsterdam). Many converted but returned to Judaism eventually; thousands and thousands were lost to the faith forever.

Nothing, however, compares to the magnitude of the death toll during the Shoah and its resultant devastation of Jewish life. Of the six million Jews who were lost, one and a half million were children. This is an important statistic when you calculate that with their deaths, many future generations died along with them.

Hitler's plan was ruthless and systematic. That anyone survived at all is a miracle, manifested by both spiritual and worldly intervention. On the spiritual level, some of the narrow escapes of many survivors have no rational explanation. On the mundane level, many non-Jews risked their lives to hide and protect Jews, to forge documents for Jews, to help them escape, and to engage in many other heroic activities on their behalf, and many of them indeed lost their lives. Those who reached beyond fear into extreme and saintly bravery are known by Jews as Righteous Gentiles and are so honored in Israel.

Just the numbers of those lost demands our attention and our reflection. How could it be otherwise? Poland lost three million Jews, or ninety percent of its Jewish population. Another million or more Jews from other European countries would meet their deaths in Poland in the extermination camps, gas chambers, and on the Death Marches. Approximately 600,000 Hungarian Jews perished.

Poland was first a home to Jews as early as the tenth century. Its first Jewish residents were merchants or traders from other regions. This is not uncommon in Jewish history. The first Jew to be buried in the ancient Hebrew cemetery on the Lido in Venice was a German-Jewish merchant, not an Italian Jew. Poland was the home of a vibrant Jewish life and culture. In Yiddish, Poland is called *Polin*, which translates into "here shall you lodge." Poland was, before the Shoah, the largest Jewish community in all of Europe. It was the birthplace of a form of mystical Judaism based on the Kabbalah, which is now known as Chassidism. It was the home of Rabbi Israel ben Eliezer, known as the Baal Shem Tov, the founder of Chassidism. Even those Jews who are not followers of this tradition know about him and recite his words as recorded in Jewish prayer books.

The destruction of Jewish life in Poland literally ripped the heart out of the communal body of an entire people. In his excellent and sorrowful book of photographs and text, Jeffrey Gusky refers to these bygone sites of Jewish population as the "Silent Places."

The horror of what happened resides in the numbers, of course, but these numbers can also numb us to the inner truths of the tragedy and take us further from understanding the reality of what happened. Included in the enormous numbers are millions and millions of individual tragedies. For each death, there is a name, a face, a smile, a laugh, a cry, a life's story, an identity, a song, a poem, a lost voice, a vision, a dream, a hope, a word, a whisper, a painting.

If we as human beings are to grasp the true meaning of the Holocaust – the Shoah – we must turn to the individual stories that survivors tell us. As the great Holocaust documentalist, anti-Nazi activist, Nazi hunter, and lawyer, Serge Klarsfeld, has often stated: the story of the Shoah is not only in the story of the millions; it is in the story of the one.

What you are about to read is the story of one woman, Lola Lieber, a Hungarian-Polish Jewess who survived and has chosen during her lifetime to tell the story of the ordeals of her survival and the strength of her faith and courage against all odds. It is also the memoir of a marriage that was a true working partnership as well as a marital bond of extraordinary depth. With her husband, Mechel, beside her, Lola defied authority, confronted the devil Eichmann in person, never giving up her faith in God and her belief that she and Mechel would be together at the end. The title of this book comes from a comment Mechel made at a bittersweet time in their lives. His words: "There will be a world after this," thankfully, would turn out to be true.

You are about to embark on a journey that begins in Hungary, in the town of Munkach, goes forward into Krynica and on into Krakow, Niepolomice, the Bochnia Ghetto, Kosice, Budapest, Debrecen, Bucharest, and finally, Munich. It is an adventure of harrowing events and many close calls. It is, in the end, the story of the survival of a woman who will go on in her life to help repair the lost tapestry of Jewish life and to become a mother, grandmother, great-grandmother, and a fine painter. Unlike Anne Frank and Charlotte Salomon, women of her time, Lola has lived to tell her tale to all of us. It is important for us as readers to understand that the telling itself is an act of a different kind of bravery.

In the willingness of survivors to relive their experiences by recording their stories, horrific as they are, we are ennobled. It is only by reading the stories of survival that the years of the Great Darkness are fully revealed to us. In some ways Lola's story is similar to other survivors' stories, but in many other aspects it is unique. I am grateful that she was willing to trust me with her heart's memories. May they serve as a blessing to all of us who are privileged to read this book.

I think it is appropriate to end this preface with a fragment of a poem by the Israeli poet Yehuda Amichai. In his last book of poems, *Open/Closed/Open*, which he wrote when he knew he was dying, he speaks of the Shoah, and he concludes his volume with a long poem. Its title haunted me throughout my work and friendship with Lola. It is called "Who Will Remember the Rememberers?"

This is the reason that Lola's story matters and must find its place within the literature of Holocaust memoir and history. It must be shared and read again and again, because we are the guardians of her memories. Who will remember the rememberers? We will, and we shall. Her story and all the survival stories are the rhythm of our prayers and a call to each of us to reach inside our own souls to find our most meaningful acts of grace and humanity toward others. Lola's past is a glimpse into the world of the now "silent places."

Alida Brill
New York, New York
July 6, 2008

[Author's Note: This is a work of nonfiction, based on events that transpired during the period of time known as the Holocaust or the Shoah. It is the personal story of Lola Leser Lieber's life experiences during that period. However, in order to protect the privacy of certain individuals and their surviving family members, some names have been changed.]

KRAKOW to KOSICE

MUNKACH to MUNICH

❧

PART ONE:
MUNKACH MEMORIES

❧

CHAPTER 1
Through the Garden Gate

I do not know why I became an artist. It is a matter of some curiosity to me. Perhaps I was on the way to becoming a painter before I could even hold a paintbrush or knew the names of the colors. I could retain the images I saw and recall them in my mind later. As a child I sometimes wondered if these scenes were being presented for my eyes alone. Whether I was destined to become a painter or became a painter because of what I saw, will remain a mystery. It would be easier for me to tell my stories in paintings, but there are things that cannot be revealed completely or accurately in pictures alone. There are also events that cannot be described adequately or powerfully enough in words. I have tried to tell my story both in words and in images.

I was born in Europe in 1923 into a Jewish family. My life is intertwined intimately with the horrible events of the mid-twentieth century, which involved millions and millions of others as well. However, let's not jump ahead to that part of the journey. My story begins in a place filled with visual delights, a place enveloped in peace. Even now, more than seven decades later, when I close my eyes I see a panorama of my family and friends spread before me. As these images settle down in my brain, I can remember it as a time of unparalleled happiness, beauty, and security – my earliest childhood memories. Many people insist they had a magical childhood; by now it seems almost as common as claiming you had a horrible one. A large portion of my girlhood was spent with my maternal grandparents, and it was in truth not only quite magical – it really was an enchanted fantasy.

Much of my early life took place within an enclosed home and a garden – behind an ornamental gate in a now-almost-forgotten corner of Europe. It was a time filled with fanciful activities, music, the wonder of learning, and family love. The gate had a decorative iron grill on top, which distinguished it from the other more ordinary homes on the street. Much of the rest of the street was gray and unremarkable, but the gateway to my early life stood out from everything surrounding it. We were on the main street of the town, just a short distance from the train station. Our residence seemed to request or perhaps demand to be recognized. Somehow I understood this from a very early age.

A few people felt sorry for me because I was living with my grandparents and extended family so much of the time instead of with my parents. Wise children and all adults will know instantly what that really means. I had certain privileges and was indulged in ways that would not have been possible if I had been living with my parents and my four siblings. If my girl cousins received presents or new dresses, so did I, because, after all, this "poor girl" was not with her "real" family. When special outings or trips were planned, I would be given new dresses or the treat of an outfit or two – or perhaps, three! I did not do anything to dispel the myth that I was "a little orphan," but I knew better.

Inside the gate, our residence nestled around a large garden. On the property were several other structures. Life behind the gate was exciting and carefully orchestrated. It was as if we were all members in a symphony and knew our musical scores by heart. Indeed music was everywhere. We had music lessons and could hear the music from Gypsy caravans as they moved through town. At times the joy of hearing their music was overshadowed by stories of their presumed misdeeds. There was the oft-repeated rumor that they kidnapped babies and children. I was only slightly afraid of them because I liked their brightly painted caravan carts and wagons and the music they played. I adored the violin music the male Gypsies played, which made me want to dance with happiness. Nothing was upsetting in those days. I did not have a crystal ball that foretold that in a short time Gypsies too would vanish from most of Europe.

But as I said, let's not get ahead of the story. I was born on March 15, 1923. I was named Esther Leah Leser, but in those days everyone called me "Leiku" Leser. The Esther part is important because I was born on the Jewish fast day that precedes the holiday of Purim, called the Fast of Esther. I wasn't the only youngster on the map of the region in that moment of history. The country then called Czechoslovakia was also only a toddler. It was created from the remains of what had been the Austro–Hungarian Empire before the First World War. Even though I was born a Czech citizen, my family retained its attachment to our Hungarian roots. Because my grandparents were Hungarians of Polish origin and had a long history in Munkach, I still think of the region as Hungarian. I have attachment to my heritage for nostalgic reasons and for very pragmatic ones. The Hungarian language was so much a part of the rhythm of our lives that I called my mother always and only by the endearment, "mammiko." I would also call family members by their Yiddish/Hungarian appellation, such as bubbe/babbiko (grandmother), zeide (grandfather), tattiko (daddy), and the like.

The garden had many secrets and there was much bustle and activity every single day. There was a statue of a big dog at the entrance to the house, as if to stand watch and protect us all. Grandfather also had his own large, black pet dog with a soft and shiny coat. He was a friendly and dear dog, and I was terribly fond of him. The dog lived in harmony with a circus of cats that roamed the house and the garden freely. The cats didn't get in the way of Grandfather's dog, nor did he bother them. Perhaps the animals understood that they were, in a manner of speaking, all relatives too. There was much to observe and many things to participate in at my grandparents' home. Harmony in all things – between the animals, the family, and the outside non-Jewish world – was a hallmark of the 1920s and early 1930s.

Munkach itself could be described as a friendly circus of friends and family. I can't imagine how or why, but at some point my grandmother had compassion for a talented but poor acrobat who had no place no live. Grandmother, with her typical generosity, offered the acrobat one of the small cottages on the premises as a home. Everyone was happy together, and there were also visits from my cousins, the four daughters of my mother's sister. Like Mammiko, my lovely aunt was elegant and refined. We ate lunch on the big porch at the side of the house, looking out at the garden. It was there under the watchful and demanding eye of our German governess where we also did our lessons. Occasionally our acrobat entertained us doing her tricks and exercises. She had to do these in order to stay in shape for her public performances.

Mammiko and Tattiko and my siblings came from Krakow to visit often. This meant my beloved older sister Goldie might be allowed to stay with us after the others returned. I loved Goldie deeply and felt sad and lonely when she returned to Krakow with the rest of the family. There were differences between my Krakow and Hungarian families, but they did not seem significant to me at that point in my life. Religious practices were observed differently in Krakow and the foods were quite different, and some of the customs were not all that similar. However as a young girl I just thought we were all one extended and connected European Jewish family that lived both in Krakow and in Munkach.

My great-grandmother Feigi, my grandmother's mother, also lived with us in Munkach. She was very old and slept almost the whole day, and often wandered the house at night unable to sleep or rest. She did not speak much. I suppose she had a form of senility or what we now call Alzheimer's. Yet she always seemed to sense when I returned from school and would wake to greet me, enthusiastic to hear what I had done during the day. I tried to make the stories of school particularly interesting for her, as I knew how limited her life had become. She was alert and happy when I shared the tales of my school activities and my friends and my lessons. Each day she rewarded my report and stories with a few pieces of delicious candy. She waited for my return and I eagerly rushed to her the moment I came home.

Munkach was lively. Although it was not a large cosmopolitan center, life there wasn't boring. Munkach had a cozy feeling as well as an international flavor. It was accessible and easy for a child to experience and comprehend. In Munkach, Jewish people got along well with gentiles. Many of us went to school along with Christian children. I am not certain everyone was aware that I was Jewish; these distinctions were not yet important to me. When I was a girl, more than half the town's population was Jewish. No wonder I felt it was cozy and welcoming! At that time the Jews of Munkach identified their "nationality" as Jewish, not Czech, Hungarian or other European origin. This was a common practice among Jews throughout Eastern Europe.

We had a private, multinational community living behind our garden gate. Grandmother had a large domestic staff that was needed because the place had so many rooms and spacious common areas. There were at least fourteen rooms in the main house, which was built in an "L" shape. There was a gazebo in the garden with leaded glass windows where we played, had our language and other lessons, and most memorably, our music lessons. Each year our gazebo would have the honor of becoming the family's *sukkah* for the Jewish Festival of Tabernacles or Booths. We ate all our meals in it during this wonderfully festive holiday. We had a full-time maid who came from the countryside and was known in those years as a "peasant." My grandparents employed a number of other part-time maids as well, and a laundress and gardener. A young Jewish girl cooked our meals and served them to us either on the porch or in the formal dining room.

We also had a stern and demanding German governess, who lived with us and was an integral part of our lives. Because my parents wanted him to speak German, my youngest brother, Naftoli (Tuli), spent more time living with us than with our parents. My middle brother, Ben (Beinish), who was born in Krakow and spent his (prewar) childhood there, did not spend much time with us in Munkach. In wealthy or middle-class European Jewish families during this era it was expected that children learn to speak "proper" German, that is, *Hochdeutsch* or High German. This rigorous course of language instruction included mastering the difficult penmanship of complex Gothic-style letters. We became conversant in Heine, Schiller, Goethe and other German writers. Our German education extended to our music lessons and we learned to play the works of important German composers. German was considered the language of culture in most circles because it was the language of the best educated and most accomplished members of the European community.

Another regular member of our extended family of teachers and staff was a diminutive and kind music teacher from the nearby town of Ungvar. He lived with us during the week and instructed my cousins Mimi and Koti, my sister Goldie, and me. He taught other students in their homes as well. Grandmother found these students for him because she knew he needed the extra income. Of course there was also a *belfer* who came to instruct us in Hebrew and Yiddish. A belfer is a young man who teaches children.

I lived in a house of women and girls. Inside the patriarchy of traditional Judaism, we were a reigning domestic matriarchy. The two men in the family – my Uncle Baruch (Bela), Mammiko's youngest sibling, and of course Grandfather – were well looked after by all the women. Although the men were in the minority, they were the actual and the religious heads of our family. Besides, we loved them and it was easy to please them.

Grandfather was well known and respected in Munkach. As a member of the distinguished Segel family he was honored in many ways. Fortunately he was able to provide the ample resources that were required to keep the family's lavish establishment up and running at all times. Grandfather had a commission from the municipal government that enabled him to collect tariffs from people wishing to sell produce and livestock. He and his partner hired a team of men who dressed in official uniforms, not unlike the police. These men controlled all the checkpoints at the borders of town. Any farmer or peasant wishing to bring food or livestock into the market in Munkach had to pay Grandfather's staff officers a tax. Grandfather then shared part of his tax collections with the town's governing council. Because he was honest and fair, he was well respected in both Jewish and non-Jewish circles.

Grandfather had a side business as well. He made a special type of slivovitz, or plum brandy, which is very strong but delicious when made properly. Grandfather Segel must have had a secret recipe for none of the others could compete with his "brand," which was much in demand among the locals. I always look forward to opening a bottle of slivovitz with the faint hope that it will taste just like Grandfather's. It never happens, of course; even the best ones are not the same – they do not have the same texture or smell. Such are the cherished memories of a beloved grandfather – and even his homemade liqueur – with whom no one and nothing can compare.

Grandfather was a well-respected leader in the Jewish community. He belonged to the largest congregation and was elected by the membership to be the *gabbai* each year. The board of directors of the congregation was known as the *kehillah* and a gabbai was the equivalent of the president of the body. We celebrated this "election" annually with a fancy meal and party at home, to which we invited many friends and relatives.

My grandmother was a bit more remote than my grandfather, who was extremely warm and affectionate. My grandmother was known as Mimeh Roshe throughout town, which would be Auntie Rosie in English. She was tall, elegant, reserved and extremely generous. She wore a wig *and* a hat. She dressed in long, finely tailored dresses made from beautiful fabrics. She was disciplined about *davening* (praying) regularly, for her devotion to Judaism was not limited to running a Jewish household only. She was an observant woman with a deep and private reservoir of faith in God.

Her best friend, a Mrs. Spiegel, had a husband who was also very wealthy. Together they were known in town as the "lady philanthropists." In other words, they organized and managed the *tzedakah* (charity) activities of the town's Jewish women. My grandmother taught me from an early age that as Jews we must help to "mend or repair the world" (a Jewish philosophical concept called *tikkun olam*). She taught us that part of any Jewish woman's life must be in service to those in need or in trouble. The two Mrs. S. were a formidable pair. "Spiegel and Segel" they might have been called because they were a non-profit business team in every way. They kept a horse and carriage in Mr. Spiegel's lumberyard just for their charity work. A coachman drove them around as they dispensed food, clothing, and money to those in need at least twice a week. Grandmother invited people to our home for meals who did not have such a comfortable lifestyle or who were hungry and in need of a hearty meal. I watched her as she sometimes quietly gave them a few coins as well as food.

Although I was separated from my parents and siblings much of the time, mostly at my grandparents' request, my childhood was not at all deprived. In fact, I lived a privileged life. My grandparents really wished we would all live together, but in Munkach not in Krakow. Poor Mammiko tried to keep both her husband and her parents happy. This is why Mammiko seemed always to be coming and going between Krakow and Munkach. No matter how hard she tried to make her parents happy, they never understood why Mammiko wanted to live in Poland. Perhaps it was some sort of geographic or regional "snobbery," but I doubt it. It was that only Mammiko, of the seven Segel children, lived in another country. My grandparents could not understand the separation of family members.

Periodically, both my parents would come to Munkach to see if Father could get a business going there. He was a gifted candy maker, but not of common candy. My father made a unique chocolate wafer that had been made popular in Vienna originally. He manufactured Piszinger brand confections. Father's chocolates were very popular in Krakow also and therefore he was a successful businessman. After much pressure from his in-laws, he decided to turn his business in Krakow over to his partner, a Mr. Rapaport. For some reason, all his efforts and attempts to make his chocolates popular in Munkach just didn't work out, and this caused great stress for my parents. Inevitably, after a time of trial and experimentation, they returned to Krakow and he went back to his company.

One part of the problem was that as a Polish citizen my father was unable to obtain proper business licenses in Hungary. Not being fluent in Hungarian was also a severe handicap for him. He tried just about everything, even buying old wine-press parts and trying to resell them. My father was a man of stature in Krakow, a successful entrepreneur. In Munkach my father was a sad man and understandably depressed without a profession or status in the community. Finally, my grandparents must have understood that my parents could not tolerate this, and they relented. That is probably why I stayed on with them as a sort of "consolation" prize.

Mammiko enjoyed and appreciated all fine things. She traveled to Budapest and to Vienna to have her couture dresses and outfits designed and made. I think often of Mammiko's beautiful wigs, which she was very proud to own. Mammiko had numerous wigs, and changed them daily. She left them on the doorstep each morning, and the shop would pick them up, refresh them, recomb them and return them to her. Mammiko's wigs gave her a more modern appearance, but they also added to her beauty. Everything about Mammiko's appearance and dress was carefully considered. I am sure my taste in clothes and wigs began with my admiration of beloved Mammiko's flair for fashion and understanding of style.

Not everything about living in Munkach was perfect, mainly because I didn't spend as much time with my siblings as I would have liked. My oldest brother, Moishe, was chosen as one of ten students to study with the Belzer Rebbe, whose *beis medrash* (study hall) was about 100 miles north of Munkach. Moishe did spend most of his vacations in Munkach, though, so we had that time together and therefore knew each other very well.

Goldie, my older sister, seemed almost ethereal to me because she was so kind and gentle, and so willing to help everyone. She thought of the welfare of others before she considered herself. When I was about twelve Goldie moved from the family home in Krakow to Munkach. Like Mammiko, Goldie also had a talent for clothing design and for cosmetics. She was very good with wigs too, and learned how to make them when she was about sixteen. It wasn't easy to construct wigs in those days. Everything was done by hand, with human hair of course, and required tremendous concentration and a steady hand. Goldie's essential nature of wanting to accommodate others, combined with her talents, probably worked against her best interests. It is a reality I would comprehend only much later in my life. Goldie was highly intelligent and exceedingly talented musically, but her life was determined by her skill with her hands. Uncle Bela was so impressed by how quickly Goldie learned to do machine embroidery on a then-still-new invention, the deluxe sewing machine, that he hired her.

Goldie was beautiful and she was able to turn out, seemingly without effort, beautifully embellished fabrics. Being such a good businessman, Uncle Bela had Goldie sit in the window of his shop to attract business. There she would sit for hours, on display, at her sewing machine, with the public observing her. There is no question that it was good for his business. In the final analysis, however, it was not good for Goldie because it meant she never got a proper education, which she deserved. At that time, however, I was jealous of Goldie. She had a skill and a craft, and I wanted to be special and accomplished at something too.

I was good at art and loved to draw and sketch. Goldie made me realize I could be an artist – she told me I already *was* an artist. So I began to take art classes. My art classes met twice a week, but it wasn't enough for me. Everywhere I went I sketched what I saw. In fact my mathematics teacher said she would not have given me a passing grade if my drawings had not been so delightful. My art teachers started to keep my assignments, and I was too obedient to confront them about it. I did not know they were entering my drawings and paintings into competitions where prizes were awarded to the best entries. I knew nothing about my teachers' secret efforts on my behalf.

I was particularly proud of one of my paintings, which was another one my teacher did not return to me. One afternoon, when I was twelve or thirteen years old, I came home and found one of our favorite cats in proud residence in the parlor. She was on Grandmother's expensive sofa, happily positioned on a precious needlepoint pillow. The pillow design was a still life of flowers intricately done with multicolored threads. There sat our favorite cat, with her four tiny, newborn kittens, their eyes still partially closed; she was nursing them. I started toward her to touch the sweet little creatures, and to let our cat know it was fine with me if she was in the parlor on the sofa with her babies. This beloved pet gave me a look more appropriate to a mother lion than to an average mother housecat in Munkach. I got the message and retreated quickly, but I did not leave the room. I took my art supplies from my schoolbag, sat down across the room from them, and quickly sketched the scene, including the background of our parlor, sofa and needlepoint pillow. Immediately after that I took the sketch to my bedroom and made a full size watercolor of the scene.

When I took the painting to school, my art teacher was stunned by the quality of what I had done. Somehow I had managed to capture the look of pride, protection and defiance in the mother cat's eyes. There was an exhibition in town sponsored by the Russian gymnasium (high school), and my teacher entered my painting. It won! It was a serious prize, not just a fancy ribbon or medal that would soon be forgotten. I was offered a fully paid scholarship to study art in Amsterdam. The painting traveled all around the region from exhibition to exhibition. I never saw the painting again, nor do I have any idea what happened to it eventually.

I was not told at the time that I won the scholarship. It was customary to announce such things to the parents or family of a student first, not to the child. My family simply did not tell me. It was many years later before I learned about the missed scholarship opportunity. A serious art education in a sophisticated European city could be thought of as an incredible opportunity. I was denied this "chance of a lifetime" because of my family's strict adherence to tradition and their idea of what was deemed appropriate for an Orthodox Jewish girl. By the time I finally knew about this, I recognized that my family's restriction might well have saved my life.

In these years after the Holocaust, I have thought about Amsterdam, the cat painting, and another young Jewish girl and her diary. I speak, of course, of Anne Frank and her now-world-famous book, *The Diary of a Young Girl*. After its original publication, the story of her life was turned into a play and then a movie. As everyone now knows, Anne Frank was in hiding with her family in an attic in Amsterdam. She perished. We have her brave words and the record of that time written as perhaps no other young woman could have done. As anyone who reads the *Diary* even all these years later can see, it is easy to believe that Anne Frank would have become an accomplished writer and journalist if she had lived. What remains for us is that she dreamed about a future life while she wrote in her private little book. Perhaps all Jewish European women of a certain age who somehow survived the Shoah remember from time to time that the spirit of Anne Frank lives inside each of us.

Little Leiku of Munkach was starting to mature. I was ready to attend high school, excitedly looking forward to playing tennis, as I was a good athlete, and so signed up for the team. I liked to skate and to ski too. It was autumn and the Days of Awe were coming. Mammiko arrived from Krakow for Rosh Hashanah. As a matter of protocol and in conformance with normal regulations, without any concern in her mind, she stopped in at the Polish consulate in Ungvar to extend her passport, which was a Polish one about to expire. She came out of the consulate in shock. The officials could not renew her passport, nor were they able to give her even a modest time extension. It was 1938. Poland and Czechoslovakia were not getting on with each other. There was at best a chill in diplomatic relations between the countries. Needless to say, this was due to the Nazi ascendancy.

We proceeded to Grandmother's house, with Mammiko talking normally and attempting bravely to keep from weeping in front of her parents and us, so at first I did not understand what it all meant. Goldie, who was already sixteen, had her own passport and was therefore "safe." Because I was listed on Mammiko's passport as were my younger siblings (who were in Krakow at the time), neither Mammiko nor we had any right to remain in Munkach, nor could we return thereafter without proper documents. When I returned from school later that day, I walked into an emotional storm that soon turned into a full-blown family drama. Within a few minutes I grasped the gravity of the situation we were in if we tried to stay in Munkach. Within twenty-four hours we would become illegal aliens.

There was no time for consolation or conversation.

"Leiku, pack up now, you and Mammiko must leave tonight."

My grandfather, usually so softspoken and gentle, was firm and barely able to contain his feelings of fear and panic. These were not emotions I had ever seen on his face or heard in his voice. This was the first of many future occasions when I observed adults with a look of dread on their faces, followed by momentary paralysis, followed by a strategy session with rapidly made decisions. It was Thursday; we would leave that very night, in order to cross over the Czech border before Shabbos began.

We had only a very few hours to get things ready. I wanted to stay. I had many friends at school. I loved the notion of attending high school in Munkach, and I wanted to continue my life with my sister and my grandparents and the daily activities and rituals of life behind the garden gate. I was also quite vain, but for a girl of fifteen that was understandable. I was worried about not having enough clothing to take with me! I ran almost the entire way to my wealthy uncle's store and got some silk fabrics from him. Mammiko and I then stuffed the silk fabrics under our coats to get past the customs officers. It would be the first time we were layering ourselves with clothing and possessions, but it would not be the last. Then it just seemed like a stupid inconvenience, and it made me angry and sad.

Before we started out, I walked through the garden slowly and alone. I must have sensed then that I might not come back to its enchantments. I did not admit it, but I was bidding a silent farewell to all of it. I was recording it visually so it would remain in my memory – just in case. I took it all in as artists do when they can't afford to forget images that matter deeply. It was the very end of the summer, and many flowers were showing their last triumph to the world. I circled the garden many times, noting the dahlias, the orchard with its apple, pear, and cherry trees. Mostly, I stood in front of the sunflowers, my favorite residents of the garden. I think I must have said a prayer in front of the sunflowers, a childish prayer no doubt, but a real prayer nonetheless. I asked *Hashem* (God) to keep sunshine in our lives, to bring our family back together, clustered together again the way the seeds of sunflowers are in their centers. Then, with a premonition of the longing to come, I had to do as Grandfather told me.

We climbed onto the coach to make the short trip to the train station. Mammiko was silent, her complexion suddenly and alarmingly turning pale. I thought she might faint. I tried to reach for her hand, but thought it was better for her to have privacy in her sorrow at our departure. As we approached the station, I heard a familiar voice call out to me, "Leiku, Leiku, don't forget us. We'll write to you. Write to us." It was one of the girls from my class, with whom I did my homework and who often came to the house. She was running after the coach and I saw tears in her eyes.

"I will write you. Of course, I will write to you." I yelled back, trying not to cry.

By the time the coach reached the station, it was no use. I couldn't stop crying. It was Goldie who consoled me.

"I have many friends in Krakow. You have to remember I know many girls there. They will be your friends now too."

I had never liked Krakow. Standing at the train station in Munkach with virtually nothing of my present life remaining, I wasn't going to decide then that I was going to like it. For the first time in my life an intense and strange anger come over me. It was anger against forces I did not understand. I had been in squabbles and disagreements with my siblings and classmates, but I had never had the feeling I did that night on the platform. I was enraged at something I could not see and could not comprehend.

Whatever it was, or whoever they were, those "others" had the power to destroy my family's continuity and to determine whether we could stay in or leave our own homes. It would be only the first of many deportations, departures, escapes, and passages filled with uncertainty. It would not be the most dangerous one, not by a long shot. But it would be the most important in many ways, because it was the first glimmer of recognition that we were no longer in charge of our own destiny. It was only a brief glimpse of the future, but it remains etched permanently in my mind, and written in acid across my heart.

CHAPTER 2
At the Three Roses

As soon as we took our seats on the train I closed my eyes. It was the only way I could blind myself to what was happening. We were headed to Krynica, a popular spa resort town in the mountains. It was a place favored by Chassidic Orthodox Jews for health and relaxation. It was often referred to in the travel literature of the nineteenth and early twentieth centuries as a place to "take the cure." In the vernacular of the time, this phrase meant the place contained fresh air and pure waters. Arriving in large groups with our Rebbes, Jews also traveled to Krynica to celebrate the High Holidays and Pesach. We were more than welcome in town. Families with ample resources chose to stay in lovely hotels or in smaller boarding houses. Both the large and smaller places met our religious needs – all establishments were equipped with kosher kitchens. In the more expensive places, delicious meals were served with style and in the graceful European manner typical of the period.

Jews were not the only people who came to Krynica. It was a vacation destination for many others living in Poland and the surrounding regions. Krynica was renowned for its healing mineral waters and uniquely picturesque landscape. Four beautiful streams fed into the valley. These were the source of the waters believed to possess curative medicinal properties. It was a prevalent and strongly held conviction that by partaking of these waters one could alleviate the symptoms of a variety of diseases. Nevertheless, there was one virulent ailment the waters of Krynica could not begin to heal. That was the malignant disease of anti-Semitism infecting the hearts and the souls of non-Jewish Europeans by 1938.

I knew we were going to a resort spa for reasons other than our health and the High Holidays. Although I did not understand fully all that was changing for Jews, I was not a complete fool. We were going to Krakow, with a stop in Krynica, because we were no longer free to make the personal travel decisions we had previously enjoyed. I was beginning to digest the fact that the life I had taken for granted was disappearing. With this transition would come the loss of many of our accustomed activities and recreational pleasures. Somewhere deep inside I sensed an important gate was closing permanently. It was the gate to my enchanted garden in Munkach and the warmth and presence of my extended family. The security I had as a protected child was ebbing away from me. A life of considerable privilege and the absence of fear were slipping forever out of my grasp.

We were among those who had sufficient money to stay in an upscale kosher hotel called The Three Roses, the managers of which were good friends of my parents. In 1938 darkness was already visible to those paying close attention to the decrees and pronouncements of Hitler. However, I was only fifteen years old and my thoughts and concerns were centered primarily on my own future. I was concerned about the destiny of my combined and extended family and the separation from my many friends. My heart must have been far more mature than my thinking, though, because on the train I suffered the broken heart of a much older person. Saying good-bye to my family and friends in Munkach had taken away a part of my soul. The clicking of the wheels on the tracks sounded like the repeated opening and closing of the ornamental gate at Grandfather and Grandmother's. I was not living in the present tense on this trip. I was living in the extended pain of the last minutes of the Munkach farewell.

The larger reality for all Jews had not yet settled into my girl's brain. It was a series of events even adults found hard to envision. In Poland alone before the Holocaust more than three and a half million Jews thrived, had families, and practiced Judaism openly. We were not aliens or foreigners living in Europe as third-class citizens, we were a robust people. Because of our traditions and our customs, many of us did live somewhat apart from our fellow European citizens, but we had chosen our way of life, and the rituals and manner in which we observed the practice of our faith, and the laws of the Torah. Who could have imagined what was coming so soon? It would have been to suspend all belief. It would have been to embrace an indescribable horror that would become a reality experienced and endured by millions.

The train ascended into the Carpathian Mountains and crossed into Poland. Through the compartment window I glimpsed a scenic view, but I was not in a mood to appreciate beauty in nature. The only image I could see was my sister's face. Goldie had been so brave when she said good-bye to me. I should have reassured her more than I did. I had not offered her as much comfort as she had given me as we made our farewells. Goldie was always concerned about others, especially about me. Her name was well suited to her personality. There was something so pure and perfectly tender in all she did. I had played the role of the "orphan" in Munkach almost as a joke, but I was a much-loved child and extremely cherished by my sister.

My world was changing quickly. Who was I now? Who would I become in the next days, weeks, and months as I progressed on this involuntary and unknown journey? The monotonous clicking of the train's wheels helped me achieve a measure of mental clarity. My life was disrupted. I was about to change my identity (for the first time). Eventually, I would get off the train to join my family, not as little Leiku from Munkach, but as a girl named Lola who lived in Krakow. I would become a Polish Jewess.

I could not know that an entirely different universe was waiting for me. It would be an underworld where I would learn to maneuver with false names, fake passports, and forged documents. This disordered way of life would become the daily rhythm of European Jewry. Moreover, this bizarre future would be only for the most fortunate among us. As the train climbed further into the mountains, I could not know that Jews would need to fight with all their wits and ingenuity. That we would give up our resources and possessions for the chance to survive. Fortunately, in His Divine wisdom, Hashem does not reveal everything to us before we are strong enough to know.

Instead, on the train I focused on how much I did not want to live in Krakow all the time. My Polish was very limited. Inside the family and our community, I spoke fluent Yiddish. During my visits it was all I had needed. I would need more than Yiddish to be a Polish resident. I knew my excellent German wouldn't be terribly useful in Krakow. Our parents had decided that Goldie should remain in Munkach. I was quite distraught at the notion of life in Poland without my sister and girlfriends. My brother Moishe had stayed in Belz because he had his own passport. These were my primary thoughts. I was just a young girl about to be deprived of all her pleasurable activities – gymnastics, ice skating, sleigh rides, tennis, life in the garden, the sight of the colorful Gypsies, music lessons, the acrobat living in the cottage, my friends, and my Munkach family. It was indeed the closing of the gate on a life of delight and enchantment. Tattiko would be joining us at The Three Roses in Krynica, but I was not anticipating the High Holidays with anything except sadness. There would be nothing sweet about this New Year. I wallowed in despair and feelings of loss. I was a big crybaby during the Holidays. My parents permitted me to indulge my sorrow. As I look back on it, it is hard to appreciate fully their amazing love and tolerance for my adolescent behavior. They were facing horrible fears they kept hidden from me. There were so many practical strategies weighing on them, which undoubtedly caused them sleepless nights. Yet they did not show me their apprehension and continued to be my attentive parents, once again assuring me that all the comforts and advantages were within reach.

We recited our ancient prayers requesting Hashem to inscribe us in the Book of Life, not knowing the profound immediacy of that prayer in Europe in 1938. When the High Holidays concluded, Mammiko and Father returned home to Krakow. I would be staying behind, alone, at their request. Krakow is located only about eighty miles to the northwest of Krynica, but it felt as far away as the Earth from the Moon. With the turning of the Jewish year, my girlhood was left behind, never to be recaptured. It would be many years before I talked about this time or recalled it without a wrenching grief.

As virtually everyone left immediately after the Holidays, Krynica became very quiet. Few of the permanent residents were young, and a sense of isolation enveloped me. The year 1938 saw the end of the Krynica where joyous Chassidic family groups came together to observe and to celebrate holidays. After my parents left, I had to get serious about learning to speak, write, and read Polish, which was the reason I stayed behind. Father had hired a tutor for me before they left. Although he was a kind teacher, I did not care for him very much. My true energies were not dedicated to the assignments he gave me. I wanted to paint and draw and sketch, not study Polish. Adding to my dilemma was the fact that my tutor's Polish was not refined or easy to listen to as he instructed me. He spoke with a rough country accent. With his help, my Polish grammar and vocabulary did improve tremendously, but I spoke Polish as he did. I still sounded like a Hungarian–Czechoslovakian speaking a strange dialect of Polish. This was fine with me, because I was proud of my identity. My accent was a form of verbal identity – the memory of my past was obvious to me in every Polish sentence I uttered.

Although I missed my parents and my family, I was happy *not* to be in Krakow for a few more weeks. Surprisingly, my stay at The Three Roses turned out well after such an isolating start. People were kind and looked out for me. Even the staff at the hotel befriended me. It was a tasteful place and I felt quite at home and comfortable. I tried to paint as much as I could. Although my Polish still left much to be desired, I could soon carry on conversations easily. I was happy to respond to the conversation offered by those around me. It was a rite of passage from girlhood to the first stages of young womanhood, even if it was happening in strange and bewildering times.

Because the hotel catered to a wealthy crowd, there were shops filled with pretty objects in its lobby arcade. I liked to window-shop in these souvenir stalls. Each day I looked at small beautiful pieces of artwork for sale; I was told the artist was a local artisan. I learned he was a young Chassidic man whose name was Arek. He earned his living making these souvenir items. There were lovely still-life paintings on glass, others painted on wood in small frames, some on leather, and other scenes were painted on wallets. They were delicate and intricate. His use of color and the exquisite detail in each one particularly appealed to me. I thought this man had great talent and should do something more serious than making souvenir items. He was, I learned, somewhat famous in town; his works were seen on display in all the finer shops. The ones I liked best were paintings of flowers and also those depicting forests. I had not noticed that he came into the hotel daily, but apparently he had taken note of me. He worked in a rented studio loft in the hotel.

He was young, but of course he was older than I. He was a nice-looking man who had light eyes, and light hair, and wore glasses. He probably wasn't tall, but he seemed tall to me, as I am quite short. I thought he was handsome in his long Chassidic coat just like Tattiko's, but as he was still young his beard had not grown very long. He was shy, had impeccable manners, and was deeply religious. He certainly did not dress or behave like a Bohemian artist. More than anything else he looked like an observant Jewish man. We did not acknowledge each other openly, but were aware of each other in an acceptable way – a most modest glance here and there. In that way alone we communicated and we each knew the other existed.

Because he was both proper and religious, he would never have approached me directly. Instead he asked his sister to meet me in order to make a formal introduction. She was a beautiful young woman and we became friendly in a short time. Accompanied by his sister, I went to Arek's loft and watched him paint. There we talked together about art, and Arek spoke about the life of the artist. It was a joy for me to connect to someone who not only painted, but also defined himself as an artist. As sister and brother, they obviously understood how I felt without my family. They were very close and gentle with each other and attached to their own family.

I was invited to their family home for meals on a regular basis, and most meaningful for me, they had me for Shabbos. I did not have to observe Shabbos alone in the hotel or be seated with strangers, however friendly they were. It was an act of great generosity. It was also typical of the way things were in this early period of distress: Jews tried to look out for one another in a time of confusion and anxiety about family separations. I liked Arek, his sister, and the rest of his family tremendously. Although it was many years ago, the warmth of his mother's welcome to her Shabbos table and to the light of her Shabbos candles stays with me. Arek's family was an echo of sweetness and momentary happiness for me in a time of uncertainty and growing chaos.

My temporary residence at The Three Roses had come to an end; it was time for me to make the short journey to Krakow. I said good-bye to Arek and thanked the family for their kindness. He asked for my address in Krakow so that we could stay in touch by mail. I happily and innocently gave him the address. I did not understand his heart had opened toward me in a way mine had not toward him. He began to write letters immediately. I think there was even a letter waiting for me at home when I arrived. I did not think I should answer Arek. I was moving into an existence I had not anticipated. I was adjusting to new conditions and a different culture. More than anything, I was flung headlong toward an increasingly frightening horizon.

PART TWO:
FIRST CHAPTER OF MY ADULT LIFE

CHAPTER 3

Krakow and a Man Named Mechel

From Munkach to Krynica to Krakow, I traveled within the space of weeks not months. Although the miles were not many, the atmosphere in Krakow was totally different. I felt like an explorer discovering a new continent of alien smells, ideas, customs, and norms. Events around me were spinning so rapidly I couldn't keep track of everything. I was living a mystery and didn't yet have enough clues to figure out how it would turn out. Within a short time of my arrival, strangely enough, an enormous segment of my adult life had been decided. Obviously, I was not aware of this. I was naïve and did not suspect how fast I would become an adult. Until I stood directly in front of that crucial life's bridge, I had no notion of how ill-prepared I was to cross it.

On my arrival from Krynica I truly saw the city with open eyes. Even though I had often visited my family, I found virtually everything about Krakow overwhelming. Where exactly was I? Krakow was a large city of about 250,000. Its Jewish population of more than 60,000 was several times greater than that of all Munkach. I was not only out of the enclosing embrace of my grandparents and their sheltered lives, but was now living in a major urban European city of cultural diversity and complexity. My father's family was firmly woven into the tapestry of life in Krakow. Here our Jewish life was circumscribed by a specific Chassidic sect, markedly different from the one I had known in Munkach. I felt like an outsider, even though I was living with my family. I would have to adjust – socially, religiously, and emotionally.

The first major change came almost immediately. A large wedding was about to take place in our extended family. Toby Berger, my first cousin, was about to marry Itche Pflancer. Her mother was my Aunt Ruzhe. She owned a successful corset shop on Krakowska Street, one of the best shopping boulevards in Krakow. My aunt and cousin ran the store and employed young girls to do the intricate sewing and handwork. In the sophisticated cities of Europe in the 1930s, elegant ladies did not buy intimate garments that had been mass-manufactured in factories. Instead, these garments were individually custom-made and fitted, created from the finest materials available. As cousin Toby's wedding date approached, my Aunt Ruzhe desperately needed someone to watch the shop, mind the cash register, inventory the merchandise, and assist the clients, and I was very flattered when they asked me to take over. I felt quite the grown-up young lady because they invested such obvious trust and confidence in me. Excited by the prospect of a wider world to experience, I excitedly said yes. I became a working girl while still in school.

As I said, the most significant event of my life happened without my realizing its importance. At Toby's marriage I met my future husband, Mechel Lieber, who was a guest. He noticed me at the wedding and took a fancy to me. He was interested in finding out who I was and he rather easily traced me to the shop. Mechel was born in 1915 in Karlsbad, the son of Hershel and Matel Lieber. Our family connection was that we shared an aunt and uncle, which made us cousins. At that time, he was a traveling insurance salesman who made a decent income. The minute he saw me, he said later, he made up his mind that I would be his bride. He did not know how very young I was. For him, it was, as it is sometimes is, "love at first sight."

How can I describe Mechel? He was an optimist and a determined man. Some might have called him opinionated, but that would miss his essential nature. He was extremely persuasive, yet managed to be humorous and light at the same time. There is no question, however, that he had the aura of a man accustomed to having things go his way. He wanted to walk me home from the store when I finished work, which startled me and really upset Father. Although Mechel was completely respectful and modest, my father would not permit this. For Mechel to walk with me in public, unescorted by another family member, was totally inappropriate. Mechel was eight years older than I. At that time in our lives, he was a man and I was still a girl.

My parents were concerned for another reason as well. Traditionally, the older sister in a family should be the first to have a courtship, engagement, and marriage. If Mechel were an acceptable choice as a husband for one of my father's daughters, it should have been for Goldie, not me. It may seem odd today, but this was common among Jewish families in those days. Father was traditional. The notion of "love at first sight" was too far-fetched for him to contemplate. Father had made a miscalculation about the comparative strength of wills, however. Mechel was not going to go away easily, or at all. My father misjudged the loyalty and commitment Mechel already felt toward me and the fact that Mechel had already made his plans.

"At least allow me to visit her at home," Mechel argued politely.

Even my strict and cautious father could not resist Mechel's reasoning. He wanted Father's permission to visit in order to get to know me and the rest of our family. Mechel was exhibiting the same personality traits that would characterize his behavior throughout life. When Mechel was certain about the correctness of his opinion, he could not be deterred. Although Mechel was charming and had a most compelling manner, he was not a smooth talker or a false charmer. It was something else entirely. I believe Mechel had an innate charm, which came from the sincerity of his heart and spirit. Father could not deny Mechel's deep devotion to our people and faith. This alone helped make him a serious candidate as a son-in-law. So Father relented, or at least he gave in – to some degree.

For a short period of time I think Father tried not to like Mechel, but that was an impossible task. There was also another important element in the decision about being hospitable to Mechel. In our community everyone knew and respected the Lieber family. So with considerable speed, it was agreed that Mechel could visit us almost every single day. I was not yet sixteen and not socially sophisticated. I was even younger emotionally than my actual years. I enjoyed Mechel's attention but did not interpret correctly the meaning of the visits and my father's permission. I did not realize by accepting these overtures of friendship, I had started down the path to the *chuppah* (marriage canopy) and to life as a wife – Mechel's wife.

I had my own dreams about what the perfect husband would look like, what he would sound like and what he would do. Like most other young girls in the world, my dreams began with "tall and handsome." Mechel was tall and he was slim, but he wasn't a truly handsome man. However, his eyes had a deep, intense sparkle that caught me off guard and pleased me from the very beginning. As I said, Mechel Lieber was a hard man to resist. Father was still not thrilled, but he stopped trying to push Mechel away. I was a pretty girl and a bit vain, as most young and pretty girls are. I did not see Mechel as the idealized husband of my fantasy life, and I was sometimes uncomfortable introducing him to friends and relatives. Fortunately, it did not take long for me to abandon such superficial feelings as I evolved into a person of more depth. I could soon see for myself what his qualities were. Mechel had won me over. The moment he smiled at me, or at anyone, glaciers melted.

Mechel would be described today as a lovable man. He had a unique charisma, a generosity of spirit, and a wondrous way with language and conversation. And he could do something that was very difficult in our world: He balanced and combined our *Yiddishkeit* (our Jewish way of life) with a touch of worldliness I did not see in any of the other younger men. This impressed me. What I would learn later is that his relatively modern attire actually masked a much stricter approach to observance than my own.

In the months and years ahead Mechel would teach me many things, and ultimately, I would also teach him. Neither of us knew then the degree to which our partnership and marriage would be tested. Hashem must have had a role in our meeting each other because it was as a team that we would face up to the forces of total and powerful evil under the Nazis. In Yiddish, the word *bashert* translates roughly as "fated" or "preordained." I think Mechel and I were blessed as being bashert (destined for one another). It was a gift from Heaven that would provide us with a special strength to go forward without giving up or losing our faith.

CHAPTER 4
The Education of a Jewish Girl

Adjusting to Mechel visiting our home each night was not as much of a jolt to my situation as the question of my formal education. There has always been a mythology that strictly Orthodox families do not wish to educate their daughters. Certainly there was resistance to girls receiving formal Torah education and training to the same extent and depth as boys. Our faith is the oldest monotheistic faith in the world, and in our Torah men and women are treated equally. Each contributed in their own way to maintaining our faith at crucial times in our long history. Sarah, our matriarch, joined Abraham, our patriarch, in leaving the land of false gods and settling in the land where our religion took hold. Of course, I was also aware from the teaching of our belfer and from my babbiko of our other matriarchs besides Sarah – Rebecca, Rachel, Leah – and others such as Miriam, Devorah, Ruth, and my own namesake, Queen Esther.

I also knew the blessings and duties required to be performed by women on Shabbos and during the Holidays. I was intuitively aware that as women we did play a significant role, particularly in what is now called "ultra-Orthodox" Judaism. It was a term I had never heard as a child. We all lived in our shtetls and everyone was the same…we were simply all Orthodox Jews living together and observing in the same ways. Labels were not necessary in those days.

By the 1930s in Poland, and in Krakow especially, a new phase in the education of Jewish girls had dawned. I am talking about the historic figure of Sarah Schenirer, a remarkable and intelligent Jewish woman, the leader of the Bais Yaakov movement. She was a Krakow seamstress (in fact her last name is the word for seamstress). Although she was unmarried and had no children of her own, she was a true Jewish mother. She became the spiritual mentor for many Polish girls. Our modern Sarah was born in 1883. By 1918 she had accomplished something few believed possible. She had opened an authorized Orthodox school for Jewish girls in Krakow. The number of her schools, which she named Bais Yaakov, expanded quickly into the hundreds.

She was taken from life in 1935. It was by the profound grace of Hashem that she did not live to witness the extinguishing of the lights of Jewish learning and of Polish Jewish life. It is told that upon her death hundreds upon hundreds of Jewish girls wept in inconsolable grief at the loss of their teacher and mother figure. How sad it is that despite the great amount of knowledge now available about women leaders and thinkers, few people, even among Jews, know of this dedicated and pious woman.

You might say that Sarah Schenirer was a Jewish missionary working for the continuation of our people. She saw that without understanding the meaning of our rituals, Jewish girls could be tempted to leave Judaism and to marry outside our faith. In nothing short of a miracle of understanding and activism, she understood what needed to be done.

In the period just after the First World War, she saw that as girls became more modern, they were somewhat embarrassed by their mothers. Mothers had old-world or shtetl mannerisms and usually spoke in conversational Yiddish. She knew this could cause a rip in the fabric of Jewish life that would disrupt the legacy of Jewish continuity. Sarah Schenirer knew that the way to a girl's heart would be through her mind. A girl who understands fully the antiquity of our faith and is able to comprehend Torah knowledge will develop pride for the critical role a woman plays inside Judaism. Feelings such as this ensure a lifetime of devotion to Jewish tradition. Sarah was able to convince important Chassidic Rebbes in Krakow of the importance of and the need for the education of girls. With their cooperation and approval she established a school and an after-school program, and later a seminary for the training of women teachers.

When I was only ten years old and spent a year in Krakow, I once met her. I did not then have any idea of her significance to Jewish life in Krakow and elsewhere. She was an unassuming woman, who wore thick glasses and dressed in a simple style. I was not enrolled in the Bais Yaakov School then because I was only a part-time resident in Krakow. In any case, I could not have done the required assignments as my Hebrew was woefully inadequate.

When we think of the Shoah, it is difficult to focus on anything other than the genocide of an entire people. However, it is also important to remember that besides all the lives lost, we lost the main threads of our history because we lost entire nations of Jews. Although the Bais Yaakov movement eventually rebuilt itself in Europe, Israel, and North America after the war, the numbers are far smaller than they would be if so many had not been efficiently and ruthlessly killed.

When I became a permanent Krakow resident and not just a ten-year-old visitor, I was more than willing to enroll in a public high school, as I had in Munkach. However my parents and grandparents in Poland wouldn't hear of it. By now I was old enough to attend one of the schools started by Sarah Schenirer. One major impediment remained for me. I might have been sophisticated and adept in other languages, but I did not meet the Hebrew language qualifications for admission. I knew only a limited sort of Hebrew: the blessings and prayers that my Munkach belfer had taught me. I could struggle through a smattering of other Hebrew words but without understanding much (this was exactly what Sarah Schenirer sought to change among girls!)

What would become of my educational development? I think everybody in the family was a bit perplexed about what to do with me. While I did love to read and to learn, there was no question my talents and true vocation resided in the world of art. I "killed time" with Polish library books, trying to further my comprehension of the language. I read them between mornings at the corset shop and evenings of crocheting. My Polish was getting better and better, but it wasn't really enough to satisfy me. Nor did it serve to replace companionship for a girl so homesick for the familiar setting in Munkach.

Then I discovered B'nos, which was the after-school organization of the Bais Yaakov movement. I fell in love with it. Their activities held my attention and made me happy again. We divided ourselves into groups, each with a leader who attended the seminary. My group leader was Reina Finkelstein, and one of the other participants was Peszka Mandelkern (subsequently Pearl Benisch), who wrote the best-selling Holocaust memoir, "Vanquish the Dragon." This is when I became officially known as Lola, the Polish version of Leiku. I had girlfriends now as well. My two best friends were older girls, who were both named Lola.

Lola Scheindorf crocheted pilot caps and earmuffs to earn enough money to purchase a proper marriage trousseau. She was extremely disciplined; she set herself a quota each day and would not stop until she had reached it. Finally I figured out that despite her strict regimen, she was never going to have a moment of life as a girl if someone didn't rescue her. Happily, I pitched in, and then we had some fun together. The other Lola was from the Petzenbaum family. She was a wholesome, dark-haired girl, whose family owned a furniture store. We were the Lola Triplets.

Even though we were not full-fledged Bais Yaakov students, as B'nos girls we were still taught some *Tanach* (Bible) as Jewish history. We also studied the weekly Torah portion. We sang Hebrew songs and danced the *hora* (traditional Jewish circle dance) together. The memory of all of us Orthodox Jewish girls dancing together still brings me joy when I recall it. At last, I looked forward to each day with the expectancy of a normal teenager. It was thanks to these girls and to the B'nos program that for the first time since our rushed and forced departure from Munkach, I wasn't so sad,

To some of the B'nos girls I appeared a bit spoiled and privileged. They were not unkind to me, but they couldn't figure me out. I did not look anything like they did. By their standards, I wore fancy clothing. More than anything else what set me apart in dress was my silk stockings. Fifteen-year-old girls in Krakow wore heavy woolen stockings, not lady-like stockings. I was modestly dressed, of course, but still, the sleeves on my dresses and blouses were a tiny bit shorter than theirs, and this raised eyebrows too. And I played the violin and spoke several languages.

But the most obvious deviation from the norm, even worse than the stockings, was my hair! I'd come from Munkach with beautiful curls, just like Shirley Temple. In Krakow, Orthodox girls all wore their hair very short or braided. At first, I brushed off their attitudes because I knew that teenagers are conformists – they all want to be alike. I was an artist; I was from Munkach; I was different. They would just have to accept me as I was. It was their problem, not mine.

What was really bothering them began to settle into my brain more slowly than it should have. They were thinking something other than what I thought they were. It wasn't that they thought I was rich or that I was spoiled or that I was a snob. They suspected that my appearance was the sign of something far more troublesome. What I saw as exhibiting a personal artistic and geographic cultural difference, these girls saw as an indication of religious laxity – or worse! They thought I was indifferent to our traditions. Krakow had such a large Jewish population of so many different leanings that things like this mattered. This was the real education of Lola. I finally realized that I was misunderstood because of something I had not thought about, yet could unintentionally bring embarrassment to my family. That is why I wanted to enroll in the Bais Yaakov seminary and become a part of the educated and Jewishly enlightened girls of Krakow, who knew more than their Hebrew blessings. I wanted to know more Torah and more about our faith. The paradox is that I wanted to become more observant, not less. Yet the others thought the way I dressed signified a lack of commitment. The girls who were "in charge" debated at length about what on earth to do with me, an alien creature from Munkach. They reasoned among themselves that if I were admitted, I might be a bad influence on the others. They were probably also a little jealous. They criticized me but they might have liked to have pretty things to wear. Fortunately, the teachers took over and held a vote. They admitted me, the nonconformist, but with some restrictions. I, too, would wear woolen stockings and a sweater to cover my shorter sleeves.

I wanted to be accepted by the B'nos girls, and I wanted to receive a deeper Jewish education, so I surrendered to the requirements. Then they went too far. They demanded that my hairdo had to go with words such as, "Why can't you just put it up into a bun?" I felt I had given up enough of my former identity, said no, and stood firm. They compromised and let me keep a bit of my old self. So with compromises on both sides, the Education of a Jewish Girl In Krakow began in earnest.

Goldie had promised me her friends would become mine, so I contacted them, but found only more disapproval. After we met, they immediately asked about my background. Most of them had turned eighteen and were marriage-minded. My responses caused them to question me even further. *Oh No!* I thought to myself, *here I go again. Am I ever going to be accepted into this Krakow Bais Yaakov crowd?* However, they were acting like typical girls and I realized they didn't dislike me. They simply had to become comfortable with someone so different. They told me small secrets about how they sometimes bent the norms a little bit themselves. Nothing they did was of any serious importance. It was just their way of saying: "Okay, Lola, we will take you at your word and you'll take us at ours." Our divergent personalities and styles met and adjusted to each other and our norms converged. Finally, I had friends and a life in Krakow.

Without the dreadful fanfare that should have announced it, the secular year of 1938 crossed quite silently into the secular year of 1939. My life had a routine that did not vary much. I worked in the morning, attended Bais Yaakov afterwards, and hosted Mechel after supper. I played the violin. In the moments I could steal from my work duties, my tasks, my school assignments, and my social obligations, I sketched or painted. There was also the continuing obligation to Mammiko's wishes. She still insisted that I must work with diligence on my German. Mammiko believed that only by speaking fluent and perfect German and reading without hesitation would I establish myself as a civilized young lady of haute culture.

Now at the age of eighty-plus, that sentence brings me to the brink of ironic tears – too bitter to allow them to spill across my face. In Poland in early 1939, my beloved Mammiko thought the road to a good future would be in knowing the language of those who would become our killers. Dear Mammiko could not know. We did not know. Who could have known it then? The German language was a part of Jewish life throughout the Europe we knew. The fact that some of us spoke German would not exempt us from their hatred.

I was educated in another area of life just then. Arek, my artist friend, arrived in Krakow without warning. One of the other Lolas alerted me to his arrival and to the fact that he was eager to see me. Arek had left Krynica and made his way to Krakow. I assumed it was probably a passport problem like ours. I was not shocked to learn he was in Krakow. Jews were on the move all over. What shocked me was him appearing at my door with an urgency that did not have anything to do with his citizenship. He was in Krakow with a specific purpose in mind and that purpose was to see me again.

By the time he reached my home, he had learned that a man named Mechel Lieber regularly visited my family's home. Arek knew this meant

Mechel had serious intentions about making a future with me. Arek would not go away without making a stand for himself. He presented me with a beautiful cosmetics case. He insisted he must meet my parents immediately. When I asked him why he was so insistent, he confessed that he had learned about Mechel from my girlfriends. He was most unhappy about the information he had been given.

The drama in my life was building into theatrical proportions. Mechel was at my house on one of his usual visits when he heard about Arek. Mechel became incredibly jealous. Who was this Arek? What was he doing coming to my house attempting to have a formal meeting with my parents? I was unprepared for Mechel's next move. He stated, in no uncertain terms, he simply could not and would not go forward with his life without me in it. In other words, he threatened dire consequences if I saw Arek again. I was growing up too quickly. Here I was, a sheltered and obedient Jewish girl in a strictly Orthodox home, being pursued by two potential husbands.

Mechel was flushed with anger and confusion: "I know that I have never spoken of marriage directly, but you know very well that is my intention."

I was annoyed and protested. "Mechel, listen to me, Arek is a lovely young man. His entire family took me in like a family member when I was alone. He has come from Krynica to see me. I must speak with him."

Mechel proposed the only acceptable condition under which I could meet and speak with Arek again. I could see him if Mechel was with me and we saw Arek together. Now I was aggrieved with Mechel. My father wouldn't even let us take a walk in the local woods or parks without my siblings as companions. The notion that Mechel would serve as my escort to meet my friend Arek was too much for me to tolerate. I was exasperated by Mechel's extreme reaction. I said as sweetly as I could, that I felt Mechel's possessiveness was quite premature, under the circumstances.

"Please, Mechel, can't you give me a little privacy?"

Mechel relented because he knew that I was not going to agree to his terms and that it would cause lasting bad feelings between us if he persisted.

I met Arek outside, standing at the building next door to our home. Arek pulled out a small box from his pocket and opened it. Inside was something very serious and beautiful. It was a ring. "Please, I must speak with your father," he said. Even today these remarks and a ring usually mean only one thing: an engagement to be married. In our world and at that time, it could not mean anything else.

"P-please d-don't," I stammered. I told him about Mechel. I was shaking with anxiety and I was perplexed. What was going on in my life? What was all this attention about for a girl who was not quite sixteen? Then I said something that still puzzles me some, but I think I was determined not to hurt the feelings of such a dear young man who had been so kind to me. Arek was clearly heartsick over me. I said I wasn't at all serious about Mechel, and I told Arek that I was not sure what the future might bring with Mechel. At that time of unknowing blindness, I thought the future meant at least five years more, or even longer.

As the words left my lips, I watched Arek's face fall with disappointment and rejection. I was unhappy with myself, unhappy with Arek, unhappy with Mechel. I was not interested in being fought over to be anyone's bride. I wanted to remain a girl. Yet Arek was so sweet and so shy that I knew what it must have meant for him to bring the ring, to approach me. When I realized he had been thinking of me ever since I had left Krynica, I felt simply dreadful. I had broken his heart although it was not at all my intention. As a moral person, I was sorry to have wounded another person, especially one as kind and gentle. He had a very different personality from Mechel's, so I was quite surprised when Arek said what he did. He did not agree to go away and forget about me.

He said, "Please take the ring and think about it for as long as you wish or need."

Of course I declined the ring, but I did promise to write him. He asked if he could have my photograph. I gave him one and he asked me to sign it to him. He left me then and said he would write. I said that I would write to him. It was a shocking moment for me. Girlhood was running away from me. But I was not going to let it go without my own fight!

I held onto to my girlhood for that last summer. Despite all the grown-up attention from young men, I was enrolled in a summer camp. It was not far from Krynica and sponsored by the Bais Yaakov seminary. It was like B'nos but more intensive; we would live in small cottages, go swimming, and do morning exercise. I was really looking forward to some fresh country air and a return to the gymnastics I adored.

I was very disappointed by what awaited me. The first morning, someone blew a whistle and everyone stumbled out of bed into the morning mist. One girl came in a delicate nightgown, another in a terrycloth robe, and a third in a skirt of the sort she would wear to shul. Others reported ten minutes late. As soon as the whole group was there, we lined up, ran in a circle for fifteen minutes, and then did calisthenics.

Well, if I was going to take control of my own life, I figured I could be a leader in something at camp. I knew about proper gymnastics even if my Hebrew wasn't perfect. The next day, I made up my own exercise routine and did it in my room. It did not surprise me when one of the girls, noticing my absence, glanced inside and motioned to the other girls and the teachers. When I was done, they applauded. Then they asked me to be the exercise instructor. I agreed and then, taking advantage of their satisfaction, laid down the law. First, I ordered everyone to wear black shorts and white polo shirts, the sort of uniform that I knew. They had to send someone to Krakow to buy these items. Second, I insisted everyone must report on time. Third, I added gymnastics to the exercise routine.

They accepted it all. This accomplished, I turned my attention to the swimming activity. A few girls had bathing suits; the others waded into the lake in their robes, or old nightgowns, or blouses. I stepped past them and jumped in at the deep end. The swimming instructor screamed in alarm. She didn't know how to swim. I treated this like the morning exercises and persuaded the girls to get bathing suits and caps. In my few free hours, I took out my sketchpad and ended up teaching some of the girls how to sketch as well. It was a welcome relief for me from the attention of potential husbands.

August wound down and I headed for home, which by then I fully accepted meant Krakow. Over the summer I had earned the respect and friendship of quite a few peers who no longer thought of me as different and slightly dangerous. My year of education had been about Hebrew, Judaism, academic subjects, sketching, and maturing. I was on the brink of womanhood.

In many ways one of the most important things that happened was not so obvious. When I got back to Krakow, life there did not seem as strange and foreign to me. It had not happened all at once, in one moment of clarity or inspiration. It happened gradually. I had opened my heart to accepting the different ways in which people, even my own family members, expressed themselves and existed inside a Jewish enclave.

When I had been a visitor to Krakow, I dreaded going to my zeide Yoikl (my paternal grandfather) on Shabbos. He was a not a member of any particular Chassidic sect, but was somewhat attached to the Czechower Rebbe. He was very strict in adhering to the observance of law and ritual. Even his work was connected with Jewish law. He sold *cholov Yisroel* milk, which is milk produced under the most rigid and regulated of Jewish dietary supervision. (Today some might call this "glatt kosher milk.") Zeide Yoikl was a classic Polish Chassid. He was neither privileged nor at all wealthy. Unlike the life in the garden of Munkach, Zeide lived in a small apartment that I thought was a bit dingy. He always sat at the head of a huge table, which was the largest item of furniture in the house. A gas lamp hissed above us, suspended from the ceiling in a precarious and undoubtedly hazardous way. On Shabbos, for *"shalosh-seudos"* (*seudah sheleshis,* the third Shabbos meal), we ate in almost total darkness, a custom that I had not experienced in Munkach.

Grandchildren and family surrounded Zeide Yoikl. There were many of us there each Shabbos. The men chanted the *zemiros* (Shabbos melodies) in sonorous and melancholy voices. As a ten-year-old I found all of this impossible to endure. I watched carefully to see when I could creep away and lie down on the couch without being called out for bad behavior. He would call each child to him by name, take a tiny bit of challah, dip it into fish broth and hand it to the child as a precious delicacy. By the time I had become a part of the Krakow community, I no longer saw these customs as unpleasant or strange.

This was another part of my life, a part of what it meant to be a Jew. Yes, the customs and the styles were different, but we were bound together by one Torah, one Shabbos. I sensed the "wings of the *Shechinah*" (the Divine Presence) present in the shadows of the dim light, in our daily life, and in our Shabbos. Shabbos for Jews is known as the "Bride of the Week," sacred and holy in its presence as it enters our souls each Friday at sundown. The education of a Jewish girl was coming to a closure, but not in any of the ways I dreamed it would. Poland saw it coming. Some members of the Jewish community saw it coming. We now know there were people in other countries who suspected things were about to happen. I did not.

It was the autumn of 1939.

Now, even to say the words "September 1939 in Poland" is to make a statement that conjures up historic horror of unprecedented dimensions, unfathomable sorrow, and total annihilation.

PART THREE:
1939 AND BEYOND

CHAPTER 5
Darkness Descends

It may sound unbelievable today, but I don't remember when I first heard Hitler's voice. The adults spoke of hearing him on the radio. His infamous book, *Mein Kampf*, certainly made his ideas clear enough. My relatives and other adults were surely reading the newspapers, which reported with accuracy the build-up of Nazi forces at the Polish borders. Uncle Shloime, who had made his home in Katowice, Silesia, had moved to Krakow during the summer. Germany had eaten up his province and he fled to Krakow, assuming it would be safer. He was well informed and did not hold back his opinion about what Hitler and his leadership circle intended to do. Hitler and his group became the subject of family conversations. I remember my uncle's stories made a strong impression on the adults and I was frightened.

Father converted a fairly substantial amount of zloty into dollars. When I expressed my fears, my family said it was always good to have U.S. dollars in case of a "rainy day." Did my parents know what was coming and decided I was too young to know, or were they also in some foggy dream of hope against hope? The truth is I was still a happy-go-lucky child, and I believed my parents when they said not to worry. I was stuck in the mindset of a young girl from a place called Munkach. I did not yet concern myself with worries about Poland, a country I was not all that emotionally attached to. I was attached to Mechel and Father, but not to their country of origin. Deep inside me I was still Leiku, but it was a flimsy disguise of protection that would vanish without warning.

Germany invaded Poland on September 1, 1939. At least two weeks prior to the invasion, Poland had started to mobilize whatever military forces they could. Everywhere in Krakow optimistic political posters announced Polish power, strength, pride, and resistance. Those in high positions in Poland surely knew the country was but a feather in front of a land-based flotilla of Nazi tanks and weaponry. I did not have the same worry many other young women in my position did. Mechel was the only son in a family of six girls. Therefore, according to Polish law, he was not drafted into the Polish army like virtually all the other men.

Mechel was inducted into the Civil Defense, wore an armband, and was put in charge of air-raid alerts at his family's apartment building. There was war activity everywhere, and I adjusted to it quickly – far too quickly, I believe now. Bomb shelters were being prepared, air-raid equipment was tested, and there were lots of drills, complete with fake sirens and bomb sounds. When a drill was announced, Mechel flew into action and competently and authoritatively stopped cars, and chased pedestrians off the streets and sidewalks into the reinforced shelters. At first it made me nervous, and then I thought it was almost comical. Thankfully, I had the presence of mind and enough maturity not to suggest to Mechel that his job was funny or amusing. Yet so it was to me, until the actual horror of Nazi conquest overtook us; until then I thought the preparations were like a school play in rehearsal.

Then the invasion happened, but I still clung to my girlhood. In Krakow most people were still hopeful, adults all around were suggesting that the situation was not so dire. I remember hearing someone say, "Our army will hold them back, and besides the British and French are on their way now to help us."

September 5, 1939, marked the official end of the life of Leiku, the innocent and playful young girl. I was sitting by the window in our home and I noticed a priest walking just across the street from our building. I admired his vestments and "costume." Priests looked so different from rabbis in their dress and I was curious about them. I watched him as he raised his hands upward, as if in prayer, to his God. I thought for an instant that all of Poland, all faiths, were praying for our successful resistance. Before that thought was fully formed, a shattering and deafening roar ripped through the cool, still autumn air.

A bomb hit a building only half a block away from us. It instantly crumbled into dust. I saw the entire event from our window as it happened. The priest had been a fake, of course. He was a German spy and his presumed gesture heavenward was only a signal to a German airplane to hit an important target. That building had housed an important enemy of the German war effort – it had been the headquarters of a major Krakow newspaper.

At this point our family and others in Krakow were filled with anxiety and fear. We trembled at the slightest sound from the outside. I watched the German soldiers march through Krakow – first came the ones on foot. They were striking in their powerful goose-stepping strides and in their immaculate uniforms and expensive boots. In contrast, the Polish army was shabby and poorly outfitted. The killers are very well dressed, I thought to myself now with an adult's sense of sarcasm. Then the tanks came rumbling in, intent on rolling over Poland and all her people. We retreated indoors. This was no longer a show or a rehearsal. We were all in mortal danger. Our entire family gathered around the radio. The news went hourly from horrible to grim to hopeless.

We lived on the first floor of our building. Across the hall and up a short staircase was another apartment. At about midnight, we heard a fierce and angry pounding at our front door. Moishe, my brother, opened the door and was confronted by six German Gestapo agents. They pushed my brother aside and with their guns at the ready, they poked at our possessions, leaving a wake of destruction behind them. Then they demanded our gold and silver. We never thought of resisting them. Quickly, we opened the family safe in the dining room and they grabbed all the family silver that was inside.

Before I understood what was happening one of the soldiers shoved me into my parents' bedroom and pointed his gun at the small nightstand next to the bed. "Open it," he ordered. I jumped to obey him, because I was thoroughly afraid of him. When I leaned over slightly to open the drawer, he slammed the bedroom door shut and pushed me. He had his rifle in his hand, ready to use on me. I didn't care. I kicked him as hard as I could and I screamed for my father and my brother. I would rather have died than to have been assaulted and victimized by him.

My father screamed to me from the other side of the door, unable to open it, "My daughter, my daughter," but his words were more of a plea for mercy than a cry of anger. Terror is what I heard in his voice, because naturally he assumed the worst was happening to me. The soldier was not deterred by my kicks and screams or by my father's shouts. I took a deep breath and with all of my force kicked out at the soldier; he lost his balance and fell down. Just as he was about to get up from the floor and probably finish me off for good, the door crashed open. His comrades, two more Gestapo men, grabbed my attacker and quickly left the room.

Almost out of my mind with fear and hatred, I ran blindly upstairs to the neighbors, gasping for breath. Two more Gestapo agents had beaten me to their apartment and had begun to loot it as well. Our neighbors' tiny infant was lying in a small cradle close by the door to a bedroom. The mother moved quickly to comfort her baby, who was alarmed by the noise and the screaming. I watched one of the Nazis observe my neighbor with cold eyes that betrayed his complete contempt for all of us. Just before the mother could reach her infant, he grabbed the baby by its feet and swung the baby around like a sack of dirty laundry. Then, as the mother lurched forward in an attempt to grab her baby away from him, he took the baby and slammed its head against the corner of the door. The baby's head burst open and its brains spilled out onto the rug.

The mother let out a wailing sound — a shriek of grief — the tone and depth of which I never heard before or since. It was truly a cry from the depths of the heart. By then we were all screaming and crying so loudly with disbelief that the walls seemed to shake with us. Perhaps it was the passion and intensity of our response that startled the Nazis. Or was it possible that they were stunned by the inhumanity of their fellow soldier's actions? They ran down the stairs in a group, jumped into a car, and sped down an otherwise silent street in the middle of the night. We were left with the evidence of a kind of killing we had witnessed but could not yet comprehend.

By September 7 our family and our neighbors were completely numb with shock. The past two days had evaporated in a blur of quiet and horrible mourning and sobbing disbelief. We were now in the hands of the Nazi death machine. Its operators and managers were very well organized in addition to being very well dressed and very heavily armed.

On September 8 circulars were handed out everywhere and posters appeared in plain view throughout the city. Every Jewish home had to be marked with a Star of David for identification purposes. By September 12 the reason was clear. Jewish homes were to be marked for as yet unspecified restrictions to their residents, and all Jewish-owned businesses were to be "Aryanized." All Jews who owned businesses were required to report to the German authorities, turn over their keys to the Nazis, and then stay on for a period of time to teach our mortal enemies how to run our businesses.

Some Jews left then, hoping to find safety in the east. In Krakow, despite its large Jewish population, there was no organized resistance; there was no "uprising." Nobody did anything to confront the enemy. The whole community was caught in the blind and fearful hope that if we did what we were told we might be spared death. Needless to say, no Jewish business in Krakow was ever returned to its rightful Jewish owners. The occupation and domination continued with relentless and ruthless efficiency.

Mechel's family had one of the finest textile stores in Krakow. They had a loyal and wealthy clientele, many of whom had credit accounts. The Nazis ordered the Liebers to give them the names and addresses of all those who owed money so that they could collect it. Somehow the Liebers managed to transfer some valuable textiles to their customers in the countryside without the Nazis discerning it. This would become very useful later to all of us.

My father was wiped out totally. By the time the Nazis had completed their expropriation, there wasn't a trace left of his business. My father handed over the keys and gave them a guided tour. Father came home exhausted and defeated. He kept saying he was glad that at least he had those few American dollars. He told us they were hidden safely somewhere, but he did not divulge the location to us and we did not inquire.

Obviously observant Orthodox Jewish men were the first to fall victim to public slaughter. They were dragged into the street, and then, to degrade them further, the Nazis pulled the men around by their *peyos* (sidelocks) and hacked off their beards. In the end they were often killed. Uncle Yoshe Berger's son, my cousin who was also called Moishe like my brother, was living in Krakow with his wife Rosie, who was then more than seven months pregnant. Cousin Moishe went out to get a bit of yeast in order to bake some *challah*. Although we all had small amounts of sugar and flour, yeast was very hard to find. It was a reckless thing for Moishe to do because he was so obviously Jewish. But the holidays were coming and he wanted to be able to celebrate with a challah. It took the Nazis less than five minutes to capture him. They accosted him on the street and shot him to death.

When the news reached Rosie, she went into premature labor. Their little girl was named Micheline, which is the feminine for Moishe. My cousin Moishe would never have the pleasure of even a fleeting look at his beautiful daughter.

Within days of this terrible loss and rebirth of hope with Micheline's arrival, I received word of Arek. I received a letter with a postmark from Warsaw telling me about Arek, so I knew he had gone to live there as he'd told me he would. He had been badly injured in a German bombing raid. The neighbors who rushed him to the hospital found my photograph with the address and wrote to me immediately, assuming I was a relative. When I reached the hospital administrators, I was told he had not survived his injuries. He was dead at twenty-two, if that. He had kept my photograph under his pillow. I cried for days and would not be comforted. Even Mechel, previously so jealous, was consoling and tender. He called the death of Arek, like the murder of Moishe and all that was going on around us, "a sea of tragedies." How prophetic those words of Mechel would turn out to be as the weeks and months progressed.

Another death, not officially announced but obvious to anyone paying attention, was the demise of Poland itself. On September 17, with a secret agreement in place with the Nazis, the Soviets occupied the eastern region of Poland. Warsaw surrendered completely on September 27. By October 6, Poland no longer existed as an independent country. The western region of what had been Poland became part of "Greater Germany," or the expanded Reich. Krakow was the capital of this newly captured possession of the Nazis and was controlled by "Governor" Hans Frank. He was a particularly brutal thug and all Jews feared him.

The Nazi high command figured out fairly quickly that if they killed all the healthy Jews in Poland immediately, they wouldn't have enough workers for their war effort. They didn't want to take German manpower away from advancing the "Final Solution," so why not use us? We were a captive work force of trapped and frightened civilians, easily apprehended. The Nazis began to round up Jews in the streets of Krakow at any hour of the day or night and send them away to forced labor camps and factories. In some cases, those people never returned; in other cases it was day-labor, but it was always humiliating and always filled with the dread of separation from loved ones and possible death. The Nazis amused themselves by giving people shovels and sending them on pointless exercises of manual labor; this busy-work served no purpose, not even to move forward their own vile plans. A common practice was to find as many young people as possible and push them into overcrowded flatbed trucks and take them out of town. When the men and women would return they told stories of being made to stand for endless hours sorting uniforms and the like.

One day Mechel and I were standing in front of my house and talking to a friend. A flatbed truck lumbered by us and suddenly stopped. The truck was already filled to capacity so neither Mechel nor I reacted with much apprehension. However, we were mistaken, as the Germans wanted us, too. In their normal abusive manner, they ordered us to get into the truck, and when I hesitated for a moment trying to figure out where exactly I was to sit, I was roughly pushed into the mass of people and so was Mechel. The Germans said nothing; this was also the rule of the day by now. We never knew for sure where we were going or what they would do to us. What we all knew was that silence and obedience gave you a slim chance of returning home. Resistance and disrespect was the guarantee of becoming yet another number in the statistics of Krakow deaths.

Mechel, however, had a way of handling even these monsters. He could ask a question in a way that was bold but not perceived as disobedient. He kept asking where we were being taken and there was no reply. Finally, Mechel shouted at them, "Where are you taking us?" Mechel scared me to pieces when he screamed at the German soldiers, but one of them must have been worn down by his constant questions and instead of beating or killing Mechel, he responded.

The soldier said, "You are going to Auschwitz." Auschwitz (or Oswiec-im in Polish) did not yet mean anything to us. It would not be much longer before the name would become synonymous with the gates of Hell itself, and would so remain for all time to come. Then it was simply the location of a rather obscure town approximately thirty-seven miles west of Krakow.

In late 1939 Auschwitz was still a fairly irrelevant railroad town that served as a crossroads holding area, which the Germans used to establish a concentration camp. Its infamy and horror were still ahead of it. In 1939 it was a detention place for Polish citizens who the Nazis thought might inspire an uprising. Its inmates were influential intellectuals, community elites, spiritual leaders (both Jewish and some Christians who opposed Hitler), cultural and literary figures, and of course, anyone suspected of being part of the resistance.

As it turned out the soldier was wrong. We were unloaded from the truck in a town called Bobowa and our job was to clean a chocolate factory that had been recently "Aryanized." It was to become a headquarters for Nazi operations; it was unclear from the rumors whether it would become a military planning base or a munitions factory. It was a strange experience for me, to say the least. How utterly bizarre for me to be included in a group of Jews cleaning a chocolate factory, when chocolate making had been my father's profession! I had often used broken pieces of chocolates from his factory as little gifts for my girlfriends. Some of the workers in our group ate up whatever leftover candy they found in the now disused factory. It was a small reward for the nasty and hard work ahead of us, but Mechel and I kept strictly kosher so we did not indulge in that small "treat." Kosher or not, though, I'll confess that neither Mechel nor I would have eaten a piece of candy that had been stolen from its owners.

Mechel turned to me in the middle of the day and asked me if I understood where we were. I thought to myself, *Has he lost his mind? We are inside a chocolate factory, working for Nazis who have taken it from its rightful owners.* A light came into Mechel's eyes as he looked at me. It was a light that would stay with me all my life and become enmeshed eventually with my own identity.

"We are very close to the Bobover Rebbe's home. Let me show you where he lives."

Mechel's father, grandfather, and uncles were all Bobover Chassidim. This meant they were followers of one of Poland's greatest rabbis, Grand Rabbi Ben Zion Halberstam. Mechel's father as well as his uncle who lived in Berlin would visit Rabbi Halberstam on the holidays. My family was not part of the Bobover sect. However, as I came from a Chassidic household, I was certainly aware of the importance of the Halberstam dynasty.

I didn't think twice about what Mechel said. I wanted to see the Rebbe's home too. Off we went, slipping away without being detected. We walked a short distance and there was the house. Rabbi Shloime Halberstam, the

Grand Rebbe's son was standing in front of his home with two lovely women who turned out to be the rabbi's sisters. We spoke to them for a few moments and I saw how easily Mechel engaged Rabbi Halberstam. We didn't stay long and our comments were few and courteous, and then we went back to work, slipping right in again without having been reported missing. What a tremendous and quite stupid thing we had done! We had taken an outrageous liberty that placed us in mortal danger. We were not caught. We were not punished. There would turn out to be a preordained reason neither of us had resisted the wild temptation to go to see the Bobover Rebbe's home. It would not be revealed for a long time yet, but it would prove to be the entry into a world that would eventually shelter us. (Fortunately, we had been chosen for day labor only and were returned at the end of the day.)

With winter approaching quickly, the Nazis had flown into a frenzy of activity. They put out a new decree each day it seemed to us. In November our traditional kehillah (Jewish community administration) had been replaced by what they called the *Judenrat*. The first task of the Judenrat was to enforce the obligatory wearing of yellow Stars of David by all Jews twelve years of age and older. By the end of November we were ordered to surrender all jewelry, personal valuables of any kind, and all fur coats, hats, anything made of fur. We were allowed to keep only a small strip of fur on our coat collars.

All Jewish schools were closed down officially in the first weeks of December. This brought my life in the seminary to a close forever. Now I spent my time reading and painting, or sketching and drawing. My girlfriends from the seminary stayed close and we met in each other's homes regularly, until word went out one day that the Gestapo knew that girls were getting together and they came into homes and took the girls away. This was happening mostly in the old Jewish Quarter of Krakow, Kazimierz, and only because of that was I spared. Our neighborhood was close to the old Jewish Quarter, but we were not in it.

Somehow my resourceful and brave father tried to carry on as a businessman. Of course, it was illegal for him to be in business. Nonetheless he wanted to provide for us and so he engaged in highly dangerous activities on the black market. He dealt a bit in silver and in used machinery. He had a partnership of sorts with a questionable Jewish man who called himself Mr. Sommerglick. He looked more Aryan than he did Jewish and he posed as a gentile. In fact, he was so convincing that he got away with living in a very elegant part of town where Jews had always been unwelcome.

Father knew better than to venture going to Sommerglick's home, but I was also someone who did not look obviously Jewish so I was appointed my father's courier. Whenever Father needed to deliver money or to obtain objects for sale on the black market, I was sent to Sommerglick's fancy house. Mechel was courting me, still over my father's protests, and he was fairly suspicious of where I was going. I was sworn to secrecy and would not betray my father. However, one day in the early spring of 1940, my father entrusted me with a very large sum of cash. It frightened me and because of that I told Mechel what my father had asked me to do. Mechel said he would accompany me as far as Sommerglick's house and then disappear.

It was a terrible risk for Mechel to take, as he was not someone who could pass as a gentile. Mechel said the journey was too fraught with potential peril for me to transport that amount of money, at night, alone, so we set out to Sommerglick's home together. When we approached, I motioned to Mechel that he should leave me.

I rang the door bell and Sommerglick was expecting me. I had never liked him. There was something about him that was shady and slick. He had a suspicious air and I didn't trust him. I always assumed he was cheating Father or at least taking advantage of him. Sommerglick was comfortably wealthy and essentially living as a secret gentile. This also bothered me and made me dislike his tactics. However, that night when he opened the door I sensed a different kind of personal hazard looming. Sommerglick was all smiles and false charm. He invited me to sit down, to have a drink. I said I had the package of money and wanted to give it to him and return home quickly. He said that I needed to come upstairs where there were not so many windows so that in case I had been followed nobody could see us transacting our business.

Like the innocent I still remained in some respects, I followed him up the stairs. We entered another room. It was a bedroom. I saw it coming. I said, "Leave me alone. Don't you dare come one more step toward me." I threw the packet of money in his direction, but he advanced toward me. I went to the door to leave the room but he had closed it and locked it with a key. I did not panic. My prior experience in the room with the Nazi had strengthened my resolve with regard to this sort of maneuver. I did not scream, but I said in a firm and controlled voice, "Open this door right now."

He said something smug like "or what?"

I had seen enough of Sommerglick and I was not about to be bullied by him or forced to do his totally inappropriate bidding. "Or what?" I said, my voice gathering volume, "I'll tell you what…" and I proceeded to the large window in the room and pulled back the drapes. I reached for the latch on the window and said firmly, "I am going to jump out of this window this minute if you don't let me out of here."

He ran toward me at first flustered and saying I had misunderstood, he meant me no harm. He quickly flung open the door to the room. I ran down the stairs and out the front door. And just around the corner on the side of the house, I found Mechel waiting for me.

"You waited for me?"

"Of course I waited for you. Did you think I was going to leave you here alone with this man?"

On our way back I told Mechel what had transpired and he saw how upset I was without my going into details. He said he was not surprised. I didn't know how to tell my father that I could no longer serve as his courier because I knew it would mean a loss of income. Mechel said to me, "Let me speak to your father privately. He will understand when I talk to him. Your father does not want you in danger and neither do I."

Looking back all these decades, it was at that moment my heart truly opened to Mechel Lieber. I began to understand how much I meant to him. He would risk his life for mine. He would be my anchor – together perhaps we would find a safe harbor in a better sea. However, at that precise time, I was primarily grateful that I'd had the courage to stand up to Sommerglick and that I had come out of that experience to find Mechel watching and waiting.

CHAPTER 6
Exile in the Countryside

1940. Spring in Krakow was a contradiction in terms. There was neither rebirth nor joy in this normally hopeful season. In April Nazi-appointed Governor Hans Frank had proudly announced his plans for the city. Krakow would be sanitized; in other words, "cleansed" of its Jews, making it the first and most completely Jew-free city within the so-called "General Government" of German-occupied Poland. The elimination of Polish Jewry was no longer simply a topic of conversation and the focus of fearful plans made for family survival. All Jews were to be removed, and we had nothing whatever to say about it.

For those born after the Shoah, it is important to remember that the Nazis were "brilliant" in planning and executing their unsurpassed evil. Their strategy was to implement the destruction incrementally; if they had come out of nowhere and begun suddenly rounding up Jews in city after city, conquered country after country, without warning, perhaps the outcome might have been different, and, one would hope, there might have been a quicker global response. One must understand that their moves against us were at first *relatively* benign, although clearly motivated by mindless prejudice and hatred. The measures they enacted were not totally unprecedented in the long course of Jewish history: restrictions on movement, prohibitions regarding certain jobs or vocations for Jews, marks on identification papers by race, and other forms of visible identification – most or all of which had been imposed on us before and thus did not immediately indicate to us that it meant our certain death.

Indeed, the forced resettlement of Jews throughout Europe into designated ghetto areas was not a novel idea thought up by Hitler's thugs. It was an unfortunate method used before to "control" Jewish populations. The first Jewish ghetto was established not by Hitler's Reich, but in sixteenth century Italy – in Venice.

European Jewry did not believe it possible that the early restrictive laws of Hitler's regime would devolve into deportations, gas chambers and the mass murder of an entire people. Of course there was alarm, and there was pervasive fear, but the genocide and annihilation of millions were concepts too preposterous either to predict or to comprehend. We had always been aware of prejudice. Who among us was not aware of the Spanish Inquisition? Our people had known endless rounds of pogroms. Our history was filled with stories of endless, intractable anti-Semitism and random acts of violence, but nothing ever, anywhere, was on the scale of Hitler's and his henchmen's "Final Solution."

Once we arrived at the moment in our history when SS troops would routinely grab infants and slam them against walls or murder them without hestitation, the height of heartlessness and depravity had been reached. Once random murders and mass slaughter became the order of the day, the fate of European Jewry was clearly in the hands of a demonic maniac and his armies and supporters.

The rumors about camps and forced labor and death were now confirmed truths. When these concepts and ideas entered our vocabulary as if they had always been there, it was too late for many things. Though it was now our daily conversation topic, it was too late to come together in a massive, armed resistance against the behemoth of wholesale death and destruction. As if mere civilians ever could have done so anyway! To the toxic Nazi soup was added another ingredient – the dispersal and systematic weakening of the Jews to the point where they were effectively unable to reach out to the world for help. This is only one aspect of the horrific "genius" Hitler's plans and of what happened during the Shoah.

They were always so many steps ahead of us, and also ahead of the ordinary righteous gentiles who cared about us. They could not resist effectively in vast numbers because they did not have much power either. The only way to survive was by your faith in Divine Intervention, your wits and intelligence and the longing hope of an eventual Allied invasion and victory, if only it would come in time.

Governor Frank was eager to show in the most dramatic way possible his allegiance to the Reich. What happened in Poland would eventually be recorded as the model of the war against Jewish life in all of Europe, not only in Germany and Austria. On May 18 the Nazis decreed that all but a handful of Krakow's Jews were to be resettled. About 15,000 Jews would be allowed to remain in the city but hardly as free citizens. They would all be confined to Kazimierz, the old and shabby Jewish Quarter of Krakow. There they would be forced to work for the Reich and contribute, against their will, to the war effort.

All of Krakow was closing in on us and moving away from our reach. Earlier in May, Governor Frank had made all the boulevards, major squares, common public areas and parks "off-limits" to Jews. We were living in Krakow, but the Krakow we had known – where our families had spent their lives and their ancestors before them for generations – was finished, forever vanished. Spring moved into summer, but for me there were no seasons. Everything was enveloped in threats and darkness all the time, every hour of every single day.

The Germans began to celebrate the beginning of the winter season and their Christmas celebrations in a most unholy way quite early in the year of 1940. Roaming bands of SS stomped all over Krakow. By now the very sight or sound of them marching down the street invoked physical nausea in me, and I know it caused dread among all Jews. December 5 and 6 that year were notable for a continuous rampage of terror, when the SS monsters raided homes in full public view, not even trying to hide the abuses and brutalities they inflicted on innocent Jewish families – a further indicator of our ultimate doom.

Entire families were thrown onto the streets without their belongings, without warning, and without a place to go. German officers and their families were arriving in Krakow in increasing numbers to carry out the orders of the Reich, and of course they had to be made comfortable immediately. Young Jewish men, healthy and strong, were among their easiest and first victims. The Nazis rounded them up and sent them to forced labor camps now scattered across the country. By the end of January 1941 Krakow's Jews had disappeared in alarming numbers. Some were expelled to neighboring towns. Some were on the run, and perhaps they survived. Others were in hiding elsewhere. The majority of Poland's Jews, as we know now, did not survive.

On March 3, 1941, our official confinement to the ghetto was announced. Notices were posted everywhere in Krakow. Any Jew remaining in Krakow had only until March 20 to leave or to accept complete and total confinement in Kazimierz, where there was already a serious overcrowding problem. We had a choice, if one can call it a choice. Jews could choose to go into the ghetto or travel to another location in the countryside. Most of the Jews who were already living in the ghetto decided to stay. They really did not have another option. Whatever presumed flexibility in the rules the Nazis professed in order to cover up their intentions was utter and false nonsense. Jews were not in a position to make decisions freely.

The choice of running from them required a substantial amount of money or items of value. To resettle in a Polish village in the countryside meant you needed connections, cash, goods to barter, or jewels, especially diamonds. Most of those living inside the ghetto had little money and not much of anything else. They were trapped. Even most of us outside the ghetto now had little left. Every Jew was locked into one form of trap or another. We were all in a prison under the mandate of the demons in charge.

Mechel's parents still did have some resources. They therefore were in a much better position than many others to make a decision, given the circumstances. Mechel's father knew people in a village about twelve miles outside of Krakow called Niepolomice. The Liebers had with great foresight already taken some valuable textiles from their store out to the village to be stored there for their use. These precious goods were safely in the hands of some of their customers who were longtime residents of the village.

For my family, the Lesers, these options were unavailable. We did not have enough money to live except day to day and that just barely. We had no contacts or acquaintances to help us leave, hide, or resettle. Tattiko and Mammiko did not consider resisting the ordinance nor did they come up with any escape plans. With very little discussion, it was decided we would go to the ghetto. That would be our fate and we would make the best of it. Although my parents acknowledged this sentiment only silently, I could feel it in the air and in my soul. They did not specifically say so, but I sensed what they believed. It was this: What had been lost could not be regained. Moreover I saw and felt something else in the texture of their movements and in their glances: They were anticipating that much more would be lost in the days ahead. They maintained their customary dignity, but they had been dramatically transformed by the ordeal that had come upon us. I was told to prepare to move into the Kazimierz Ghetto.

Before Tattiko and Mammiko got very far along in their practical arrangements for our move, Mechel intervened with fierce determination. Mechel was not going to give in to the Nazi plan for our lives without a fight. His strength of character was becoming clearer and clearer to me. Mechel was not a dreamer, or driven by imagination against reason, but he was propelled by the deep strength of his faith that led him to believe that somehow, despite all evidence to the contrary, we would survive. Mechel did not want to be separated from me, and he knew his parents could not endure it if he were to stay in the ghetto in Krakow/Kazimierz in order to be close to me. Mechel had a simple solution even in such complex times. He proposed to Father that he permit Mechel to rent a place in the country for our family. Mechel's solution would allow for both our families to be together in Niepolomice, and for us to be close to each other, and for all of us, hopefully, to be safe. This was not the time for false pride in such matters. Father accepted Mechel's generous offer immediately.

So we too would be leaving Krakow behind. We would be living in a strange place but we would not become a part of ghetto life where our every move could so easily be tracked, and where we could be rounded up so effortlessly and taken away. Mechel found very modest quarters for us. We would have one room in a typical, thatched-roof peasant cottage. Mechel and his family, he explained, would be just about the distance of a city block away from our cottage. We proceeded to make decisions about what few things to take with us into exile.

Mechel hired a horse and wagon for us. It was decided that our departure would be less obvious to anyone that might be watching if we followed his family out of Krakow by about two hours. Perhaps by paying outrageous bribes or giving away more of their valuable goods, the Liebers were able to pack their cart with substantially more than the Nazi orders permitted. They were not detained nor were they arrested, which makes me think it must have cost the Lieber family a great deal to leave with so many of their possessions. We were not so lucky in that regard. We would obey the Nazi's rules to the letter in order to avoid harassment and get out of Krakow without any more sorrow. We picked out our best clothes and packed them. I dressed in layers of clothing, dresses and blouses on top of one another, piling my clothing on in this manner to leave more room in the suitcases for other things. What wouldn't fit in suitcases, we tied in bundles.

Mammiko said to Father, "Remember to take extra shirts and your winter coat, and of course your *tallis* and *tefillin* (prayer shawl and philacteries)." Father had a problem with Mammiko's suggestions. He refused to take his winter coat, which he needed desperately, and instead chose to fill a large sack with *sefarim* (Jewish sacred books). Mammiko was exasperated with what she viewed as such an impractical decision and she expressed her feelings forcefully. Father responded with equal force. "Don't worry. *Der Eibeshter* (the Almighty) will protect me."

There we were with our belongings, some in tidy bundles, some in mere heaps, with suitcases jammed with things that mattered and things that did not, but that we thought might be useful. And, of course, we also took a few objects that reminded us of the life that was moving rapidly into our memories. A towel, a dish, a vase or a fragment of something that might be touched in a moment of despair to give us hope and to remind us that we had once been whole unto ourselves and part of a community – and that, with love of each other and our daily prayers to Hashem we might again, at some future point, return to wholeness.

Hitler was now issuing decrees quickly, one after another, and his minions dispatched the orders of the Fuhrer with enormous efficiency, all of them building up to the carefully planned and sequentially orchestrated crescendo of the Final Solution. By now, we were in a panic and knew that we were literally running for our lives. Millions of Jews were on the run from a centralized force of mass destruction. How the Jews knew that there was a Final Solution in place and when they knew remains a debate among scholars of the Holocaust.

By the time we were on our way to the village to join Mechel's family, I had grasped that Polish Jewish life as we had known it was being taken from us, but I still did not understand that we and every Jew on European soil were in mortal danger. If my parents understood the scope of the diabolical plan, they did not speak of it. No one spoke of events as being part of a larger plan of "extermination." We were simply trying to walk or run faster than the brigades of black boots that were marching forward to trample us and crush our civilization.

Our cart swayed and bounced along the road, just as cartloads of refugees had in previous times and, Heaven forbid, in times yet to come. We felt as wretched as we looked. We had to get out of the cart at one point and ended up walking most of the twelve miles, because even with only our limited possessions, the cart was still too heavy for the horse to pull safely. When we were just a short distance from Niepolomice, we reached a bridge over the River Vistula. There we saw what we all feared the most: a German checkpoint. Soldiers surrounded the wagon and demanded we take all of our things out for their inspection.

Father looked at the side of the road and saw hundreds of books that had been thrown into a huge pile. Even from a distance we could tell they were all Jewish sacred books, which undoubtedly were going to be burned in a giant bonfire, probably to the accompanying laughter of the Nazi soldiers. Ironically, the books were piled up in the middle of a schoolyard. Books of Jewish knowledge and Torah commentary were waiting to be burned in a place of learning. Nothing made sense any longer. One could only do what they told you to do. They were all-powerful and merciless. Father saw what was coming the instant we spotted the checkpoint. He was right. Determining that his sack was filled with sefarim, one of the officers ordered the soldiers to hurl them onto the pile with all the other sefarim.

Father was in despair. He wailed in a deep aching voice, "Now I have lost everything." I tried to comfort him and so did Mammiko, but he said to us very quietly, "I had stuffed all our cash between the pages. I thought the money would be safe inside the sefarim."

That was the moment when I became a person of action, instead of a passive and frightened girl going along with events and in constant terror of the next calamity. I did a brave and quite reckless thing. I ran like the wind after the very officer that had seized Father's sack of sefarim. I lied easily and shamelessly. I was going to get the books and the money back for my family and for my father's honor.

"Please! Please understand," I said to the officer in charge. "You see my father is a writer. He is a scholar. He needs his books. You can take everything else we have, please do that, but would you please permit me to go into the yard and get his books back for him?"

The German surprised me by speaking in a normal tone of voice. He looked at me with an expression that was mixed with contempt and some pity, but without compassion. "Well, go ahead, then," he replied.

I ran into the yard, and only then saw the massive numbers of books. I knew it was a fool's errand without my father next to me to identify his books. They all looked the same to me. I implored the German one more time, "I can't tell which are my father's books. There are too many. But my father will recognize his books right away. Would you permit him to come with me? May I call for my father to come to join me?"

One word settled our fate.

"*Nein*," he said roughly and aggressively. Any notion I might have had that a human heart beat inside the soft-spoken exterior disappeared in that moment, along with all that we had. In order to keep from being arrested, I did not argue with the officer. I did grab just one sefer. It was not Father's. I did it for an emotional reason and also as a symbolic gesture. It was a small act of defiance aimed at them all. I thought to myself, *you might burn all of these sefarim, but you will not burn this one. I have saved this one at least.*

Now we were completely impoverished, truly destitute. All that was ahead of us was the single room in the peasant cottage that Mechel had paid for. Father was stoic. Now, without any trace of emotion left in his voice, he told us firmly, "Der Eibeshter will help us. We will make it. We must not worry."

CHAPTER 7
Pretzels and Straw

My first view of Niepolomice was unexpectedly pleasant. For the first time in so long I was able to see the world again as a painter. It took me back to the more tranquil period at The Three Roses, when the troubles were beginning but before tragedy had entered my life. For a few seconds I allowed myself a tiny pleasure. I remembered Arek and his paintings. I thought about what it would be like to paint again, even to paint this village in southern Poland on the banks of the Vistula River, on the edge of a legendary forest, while on the run. The village had a lovely square, an authentic medieval castle of course, a church, a marketplace, and beautiful gardens called the Italian Gardens, which were really the gardens of a queen from an earlier century.

Niepolomice was a Gothic nobles' village, originally a royal playground for members of the Polish ruling class. It had been established early in the fourteenth century with the beautiful castle built by King Casimir III. Even the Polish queens loved to hunt the bison in the forests. It must have been the background of the stories of fairy tales for children all those centuries ago, but it would be the setting of different stories for children now. There had been Jews in the village as early as the mid-eighteenth century, numbering a few hundred. By the twentieth century a few Jews still lived there, among them some families that had been there for many decades. Now, there were several hundred Jews like us, all refugees, and all living with very little or next to nothing.

We felt we would be safe here. In truth, we would be in hiding but not in bunkers or hideouts like others would soon be in Germany, France, Italy, Holland, and elsewhere. Still it was exile. We weren't there secretly, but we did not have the run of the place either. Unlike those in attics or basements or in barns, we could at least walk in the woods and breathe fresh air. That much we had known before we left Krakow. So we entered the village with some anticipation of relief.

We were grateful that the episode at the German checkpoint with the sefarim had not turned into a major tragedy – how easy it would have been for all of us to have been lost forever right there. How easy it would have been to murder me when I ran after the solider and asked to look through the pile of sefarim. I had the sefer from the pile at the schoolyard tucked into my little bag. I would give it to Father as soon as we were settled into our new quarters. But I held it close to me for a bit longer to remind myself to be strong, to never turn from my faith in Hashem, in my belief in the strength of the Jewish people – and to remind myself that even I could be brave.

Any momentary feeling we had of finding a true retreat vanished when we were shown our living space. The cottage itself was very modest, but our room, the one room we were to live in, all of us together, was a hovel. It wasn't Mechel's fault; it was the very best that could be obtained, and it probably wasn't so cheap either. But we almost fainted when we saw it. Mammiko silently grieved at our fate. I was frightened to even touch her. I was afraid she might break apart.

How could this elegant and beautiful woman, so meticulous in her appearance and her way of running a household, endure such utter deprivation? Mechel had been waiting for us. We must have looked a mess to him after all we had experienced at the hands of the Germans at the checkpoint – and Father's loss of all his money and therefore our options, and now the hovel. Mechel's eyes were able to pierce through to the truth and see one's soul, and he quietly took it all in. Those eyes of his, which were connected to his heart and his brain, came to an instantaneous, impulsive decision, one that might have cost him his life. He decided that Mammiko and Tattiko needed to have something that resembled a real home, however humble it might be.

Mechel rushed back to Krakow! It gives me the chills to think of that decision now, but that is what he did. It was only a few hours since we had left Krakow. He went back to bring a few things to us from our old home. When he arrived at our former residence, everything was gone. Not one thing had been left. Not a blanket, not a mattress, nothing. A picnic had been made from our despair. Mechel returned to Niepolomice totally defeated, holding only one torn, striped linen towel. It was all that had been left behind by those who must have looted everything within minutes of our departure. We had left in such haste and with so few things that the opportunity to pick over the remains of what had been a family's life was too great a temptation.

Mechel did not like to be defeated. It was not in his nature and he couldn't handle it as well as some others might. He was clearly not himself when he came back to announce what he had found, or I should say, what he had not found. Then it was my own father who rose to the circumstances and gave us all a good lesson in survival.

"Look," he said. "We don't have much, but we have an oven. I will make bread. I will become a baker. Things will get better. You'll see."

We all looked at him with admiration and some disbelief. The name of the village we were in was derived from the name of the forest in which it was set, Niepolomny, which means "unbreakable." It was Father now who was unbreakable. Mammiko and the rest of us took the measure of our Father and we decided that this would be our life; we would be unbreakable as the forest, as unbreakable as Father.

There wasn't any flour, of course, and we didn't have money to buy anything, not even flour. So Mechel bought flour and gave it to Father. Father made a deal with our landlord and was allowed to use the oven in the cottage, which wasn't much more than a hut. He was only permitted to use the oven a couple of hours during the day, but it was enough. Father had decided that he would not make bread, which required more ingredients, but pretzels.

Once he had made chocolate pretzels, but they were part of his past and were now family history. These would be pretzels of survival. He had, oddly enough, a competitor in the village. However, Father's pretzels were far better and the word spread quickly, so we were once again engaged in a family business. However diminished our situation, we were on our way to a new life, hopefully without the thud of boots in the streets and the terror of the knock on the door. Before the pretzel business was under way in the hut, Father made delicious bread for us all to eat. We made the blessing on the bread before we took a bite. But it was the baking of the bread itself that was the blessing – Father's blessing to his family and evidence of Hashem's abiding presence with us in our struggle.

I speak about Hashem often, but I don't do so in a childish way or in any casual manner. We felt His protection in a very real way. We felt it when we prayed. We felt it in our daily movements. Hashem was woven into the very fabric of our lives, as He had been present continuously in the lives of His people down through the centuries. We did not have to convince one another that we should not abandon Him because the world was turning against us. We simply knew that we remained under His protection. We would never need to tell each other not to forsake our faith. It was too deeply imbedded inside each one of us, which was, despite everything, the biggest blessing of all.

We barely got by with the earnings from the pretzels. It was abject poverty. Somehow, we moved through each week – from Shabbos to Shabbos. There would be tiny bits of chicken to eat on Friday night, really just scraps of chicken. The landlady gave Mammiko the rough leavings from the wheat after she had ground it to feed her livestock. And here is the hardest thing to recall and to write: the good part of the wheat that the landlady so carefully ground was to feed her pigs. So there we were. Human beings, Jews, were living on the left-over wheat-straw that was not even fit for the pigs but good enough for Jews.

Mammiko took the straw and cooked it and cooked it in lots of water, trying to make it into something we could swallow without choking. It eventually became the consistency of rough oatmeal, but it scratched our throats as we ate it and was extremely hard to swallow. It also stuck in our throats because of what it represented: pigs' leavings.

The decent clothes I still had left I saved to wear on Shabbos, and that is when I wore the one pair of shoes I had brought with me. The rest of the time my siblings and I went around the village barefoot. Mechel got me a few things to sketch with and I thought I would draw some lovely scenes of the area, of the forest, the river, and the village. In my delusional state of mind, I thought people actually would buy my drawings. How foolish to think that anyone could be interested in buying art in a village during a hideous war.

However, I did produce a small amount of income for the family by making practical things that people did need and could buy from me. I knitted hats and mittens and I made some dolls for children and clothing for the dolls.

Whatever flour Father could afford to buy went into the production of the pretzels. He found someone who baked and sold bread for Shabbos on the other side of the village, but you had to cross a field to get there. Once Mechel and I, along with my brothers Ben and Tuli, all of us barefoot, crossed the field to buy our challah. Father had given me some coins to purchase the challah. I gave my brothers the coins so that they would go on ahead and get the Shabbos loaf. Maybe I wished to spend a few minutes talking to Mechel alone, or maybe I thought it would be nice for my brothers to feel they had done something for Father.

Before Mechel and I could catch up to them, they came racing back across the field with the challah in their hands. They had torn it apart and were gobbling it down. I wept with anger and with fear. Mechel saw how hungry they were and how young they were. We both knew it was not my fault, but I felt I had disappointed Father. Arriving back at our shack, I cried when I told my father it wasn't my fault. He was not angry with me but he was angry with my brothers. "You will not eat anything tomorrow," He scolded. They did not care; there was so little to eat on any given day anyway. For those few hours, they felt satisfied because their bellies were swollen with the bread they had eaten.

Not all the Jews were in the same misery that we were in. The native Jewish population of the village had not been robbed of all their possessions by the Nazis so they still had some money and goods to barter with the non-Jews. Mechel's family had put away a sizable quantity of textiles to trade for food and provisions. For other residents, it had come down to swapping their furniture and valuables for enough food to stay alive and enough wood to cook with and to stay warm.

Even in this remote village there were restrictions on Jewish movements and activities. We could not congregate in groups. This meant we could not use the village shul without risking our lives. Families or extended families could not walk together in the town square or the marketplace. The Nazi command did not remove the Polish mayor, as they had in other regions, but all decisions of significance were handled by the few Germans who had taken over the police station.

72

Father stayed glued to a radio he had managed to get out of Krakow. On it he heard the "news" but most of the time it was more rumor than news. And when it was the truth, you didn't really know how to assess it because we were so far from any urban area that might have given us access to more reliable information. We believed that by being far from a major city we would be in a zone of relative peace. It was a false sense of confidence in our future, and it was short-lived. All too soon, Father began to report the alarming things he heard each day. Now the rumors were real news reports. The ghetto areas were being sealed off throughout the country. And the Nazi troops were abducting people for forced labor, without warning and from a variety of locations.

The darkness that had descended in 1939 as Poland had crumbled instantly under the Nazi onslaught, now appeared to be a permanent night of fear, and worse than that, we all suffered from the most paralyzing of all human emotions: the fear of fear.

CHAPTER 8
A Bittersweet Wedding

I was seventeen years old. I had seen too much, experienced too much and yet I understood so little. My young brain already was filled with memories and images of terror and death. I was afraid to think about tomorrow, let alone the rest of my life. Mechel had a different approach. Each month his love and devotion for me grew deeper and more intense. He took care of things for my family and for his own. Ever resourceful and refusing to be swept away by the tidal waves of fear flooding other Jewish families in Niepolomice, Mechel was pragmatic but also oddly optimistic. Against this backdrop, Mechel asked me to be his bride. Not just to be his wife, but to be his bride.

What unthinkable language it seemed to me then. We were like little mice scuttling around looking for food, for bread, or for the mere crumbs, eating scraps not fit for livestock. We Jews were in hiding for our survival, or scurrying from place to place, families separated, all of us just trying to outthink, or maybe even outwit the ever smarter and increasingly efficient and powerful Nazi machinery. A wedding? We could not even gather together a *minyan* (quorum of ten Jewish men) in order to hold a proper Jewish wedding ceremony. What could he be thinking of with talk about a wedding? And what about Goldie? It was sad enough that she had been left behind in Munkach and was not part of our daily life, but to marry before my older sister was to forsake tradition – the gracious Jewish tradition of an older sister preceding the younger one to stand under the chuppah in marriage.

Mechel, as usual, was determined and would not let go of his notion of what was right and what was not, not only about our love but what was a strategically intelligent course of action. He made a flat and unemotional statement: "Things are only going to get worse, not better. We'll be sent off to some ghetto in the future, not to small towns like these and Lola will be safer married to me."

This was correct. The news we did get was increasingly grim and hopeless concerning the conditions and dangers for Jews all through Europe. Mechel's realistic statement about the shortened horizon ahead of us convinced me. Then, as he would do throughout our lives, Mechel surprised me. He turned again to emotion, to matters of the heart. "And we are in love," he added emphatically. I looked into those eyes, and knew at least one part of my future had been foretold. The rest would be a mystery. If there was even to be a future for any of us.

I knew how much Mechel loved me. I was then too immature to understand that what I felt for him even within the confines of our moment in history was indeed real love. There was not any question about his appropriateness as a husband. Besides having held a good job, he had been accepted at the legendary Lublin Yeshiva. By this time I knew him well, and we had already endured so much together. I had become more than fond of him. But no, not a wedding, not a commitment for an entire lifetime, not then, and not yet, as far as I was concerned. And a bride? Who, in her right mind, would wish to be a bride in such times?

I agreed to his proposal to the extent that I said he could speak to my father. What did I really want Father to say to Mechel? It is too long ago now for me to recall clearly. It is probably safe to say that I was ambivalent. Daily life and the anxiety of each morning and each evening had exhausted everyone. My father too was so worn down and tired and fearful that not surprisingly he agreed to Mechel's request that we marry. He was undoubtedly relieved that I would have a husband. Although he tried and mostly succeeded in managing to hide it from us, Father was not a vigorous man any longer.

My mother was also weary and walked around in a kind of perpetual state of traumatic shock. Her hair literally turned gray overnight. As an observant woman her head was always covered in public, but her hair had been a beautiful color. My parents had become old, seemingly in an instant. Sometimes, in a series of surrealistic visions, I see their transformation still playing itself out in my head. One day Mammiko, in resignation and defeat, asked me to cut off her hair. She meant she wanted me to chop it off, practically down to the roots. I did but wept silently as I did so. She said nothing, just sat, as I worked an old pair of scissors to the best of my ability. She looked off into the near distance with a mysterious and grieving look of longing. I did not think that her eyes were focused on anything in the room, but perhaps she was seeing a great deal, her knowledge and her wisdom allowing her to foresee what was coming next.

Marrying Mechel was like this for me: Everything was right and everything was wrong, all at the same time. He came from a good family; he adored me; he was a religiously serious man; he wanted to make life better for me. He was generous and kind to my family and dutiful, loving, respectful, and kind to his own. These were all good things. The conditions we were living under were utterly impossible and Mechel was right, they were going to become worse. We could not have a real wedding. I was too young and completely unprepared for the unknown sanctity of marriage vows and obligations. I did not think I could make a good wife, or even a real wife. These were all bad things and I thought should stop Mechel from persisting in his rush to make me his wife.

However, girl or woman, there would be a marriage. A woman of any age who is getting married, wants a real wedding, with food and family, and a lovely dress, and happiness and joy floating in the air around her. This could not be. I did not see how anything that even resembled a wedding could take place. Yet I knew that I had only one morally right answer to give Mechel. The answer was yes. I would become the bride of Mechel Lieber. Soon I would undergo yet another identity transformation. I would become Mrs. Lola Lieber. Urgency was the way we operated then in all things, from foraging for food to deciphering the news, to making a plan for a sad little wedding. We would do the best we could, and we would do so with faith and together as man and wife, as we tried to push to the side the ripples of apprehension that were as ever present as our daily prayers to Hashem.

Mechel was now operating with a new identity too. He was called a *chassan* (a groom). Despite it all, he would not be gloomy about our upcoming marriage. Mechel had joy in his heart and he arranged things so that they might look and appear at least on the surface as normal as they could be. The custom of our engagement ritual was different from that of other

Chassidic sects. We did not drink and toast a *l'chaim* as countless other Jews did and still do. Instead, it was understood that the chassan present his intended bride with an engagement ring. The bride-to-be then reciprocated with a gift of similar value. It was generally a watch or a gold cigarette case. Father had nothing to give; nothing was left.

Mechel, with an easy grace, without in any way humiliating my father, purchased a gold cigarette case, which he gave Father so that I could present it to Mechel as my gift of betrothal. Mechel had a diamond for me but he dared not have it set into a gold ring, as there was a regulation that Jewish people could not wear or own gold and silver jewelry. So Mechel presented me with a diamond and I sewed it very carefully into the shoulder pad of a coat. Mammiko gave me a simple ring with a diamond so tiny it would escape notice.

The wedding date was set for August 5, 1941. Because our engagement was now official, Mechel and I could walk together in the beautiful forest that surrounded Niepolomice. We enjoyed our walks together and I particularly welcomed the time to be alone with Mechel and talk with him. Father, however, was so strict that he sent my brothers out after us, and they would try to hide from us. They could not trick us, though, and Father could not be persuaded to stop sending child-chaperones to accompany us, even if he did not admit he was doing it. After the first few times, Mechel and I and my brothers just took it in stride, as a family joke of sorts. Father was very strict and nothing would alter that, not even an engagement.

We would marry on a Tuesday, the day in the story of Creation where Hashem states twice, not once, that what He has created is good. The date was set for after the Fast of Tisha B'Av (Ninth of the month of Av), which is the commemoration of and mourning for the destruction of the First and Second Temples. It marks the beginning of the scattering of Jews into foreign lands or what is called the Diaspora. For me, the wedding might just as well have been held on the day of Tisha B'Av, except that it would have been forbidden. But that is how sad I felt as the day drew closer for the ceremony. Looking back now, it seems incredible that we would marry even in that permitted time of year, because the scattering of Jews was happening again with a renewed kind of ferocity and destruction not dissimilar to that which our people endured in ancient times.

There was a little shul in the village. Rabbi Glazer agreed to marry us, but we would have to be married in the backyard not inside the shul. It was too dangerous to be married inside the shul. Jews were not supposed to gather together in groups of any size, but Mammiko and the rest of the family decided that we should have a proper dinner for a small number of family and friends. Probably in an attempt to add a cheerful note and the illusion of a true wedding celebration, the decision to serve duck was made. Everyone in that part of Europe loved duck, a true delicacy.

Well, we thought we had found the person who could get us duck. And so money was paid and the duck was to be purchased and prepared for our wedding supper. I did not have anything to wear. Even if we had been able to find a wedding dress in the town, it would have been a fateful mistake, as it would have attracted attention to us. So, I wore a suit I still had that looked fairly decent, and I wore a pretty flowered print blouse under the jacket. A kind young woman named Zosia loaned me a bridal veil. I was beginning to feel a little bit of happy anticipation: the Rabbi was kind; I had a nice outfit with a veil; we would have a dinner.

Ducks could only be brought into our area for Shabbos, so we had to pay our non-Jewish poultry agent in advance. Unfortunately, we had not chosen wisely. The peasant was so thrilled, we were told, by having some extra money, that he drank away our wedding duck dinner in a pub. We never saw him or the duck again. The money was gone, and there was no duck. Quickly, the wedding menu was changed and we would have fish. The women would make a nice fish recipe. A fishmonger was found and again precious money entrusted to him. Just as before, the money disappeared, the fishmonger vanished, and we had nothing at all.

It was Tuesday, the day of the wedding, and we had no food to serve. I began to sob. I did not know how I could stand under the chuppah in a rabbi's backyard, not even in a shul, and in addition have no wedding dinner. I was sure that I could not look at Mechel without crying throughout the ceremony. I began to sob uncontrollably. Frieda, my brother Moishe's wife, who loved me dearly, did not even need to ask why I was so depressed. They had risked a great deal to come to be at my wedding. She reassured me that she had a special recipe for sweet and sour eggs that would taste just fine. She explained that she would cook onions and carrots with salt and pepper, and vinegar and sugar, and then poach the eggs in this broth. The result would be "eggs that taste just like fish."

The entire family was willing to do anything within their power to reconcile me to reality and also to convince me that this would be a happy day. I am not particularly proud of how I behaved then, but I was barely eighteen, and it was *my* wedding. Despite the heavy anxiety and fear ever present in our daily lives, somehow my family devoted time and energy to ensure that I would become a bride according to our traditions and that there would be some joy as well.

Mechel's family had been in the textile and linen business, and as I have said, they had been smart enough to take plenty of material with them to our new location. They used their goods to trade or barter for food, and undoubtedly for that gold cigarette case. Mammiko and my mother-in-law were not especially close friends. They respected each other, each in their way, but they were different women from different cultures within the larger Judaic culture. Mammiko was warm and embracing and generous of heart and spirit. My mother-in-law had more difficulty with these sorts of emotions or, let me say, in expressing them. So, of course, it is easy to understand that a woman who is not naturally at ease or completely generous would find such times especially difficult. She was constantly worried about whether things would get so desperate that they would have nothing left to barter.

Mammiko was determined that I should have a fine linen cloth on our wedding table. She felt that at least there must be a right and proper setting for the meal. And it was important to her personally as Mammiko had so loved and appreciated fine and beautiful things. So she went to see Mechel's mother to ask if we could borrow a tablecloth. My mother-in-law simply could not rise to the moment. What would happen if it became stained at the supper, and then they wouldn't be able to sell it if things got that bad for them? I am sure Mammiko must have tried to reason with her in the way that only Mammiko had of dealing with people, but even Mammiko could not convince her to part with the tablecloth for the wedding.

When Mammiko came back and told me the news, I was angry as well as sad. In a pique, I dramatically stripped a sheet off the bed, washed it and said, "So fine, this is what will be. A sheet for a tablecloth and a feast of sour eggs." I had to walk through the fields to get to the home of the rabbi, and I did so barefoot. This was hardly a pretty picture. An angry, weeping, confused and terrified young girl virtually running through the fields without shoes to attend her own wedding!

My mood did not improve when I arrived for the wedding. I wept constantly. I really recall almost nothing of what was said. The only words that come to me are those of my father, who still called me by my little-girl name of Leiku and said to me, "If Hashem gets us through this war, I promise you, Leiku, I will make a wedding for you as no girl has ever had. Please remember my promise to you." He said it to me repeatedly but it did not stop my crying and the last times he said it his voice trailed off into the air. Nobody should have been promising anyone that they would have anything in the future and Father knew it as well as the rest of us.

When I sat down to the feast and tasted the eggs, I almost became violently ill. Poor Frieda! She had worked so hard on them, but they tasted terrible to me. I did not like their bittersweet flavor. I tried to turn away so that I could conceal the disgusting taste I had in my mouth. I hope that I did so in time to keep from hurting anyone further. Even now, it is a taste I try never to remember and if I smell anything that reminds me of those sour wedding eggs, I leave quickly!

The mayor of Niepolomice was a good man. He rented us, now a married couple, a room in his home. There at least we felt safe. I wept that night after the wedding. I said that I had been married without a minyan, outside of a shul, had not worn a real wedding dress, and that our wedding feast was nasty and sour, and that his own mother would not loan me a tablecloth. When I had calmed down, Mechel put things into the perspective that was required for me to start down the road leading to me becoming the woman I would eventually become. He soothed me and was not at all cross with me for the rash way I had been complaining. This is what he said: "We will survive this era. It is temporary. There will be a world after this. And, if we don't survive, Hashem forbid it, but if we do not, at least, Lola, at least we have been married."

The first thought that went through my mind was what an awful and ghastly thing to say to me on what is supposed to be the happiest day in my entire life. Then I was truly quiet for the first time in days, and finally understood how realistic his words were, and how compassionate a man I had married. I stopped crying and just fell asleep, secure and content that this wise and tender man – was my husband, Mechel Lieber.

CHAPTER 9
Autumn Leaves of Loss

1941. The summer of my wedding moved swiftly into an unusually early autumn. The air was cooler; the trees started shedding their leaves sooner. First, the leaves turned a bright, fiery red that would become a significant metaphor for us as they then dropped to the ground, dead and useless.

My parents had gone to Plaszow, a town near Krakow, to be with Frieda and Moishe. They were taking an enormous chance to make a family visit to Frieda's family, the Singers, at such a time, just as Frieda and Moishe had taken a chance to come to my wedding, but we could not persuade them to forgo the trip. They dressed in peasant clothing, which had become the costume of choice for Jews on the run. During their absence, the reports of Nazi advances continued to cause alarm among the community in Niepolomice.

We were in the process of determining the accuracy of the information. Were the Germans really coming into the provinces, to places as marginally Jewish as Niepolomice? We did not have to wait long to receive confirmation of the reports. Early one morning, without any warning, as was their system, Nazi soldiers appeared at the home of my in-laws. My father-in-law, Hershel Lieber, was ordered to board a large flatbed truck. They were taking fifteen or twenty able-bodied men away from the village to work, but only for the day, they said. Hershel Lieber would return that night.

My father-in-law was a man with merry eyes. He smiled a great deal of the time, and his eyes smiled right along with him. I thought in the time that I was permitted to know him that much of Mechel's personality and character came from his father. He loved Torah study. It wasn't that he did it because it was an obligation; he studied for the love of it. He had a well-groomed, square beard and his eyes were an unusual color, a sort of blue-gray. In Krakow he had owned a fine linen and textile store.

Their home and their store had been in one of the finest areas of Krakow before the darkness of Hitler's reign. By the time we got settled into Niepolomice, he had aged in accelerated time like my own father. He spent most of the time during that exile studying and taking naps. He no longer had any work and no professional identity. However, his Jewish identity and his faith in Hashem were untouched, despite it all. I do not remember my father-in-law ever uttering a cruel word or complaining about our situation. Of course, his face was etched with the same lines of loss and anticipation of loss as the others'.

As the Nazis hustled Hershel off to the truck, my mother-in-law ran after him, frantically screaming, "Give me your sefer. You need to work. You won't be able to work if you are studying." In that instant, I forgave my mother-in-law completely for her ungenerous behavior about the table-cloth. She knew that he was already too old to work and so it was unlikely he was going to a labor camp. Maybe she thought that by not having his sefer, he might somehow convince someone that he should be spared. I cannot know what she thought in those seconds, except that I am sure she had the same fears that consumed the rest of us.

Hershel Lieber would not return that night or any other night. He had gone off into that seemingly endless night that had fallen upon us. It was as if we were in a suspended state of permanent autumn, where all we would ever see would be the leaves falling as our families were taken from us, one by one, forever, unto eternity.

The last image I have of my father-in-law is him refusing to give back the book. "The sefer will protect me," he said. It did not protect him from death, but I understood even then that he meant a more important and spiritual form of protection than the black-and-white temporal reality of life and death.

The truck drove away. My mother-in-law was hysterical and could not be comforted. Each man on the truck had been given a shovel. It was not long before the rumors came to us that the men were commanded to dig their own graves with those shovels. And then we heard that the Germans had executed them all in the woods near Niepolomice. These were the very woods where Mechel and I had somewhat playfully courted just a brief time before. It was now a forest with blood-soaked earth – they had become the woods of death. It was a season of the leaves of loss, of powerlessness, of senseless mass murder.

We continued to tell Mechel's mother that as no bodies were found, perhaps Hershel Lieber really was in a work camp somewhere and someday we would all be reunited. She would not be consoled. She was not a stupid woman. She had deep faith but there was really no hope, and we knew he would remain forever absent. We could not state that aloud, even though we all felt the scorching burn of the truth in our hearts.

It is now known that an execution of Jews in the Niepolomice forest occurred on or around August 27, 1941. A small gravestone records the names of only thirty-eight victims. Hershel Lieber's name is not among them, but Eliyahu Richter testified to Yad Vashem that in fact 612 Jews from the area were murdered, including his own father. My dear father-in-law, a pious and good-natured man, who might have become a treasured member of my extended family, was undoubtedly a victim of that massacre.

Autumn advanced inexorably in somber tones and a sense of unremitting despair settled on all of us. Our landlord, the mayor, came to Mechel one night and said that he had been informed of the Nazis' next planned move on the Jews of Niepolomice. They intended to dispose of us like garbage, since that is how they thought of us. We would disappear, truckload by truckload. They would come back for the men, just as they had for my father-in-law. Again, they would say that they were only taking the men away for a day's work. Then, once all the men were removed, they would come and eliminate all the women and children.

The mayor was well informed. Jews were fleeing the countryside now in fear and moving back into the urban areas – to the Jewish Quarters, the ghetto areas. However, there was no more room in the designated Jewish Quarters. The Nazis wanted to simplify things. They wanted to kill us before we could reach those fragile and temporary havens inside the cities. The mayor took enormous risks when he told us that he would help us escape. Landlords, mayors, and other municipal officials were turning Jews over to the SS throughout Europe. His actions, had he been caught, would mean his own death, or deportation followed by certain death.

He said we could either go back to Krakow or into the Bochnia Ghetto. We would, he said, have to leave in the darkest of night, by train, again dressed in the fake peasant attire everyone was in the process of acquiring. The Bochnia Ghetto had been established in the spring. Mechel and I reasoned that it might not yet be overcrowded, and we might be saved if we could get there without being arrested. We asked that he allow my now obviously widowed mother-in-law to leave with us. And, of course, we asked that he somehow find a way to get my parents to Bochnia. He said he would help our entire family, but that he had to do it gradually, one by one and two by two, in order to avoid suspicion.

The mayor told us which night we would leave and reminded us to be sure we looked like peasants. He said he would personally drive us to the station because as the mayor, nobody inspected his car to see if he were engaged in illegal activities. He might not have saved all the Jews of Niepolomice, but what he did for us was indeed a righteous act and one that he did at mortal risk to himself and his family. We prepared to leave the village forever. We gave away whatever we had – clothing, dishes, a few miscellaneous articles, a bit of household bedding. We did not want to appear to be what we were: Jews running away to the next hoped-for refuge.

I kept two towels. One was decorated with a pretty fringe; it was a lovely piece of linen. It was the only possession I would retain from my Krakow life. I dressed in many layers of clothing and looked convincingly like a chubby little peasant girl, padded as I was and carrying a basket of eggs to sell at the market. I did not look back at the station or take even a fleeting last glimpse at the village. Neither did I say good-bye to Niepolomice in my heart. Instead, I uttered my own fervent and silent prayer to Hashem to bring all of us together again inside the Bochnia Ghetto, whatever its conditions might turn out to be.

Today Niepolomice is a suburb of Krakow. About 21,000 people live there now. It enjoyed a temporary spurt of tourist activity following the release of the movie *Schindler's List*, because it was the location chosen for the film. It continues to attract a fairly steady stream of upscale tourists with a well-advertised, half-hour bus ride from Krakow, combined with a fine dining experience at the old and famous royal castle. Throughout the 1990s it made a successful transition from communism to capitalism and a number of large international industrial conglomerates set up their operations there.

The Jewish population today is, at last count, exactly zero.

PART FOUR: INTO THE GHETTO

CHAPTER 10
Bochnia

I slept for much of the way to Bochnia. Mechel stayed awake and alert, ever aware that danger could arise at any moment. I woke up and asked him if we had much further to go, and he answered, "Lola, we are very close now. We are almost there." I wondered how close we were to destinations worse than Bochnia. I was consumed with worries, large and small. How would we find the ghetto? How would we arrange for a place to stay? What questions would be asked? I was afraid that even among Jews there would be too much fear and desperation to permit generosity. Privately, I questioned whether we should have stayed in Niepolomice and taken our chances.

We got off the train at the Bochnia station. It was immediately obvious that we would not have any trouble in finding our way. The ghetto was fewer than two blocks from the train station. Its presence screamed its location to us: "Here it is – a segregated encampment for the unwanted!" It was enclosed within a wooden fence at least seven feet high, with razor-sharp barbed wire sitting on top of it all the way around. I couldn't help thinking as we made our way to it what a far cry it was from the beautifully decorated ornamental gate of my Munkach garden. Several Polish guards were posted at the main gate. They looked menacing to me and I feared we would be stopped and turned away. In fact they were totally indifferent to us. We just walked into our new and circumscribed "Jews Only" ghetto community.

We knew Mechel's sister Baila, who lived there had already taken in their mother. She had also made room for two of Mechel's unmarried sisters and another sister with a tiny baby. I had no expectation that they would have space for us, but Baila didn't think twice about it. She welcomed us into her home, which was only a shack, as if it were a palace. "*Hashgachah pratis*," Mechel said quietly, which means God's personal providence or His protection had accompanied us on our journey.

The one redeeming feature of Baila's little house was that it stood on the edge of a field. This gave us an illusion of freedom rather than the constant reminder that we were in prison. If we were not on the run from the hounds of death, the Bochnia Ghetto, modest and cramped though it was, had an almost comfortable feeling. This sounds impossible, but it was because of the imposing presence of the Halberstam family, who also lived in the ghetto. Bochnia had long been one of the Bobover Chassidic centers. All Bobover Chassidim were an extended "family" with many branches in many cities. The main branch had in turn propagated many Chassidic off-shoots, one of which was securely in place in Bochnia. Mechel, I knew, had strong family ties to the Bobover Chassidim. I had met some of them during our enforced day of labor in Bobowa.

As it turned out, a young but important Bobover rabbi led the Chassidim in the ghetto, thirty-four-year-old Rabbi Shloime Halberstam, the grandson of the founder of the Bobov dynasty. Even though Mechel was not formally a Bobover Chassid, the presence of the young rabbi comforted both of us immediately. Within a couple of days we found that many others in the ghetto were also strengthened in their courage to survive just by the knowledge that he was there, living among us.

Bochnia, now a place of sorrow and loss, had a complex Jewish history. It was then about 700 years old and had been part of the lucrative salt-mine trade in the area. Jews were expelled from Bochnia in 1445 for allegedly criminal behavior in commerce. However by 1555, under King Sigmund Augustus, Jews were invited to return under a formal treaty that permitted Jewish trading in the salt industry. A mere fifty years later Jews were again expelled, due to another series of trumped up accusations of illegal dealing. Jews were excluded from Bochnia until 1862 when, under Kaiser Franz Joseph I, new legislation, which was part of a general emancipation in all of the Austro–Hungarian Empire, granted Jews the right to live and work in the city.

Mechel's sisters gave us a tour of the ghetto and we learned many things we had been ignorant about until our forced residence there. Before the war the entire population of Bochnia was 18,000 and of those, 3,500 were Jewish. When the Nazis established the ghetto there in the spring of 1941, it, unlike the Krakow Ghetto, attracted people. Thousands of refugees crowded into the area, which became a petri dish of disease and germs. Jews who were expelled from many other places thought of Bochnia as a destination of last resort. By the time we reached the ghetto we heard daily reports that Nazi extermination squads (*Einsatzgruppen*) were murdering people en masse in Krakow.

Bochnia's ghetto had a Judenrat and also a Jewish police force called the *Ordungsdienst*. These Nazi-driven agencies expected the Jewish "overseers" to carry out their orders against Jews. The Jewish officials and policemen tried to *not* obey the Germans and to *not* get caught at it! The Judenrat established workshops to turn out goods for the Germans. As usual, our survival mentality told us that if they found us at all useful they would not kill us.

Mechel and I were evidently part of a larger movement of people into Bochnia. The population of the Ghetto grew to 15,000. As overcrowding worsened, people had fewer and fewer choices. The Judenrat decided where we would live and with whom we would live. Several families were crowded together in two- or three-room apartments. All cooking stoves were removed. Basements became apartment dwellings. Furniture of any substantial type was forbidden. We ate in a communal kitchen, tiny rations of wretched and often spoiled food. People smuggled and traded in order to "buy" more rations and eat food that was hardly fit for animals. As if to finish off any attempt to maintain a civilized or dignified existence, we had to bathe in a public bathhouse.

Yet to the best of our abilities we courageously tried to continue our life and maintain our sanity and our civility. A number of the secular Jews were unionists and were in touch with left-wing Poles. Many of them were helpful to other Jews and some of them became part of the tiny Polish resistance movement. Zionists continued to find one another and to train for emigration to Eretz Yisroel (still pre-state Palestine at that time). There was a rumor the Zionists were planning an "armed" physical resistance against the

Nazis and their Polish collaborators. We all assumed it was only a fantasy, however intense the desire was to fight back.

Traditional and more observant Jews practiced a different form of resistance. We considered the strongest form of protest as the attempt to practice as many mitzvos as we could in whatever ways we could manage. There were secret minyanim, and even a Talmud Torah study group. This may make it sound as if the "resistance" was calm and efficiently organized, but it was far from that. At any hour, we could hear the weeping and shrieking all around us of those who had lost another family member. Sometimes the worst sounds of distress were from those who simply could not bear to continue any longer.

From August 25 through August 27, 1942, the Nazis swept through the ghetto in what was called an *Aktion* but which I preferred to call a pogrom. Much of the ghetto's population was taken away. At that time we did not know where they were taken. Later we learned that thousands had been taken to Belzec and all had been murdered. We lost the chief rabbi of Bochnia, his wife, and two of their three children then. About 1,000 people were left behind because they had labor permits known as *Kennkarte*. Several hundred more had survived by hiding. In a short time, the ghetto was again overflowing with refugees on the run.

By now, another word came into use: *convoy*, which became part of our vocabulary of survival and existence. The new inhabitants had escaped from the convoy trains of cattle cars taking people to certain death. Others had arrived for other reasons. Mechel and I were part of the latter group. The Judenrat was reorganized and the Bobover Rav was put in charge of the Hygiene Department. Not only did this protect him, it enabled him as the director of hygiene to turn a public bath into a *mikveh* (ritual bath). He was the chief rabbi of the Judenrat in many ways. He made sure that Mechel and I received a civil marriage certificate.

Although completely illegal, trading and bartering with the Poles continued. People pried loose boards from the surrounding fence and slipped in and out. Forced labor continued, but at an increased pace of operation. We observed these wretched workers on our first day in the ghetto, slaves really, filthy, starving, and exhausted. People talked of "being prepared" and building "bunkers" before the next Aktion could claim more lives.

The rest of my family had gone to Plaszow but I had no word from my parents. I was terrified lest they had perished. We wrote letters and more letters. I felt we were throwing pieces of paper into the wind. Then someone inside the ghetto's network of operators informed us that there were clandestine couriers. These were people who knew exactly how and when to slip in and out of the ghetto undetected. When a courier was about to leave on a mission to deliver or barter goods, you were told where the courier was going. You could ask him to help you. We asked one going to Plaszow to deliver a message to my father and to bring one back from him – if my family could be found. These couriers or messengers could be relied on to bring true news back to the ghetto about the fate or the whereabouts of loved ones.

Concern about my family weakened me. Mechel was concerned about our own fate as well. He felt certain that we were slated for slave labor. After only a short time in the ghetto, Mechel felt that we had made an error and that we should have headed back to Krakow and into its ghetto. Part of Mechel's thinking derived from a piece of information he had obtained. A friend of his named Lazer Landau had influence in Krakow. Someone inside the Bochnia Judenrat made a deal on our behalf, probably with a bribe, so that we could venture outside Bochnia and return to Krakow again.

I found the very basis of the trip puzzling and the notion that Landau could help us dubious. However, Mechel's ideas and strategies had been the means of our survival until then and we ordinarily worked as a team. I thought it unlikely that we would want to associate ourselves with Landau, who could only have influence with the Nazis because he had become a *Kapo* (Jewish policeman). When we reached Krakow all my worst fears were confirmed. Lazer Landau was a pompous and unsavory man. He greeted Mechel in an overblown manner. He was indeed a Kapo dressed in the showy and disgusting white uniform of a Kapo.

"Mechel, Mechel, where have you been all this time? I've wondered about you." It was as if he was playing for an audience, and I guess he probably was. Mechel took him through our journey up until then, and introduced me as his wife. He said that officially, nobody knew that we were not still in Niepolomice, because we had not been officially registered yet in Bochnia.

"No problem then," said this unctuous man. "I will get you an apartment and you can become one of my special deputies."

With great drama, he officiously called over one of the Jewish police-men working under him to arrange immediately a good apartment for us. I stood frozen in place unable to speak, move, or look at Mechel. Had Mechel broken down? Was it all too much for him? I couldn't imagine that this was my Mechel. My husband would not be a toady to a Kapo.

Just about when I was gathering the words to ask Mechel to step out-side with me to have a word, Mechel took my arm. He motioned to his friend Landau that he would be right back.

"Lola, I had no idea he would be this bad. I want us to be safe and to live in an apartment that is decent and of course I need and want a job. But Lola, no, not this, to be a Kapo's assistant? Never."

I had tears in my eyes and Mechel did not know why, and I did not tell him. I was crying with relief because I had no reason for concern. Mechel would never do anything dishonorable. I told him I shared his revulsion. I added that I thought Landau was completely repulsive.

It was Shabbos, but Mechel and I had our priorities straight and we knew Hashem would want us out of there as fast as we could go. So we ran to the train to get away from Krakow and returned to the Bochnia Ghetto determined to try to make the best of it. Mechel was committed to finding a way not to end up as a slave laborer. Mostly, we were in constant apprehen-sion about another communal slaughter in the ghetto. Not long after our bad experience in Krakow with Kapo Landau we learned that he had been murdered. He had been hanged.

At the same time that we learned of Landau's fate, rumors increased about Plaszow. It was now clear that Plaszow was being "cleansed" of its Jews. Everyone was being deported either into the Krakow Ghetto or to Auschwitz. Because of the age of my parents, Mechel and I were certain that my parents would be sent to Auschwitz. I could not speak for several days as the rumors began to contain more details. I was polite to Mechel's family, but I was withdrawn and depressed.

November brought the news we had hoped wasn't coming. The Jewish police officers and the Polish guards spread the news that Gestapo forces were getting ready to surround the ghetto. This was the signal for another major Aktion. Everyone said to one another, "We must hide. We need plac-es to hide immediately." I thought it was a ridiculous idea. Where would we hide inside the ghetto?

"We must dig real bunkers," the men said to each other. I thought that was even more impractical. If you dug bunkers you had to do something with all the dirt you excavated. Where would we dispose of barrows full of fresh soil? A novel idea was presented during a family conversation; I don't remember who presented it. I think it came out of a more general discussion that we would be doomed if there were another Aktion. Even though we were getting frantic and our nerves were fraying, we were in survival mode. Close to our shack was another shack and next to that was an old shed, which stood right by an old chicken coop. Needless to say, it was empty of its chickens. We decided we could dig a deep hole between the shed and the chicken coop. Because the coop was lighter than the shed, the men would pull the coop over the hole as camouflage. This would be our bunker where we would tough it out and survive – just like those who had escaped the last Aktion.

Everything was done secretively and mostly after dark. Everyone in the family participated in some manner. Most of us helped dig. Right behind the backyard of our shack was a frozen pond. Gentiles used it as an ice-skating rink. We waited until it was late at night when there were no skaters left to watch us. Then one by one, we crawled through a hole we had made in the fence. We made holes in the ice with our shovels and carefully poured soil into the hole in the frozen pond. We did this slowly so that there would be as little trace of earth on the surface of the ice as possible. I think we deposited tons of soil. Maybe we did. When we were done, we had a bunker with room for seven people.

This was an amazing accomplishment. We "furnished" it with bedding, medications, food rations we had hoarded, blankets, and pillows. I made a rag doll for Marilka, Baila's three-year-old daughter, and tucked it into her pillow hoping it would comfort her. The family complimented me and said they were impressed that I was so calm. I wasn't calm. I was frightened to death but too exhausted to express any emotion. We had become slave workers for our own survival.

Our construction work was completed just in time. On November 10, 1942, the ghetto became silent and absolutely still. That was the way it was before an Aktion. Rumors spread, people scattered into hiding places and holes. By mid-afternoon we knew the Nazis would come that night. Just before sunset their troops gathered at the gate and moved in, quickly deciding who to arrest and deport. With grim and swift determination we headed for our chicken coop's "basement" earth bunker. Steps before we reached it, a man in his twenties startled us, saying that he was Moishe Schiller. He claimed he was a Belzer Chassid and a friend of my brother Moishe. This seemed plausible to me because Moishe had spent so many years studying in Belz.

However this Moishe was no longer a serious Torah student. He had turned into a Jewish informer to the Nazis. He admitted it without any shame. I was breathless with disgust. My spine tingled with fear and hatred. He was the worst possible form of a Kapo, and our fate was as much in his hands as in the hands of the Nazis. Was it the taste of power and authority that had corrupted a man like Schiller? Or was it his way of deciding for himself that he would survive whatever the means? The mentality of the Jews who became informers and Kapos for the Nazis remains a wound in the soul of all Jewish people. I wanted all of us to live, but I knew none of us would slip to these depths. I wanted to harm him physically, but I knew better. Such behavior would only take me to the same unholy gutter he was in – and besides, what damage could a petite young woman do to a strong man?

He was talking quietly to Mechel. From Mechel's face I could see that whatever Schiller had said alarmed my husband. Schiller raised his voice so that we could hear his threat clearly. "Look, I know all about your hideout. I know where it is and how you built it. Unless you take in my mother and my sister, I am going to turn each of you in to the Germans, right now."

I walked the few feet to where they were speaking and stood next to Mechel. Silently we looked at each other in utter helplessness. We had no option.

"Okay," Mechel said, as if he had another choice. I nodded to Schiller so he knew I would not try to trick him. There wasn't enough room in our bunker for more than our own family. I did not know what we were going to do, but I knew Schiller's family was going to benefit from our hard labor. I thought perhaps Mechel and I could find a tiny hole somewhere else. But we had to make sure the rest of our family got into the bunker.

My mother-in-law spoke first. "I am an old woman now, and my life is not that meaningful. I will stay in the house. Whatever happens to me now is meant to be – it is not in our hands – it is all in Hashem's power. You must use the bunker."

I began to dispute my mother-in-law's reasoning. I did not want her exposed to the Nazis. Then another of Mechel's sisters, also named Lola, who was single, spoke right after my mother-in-law, "I will stay with Mama. You have only been married for one year. You must have a chance to live your lives. You have an opportunity to make a new life. There will be years ahead of you when this ends. Please, understand it is our wish that you go into the bunker."

We stood together without speaking. We knew they were making the ultimate sacrifice. They were trading their lives for ours. Their view was that their survival wasn't as important as ours. How can one respond to such a sacred action? One cannot. On one side of us was the traitor Schiller, and on the other side our family members, ready to die for us. I couldn't tolerate the idea and I spoke.

"No, we are young and we can work. They will want us as workers. Even slave labor is better than nothing." I didn't convince any of them with my arguments, for we all knew that in the last Aktion the Nazis had scooped up young and able people as readily as the old and fragile ones. I insisted again we would not go into the bunker. I was adamant and Mechel did not object.

With love and tenderness, we got our family members settled into the bunker. As soon as she crawled into her space I made sure that Marilka found the doll. With bitter resentment I watched Schiller's mother and sister get into the bunker. I locked my jaw and ground my teeth in order to keep from talking. Mechel's face flushed with the same rage as he yanked the chicken coop securely over "our" bunker. We turned and walked away aimlessly, not having any idea what to do next. We had no place to hide. We were defenseless. Just then we heard the voice of someone we knew. It was a member of the Jewish police whose last name was Farber. "What are you doing outside now? Get into your hiding place. You must have a bunker or something. Everybody has been working on places for weeks. Don't you know the Nazis are here? They are upon us. They will catch you immediately."

We had different feelings about Farber than about Schiller. Farber had been drafted into the Nazi-controlled Jewish police. He had not volunteered. I was crying, "Farber, we have no place to go. We do not have a hiding place now. We had one but Moishe Schiller took it away from us." Farber spoke without emotion but with urgency. "You must come with me. I am going to take you to where my sister and her children are hiding. I will warn you that it is not completely safe or secure. The concierge knows about our place."

It was a choice between nothing and a sliver of a dream that we would live past the Aktion. "Alright, we will go to your sister's hiding spot," Mechel said.

Farber explained exactly where to go and what the signal was that would permit our entry. The Farber family owned a tannery on a brook. As in all tannery operations, it had a large round metal tank outside. We were to climb the ladder on the outside of the tank and then knock in a special sequence that was the same beat used by soccer fans of a particular team. His sister was already in the tank with her small daughter and a baby. We waited a bit longer than was prudent because I was hoping to get another invitation. If the concierge knew where Farber's family was hiding and there were babies who cried, it seemed like a lost cause. However, as sunset approached we knew time was running out, and so we went to the tank.

Our knock was recognized and we were admitted. We lowered ourselves into the tank. We were crushed next to Farber's sister and the child. Water was up to our knees. On the bottom of the tank we felt water rats scurrying past our feet and legs. However disagreeable rat bites might be, the rodents were the least of our problems. Farber's sister was very intelligent in survival skills. She had breast-fed the baby and given him sleeping drops so he would not cry. However, she was having trouble holding both children at once. The little girl would have drowned if her mother had lost her grip on her. Mechel immediately grabbed the little girl and held her tightly. I could see the child cling to him with relief and with perfect faith in Mechel. Now we waited silently. I felt the rats nibble at me. I shook my legs, one at a time. It was happening to all three of us. We did not speak. We just waited and waited.

The night passed. We could see the morning light coming through the cracks of the tank. The day went on and on, and another night came. There was nothing to do. Perhaps this was how it would end for us. Maybe the Nazis had liquidated the whole ghetto, including Farber, the entire Judenrat, and all the Jewish police. We did not know what to think and we could not talk. We assumed that even whispers might echo to the outside. Finally at 2 a.m., gunfire pierced the silence. Then we heard shrieks and wailing that could only mean one thing. We heard the German's guard dogs barking as they moved around sniffing for humans. At one point the dogs were outside the tank, barking. They had our scent even though we were standing in water. We heard a German scream, "Here. Some of them must be in here."

We stood absolutely still. We did not want to ripple the water, in the event that even a drop would spill to the ground from a small opening. We held our breath. After what seemed hours, the dogs and the Germans moved away. I heard one shout out the command, "Let's go. Come on. We're getting out of here." There was a long interlude of absolute silence again. Finally we heard Farber's knock, or what we hoped was Farber's knock.

It was Farber. We had not been detected. We were alive. We climbed out of the tank, helping with the child and the baby. My hands were frozen and the rope in the tank had cut into my skin. My legs were swollen and my feet felt useless. I did not think I could walk. Farber put the ladder back up at the tank, which we had thrown down, once inside, at his instructions. He took us back to his place and we sat in the kitchen. We asked how bad the Aktion had been and his reply was that it had been terrible. "Many have been killed."

He stopped and looked at us. I knew that he was in shock about something that involved us. I realized Mechel couldn't speak, so I asked Farber, "What do you know about our bunker? Is everyone safe?"

"I saw something." He said it in a faint whisper. "I want to blame Schiller, of course, but why would he want his own mother to die?"

"WHAT?" Mechel screamed. I had never heard Mechel scream before that moment.

"Mechel, Lola, I saw bodies. I don't know…I don't know who they were, but I saw dead people around there. You know the Germans had the dogs out everywhere. They were sniffing people out of deeper holes than yours. The Germans found lots of people."

We sat for a short time more with Farber and his sister and her family. We knew what we might be facing. If the absolute worst had transpired, we knew what our faith would require of us. We slowly began to walk to our bunker. It was sometime between three and four in the morning. It was still dark. I thought if the Nazis had found the bunker, they discovered it because of the massive amount of dirt we had poured into the frozen lake. On the other hand, if Schiller knew about the bunker, it wasn't really much of a secret. I did not continue further with my internal debate. I consoled myself with the thought that since we were safe, and they had been willing to sacrifice their lives for ours, everyone else would be safe and alive.

I was concerned about something else. Farber said he had seen dead people. According to Jewish law, you must stop if you find a corpse, no matter what or where, and provide proper burial. This is the commandment of the Torah and an especially important one to all Jews, even those who are less observant than we were. We knew what would happen if we did not take care of the bodies, even of strangers. In the previous Aktion anyone not buried was thrown into a common furnace and burned up like debris. I saw an empty pushcart and said to Mechel. "Let's take this with us. It's dark and nobody will see us. We are going to need it if we must bury the strangers in the Jewish cemetery." Mechel nodded and we proceeded to our bunker, with Mechel pushing the cart.

CHAPTER 11
Kaddish

Everything was gray and frozen. The odor of death hung in the air, stinging our nostrils. As we turned the corner toward the chicken coop we saw at once it had been pushed over, exposing the hole. We ran across the frozen ground, sliding and almost falling. Mechel held tightly to the handles of the cart, as if that alone would keep him upright. We looked into the bunker pit and saw Mechel's mother, Baila, Marilka, and seven-year-old Itche. Each of them had a single bullet hole in the head. Their bodies were frozen in death and by the winter's cold. What I remember most vividly is that their last and final living expressions were also frozen in place. Each face bore testimony to the eternal silent scream of all the millions of Holocaust victims. Marilka was clutching the tiny doll. Even as she died, the doll had stayed with her. I dropped to the ground, put my hands over my eyes, and began to scream.

Mechel grabbed me, stood me upright and whispered. "Silence! Do not utter a word or we will be next."

It took all my self-control not to continue weeping. Then I witnessed my Mechel as he absorbed the loss of his second parent and other family members. His courage was without limit. My mouth and face twisted into a silent scream mirroring our deceased family members, but Mechel and I remained absolutely mute. The crush of grief inside me was so great I thought my heart would burst out of my rib cage.

Mechel said in a flat and soft voice. "Be strong please, Lola. We have work to do."

One by one we loaded our dead family members into the cart. I had thought we would be using the cart to perform this act of mercy for strangers. We had a short time to get uphill to the Jewish cemetery and dig graves and return before dawn. The cemetery was in the ghetto but up a steep hill. We would become visible to the Nazis and their accomplices by daybreak. Mechel found an old shovel close to the coop. It was probably one we had used during our valiant construction efforts. He wheeled the cart, slipping and sliding on the ground. I carried the shovel, and kept one hand on top of the bodies, so that they would not fall out. This was the one and only thing we could do. It was not a great thing, but it accorded dignity and respect to our beloved dead.

Sobbing together, we began to dig a common grave. We determined very quickly that as we had only one shovel we could not get more than one grave dug before dawn. Mechel broke the frozen ground with the shovel, and outlined the dimension of the grave. He shoveled out clumps of frozen earth. We took turns using the shovel. One of us would shovel out more dirt, and the other would use his or her hands, which soon became painfully frozen. Our adrenalin was running at abnormal levels to enable us to dig a grave large enough and deep enough so quickly. As we finished I said to Mechel that even in this we had been given extra strength.

Just then who should appear at our family's grave but Moishe Schiller! He was no longer filled with arrogance and bravado. He looked gaunt and pale. We stared at him but said nothing. His first words were like a slap in the face reminding us too clearly of what he had become, as a Jew and as a human being.

"It is not my fault."

He was guilty and felt he needed to defend himself although we had not accused him or spoken to him. "The dogs found your bunker and one of those gentile kids out ice skating probably told the Nazis. It isn't my fault," he repeated the phrase several times. We turned to continue working on the grave. He continued, "So that's how it must have happened. Look, it also happened to my mother and to my sister."

The word "it" was the most upsetting thing he said – as if "it" were a random accident at the side of the road, or something as simple as breaking your ankle ice-skating. He had not come to express remorse or regret. He was on another mission. "You are digging a grave for my family too. They must go in here. You will bury them too."

Mechel had the shovel in his hands and turned and glared at him with a murderous look. At that point, may Hashem forgive me; I could have killed Schiller myself. In moments of profound despair and rage, morality is tested. For a moment Schiller appeared to be frightened of Mechel but quickly got nasty again. "You will do this – or else."

Mechel turned from him without response. He motioned to me to move a few feet back to find a location for our family's common grave. With renewed vigor, Mechel began to dig again. We started all over. Turning his back on Schiller and refusing to speak to him or face him was a stronger indictment than killing him. We are accountable only for our own deeds on earth. So we did again exactly what we had done before: we dug with the shovel and our bare hands. By now our hands were not only frozen but blistered and bleeding, and the flesh was shredded. When we finished it looked as if we were wearing red gloves. But we were in such agony from the tragedy that we could not feel our own physical pain.

I did look back once to watch Moishe Schiller bury his relatives in the grave we had made. He was using his hands to cover them up with the earth we had dug. Suddenly, we heard loud German voices. We were far back in the cemetery and were able to back up against the fence in a spot where the Nazis could not see us.

"Moses Schiller," they screamed. Obediently and immediately he ran to his masters, dutifully and respectfully bowed, and said, "*Jahwohl*." A moment later we heard one gunshot followed by a second. In the still hazy light, we watched two Nazis toss Schiller into the grave with his family – the very grave we had dug. The Nazis got back into their automobile and sped out of the cemetery. Schiller had served his purpose. The Nazis no longer needed him. He wasn't any more important to them than any of the rest of us.

We gently placed our five family members into the grave, a common grave that would never be marked with a gravestone. We buried three adults and two children. I stooped down and placed the doll back in Marilka's arms, just as it had been when we found her dead in the bunker. It is not a Jewish custom to bury people with objects, but I knew that there would be no objection from anyone in any Jewish community to what I had done. I knew that Hashem would understand my need to do this.

Dawn was breaking and we had to return or we would be detected and killed. We took each other by the hand and started our descent back into the central part of the ghetto. Before we left the cemetery, Mechel and I suddenly looked at each other in wordless reproach. We had forgotten something essential. We had not said *Kaddish* at the grave, our prayer for the dead whose very words celebrate and revere life. We crept back to the freshly made grave and, in unison but silently, we began to recite the words of the Kaddish. However, when we reached the words that begin "…*oseh shalom*…" we spoke out loud in soft but clear tones. The Nazis had taken almost everything from us, but they would not take this. We would say at least a few lines of the Kaddish audibly and fearlessly.

As we left the cemetery we heard a car coming up the hill and quickly hid in the low bushes. The car was looking for Jews burying their dead in order to kill them just as they had executed Schiller. The Nazis in the car did not see us. We waited until we were certain they had gone. We had intended to take the cart back with us but now decided to leave it in the bushes. Jews returning to the main part of the ghetto with bloody hands and a pushcart was not a wise idea.

Entering the residential streets of the ghetto, we saw the same car a few yards away. The Nazi in the passenger seat screamed a warning over a loud-speaker. "Do not go to the cemetery. Anyone caught going to the cemetery will be shot." We had escaped death by a hair's breadth. As we came to our shack an old man came out, delirious with starvation and loss. "Bread? Do you have a piece of bread for me?"

After what we had just been through, and all that had happened in the ghetto, I wondered how anyone could think about food. When I looked at him again I felt compassion. He was old, frail, and practically near death himself. He was undoubtedly alone in the world without anyone to care for him or love him. I said quietly, "No, we do not have any bread. I am sorry." The poor soul shuffled away asking the few other mourners that had come outside if they had any bread. He was literally out of his mind from both starvation and fear.

As the day became brighter we felt a new bleakness confronting us. The streets of the ghetto ran red with blood. There were bodies and parts of bodies everywhere. It was all-out war and we were on the battlefield, standing in the front lines. A few others began to emerge from shelter. There had been more wanton killing than ever before. The last Aktion had been terrible, but this was a massacre. So many dead! With the exception of our family and Schiller's, there would be no proper burials, and no ability to sit *shiva* (mourn) for anyone. We had been deprived of our families and of our rituals. Thousands had vanished. Those who had not been killed on the spot were on their way to their deaths. Those not slaughtered inside the ghetto or who had not starved to death were loaded onto open freight cars and transported to the camps.

Farber found us and told us everything he knew. The Nazis had not bothered to take the sick and the elderly out to the forest to kill them this time. They simply shot old people in their beds and slaughtered the sick inside the hospital wards. Thousands had been marched into the central marketplace for selection. Only about 1,700 were deemed fit enough to become "essential workers." In many cases the Nazi commanders lost patience with the lengthy process and randomly killed hundreds more. They lit a fire for mass cremation, throwing bodies onto the pyre. Farber told us he could tell from the screams (which we had heard in the tank at the tannery) that many had been burned alive.

Mechel and I looked at each other in disbelief and in gratitude. We had become "survivors." We did not know how much longer we could stay alive, but we had been spared when thousands of others had not. This caused us to feel what so many others who were "lucky" would also feel: survivor's guilt. Inevitably we asked ourselves why we had been spared when so many had not, when all our own family had perished. It weighed on us and would continue to haunt all of us who were saved from the bloodbath. We were now eyewitnesses to the "Plan" – namely, the liquidation of all Jews.

We went into our shack to clean up from digging the graves. The Nazis had not looted it. Whatever we had left had not been taken or disturbed. This time the Nazis were looking for humans, not silver, because they knew none of us had anything left to steal. *We* were the objects they were seeking to dispose of as efficiently as possible. Having lost so many family members, our little hovel suddenly looked spacious, which made me start weeping again. What a paradox! We had more space because they had killed our family. We were starving too. I was sorry I had been harsh in my first judgment of the old man who had begged for bread. I now thought we too needed to eat some bread, but I had no flour or yeast.

We knew there would be a period of calm after such a massive Aktion, so I went outside without fear. I knocked at the door of the place next to ours. It was empty. I opened the door. Everyone was gone. It was obvious what had happened to the family. Either they had been slaughtered on the street or were in a freight car. I saw a sack of flour in the pantry. I took it and went to the communal kitchen, and baked *bilkelech*, rolls made of challah dough. It was a Thursday and I had made enough for us to have for Shabbos too, but we were so hungry we ate everything I baked. I made another batch to barter for provisions.

Thursday we had buried our family. Mechel and I had miraculously survived. Friday I baked challah. We did not "celebrate" Shabbos, but to the best of our abilities and resources we kept the day sacred, a tradition whose lights we saw dimming before our eyes with each new week. In the Bochnia Ghetto, Shabbos at least was a constant living and breathing prayer to our continuing existence; it was testimony to the thousands of years of our people's survival and to our covenant with the God of Abraham. Observing Shabbos and keeping it holy was also our way of honoring the lives of all of those who had been taken from us in the Aktion.

More than anything else, we were saying, "Hashem. We will never depart from You or lose our trust in You."

CHAPTER 12

A Modern-day Queen Esther

A day or so after experiencing such horror and loss, I was standing outside of our shack and looked up to see my father walking toward me. I couldn't believe my eyes. Tattiko and Mammiko had heard the rumors of the Aktion in the ghetto and made their way as quickly as they could to Bochnia, bringing with them Moishe and Rosie and Rosie's parents. Words cannot convey the immense relief and gratitude I felt to be reunited with part of my family. It was Sunday and we had started to move around outdoors – but with extreme trepidation. Except for the joy of being with my own family, however, we continued to feel depressed and filled with anxiety. There were ominous warning signs of worse to come – new posters were pasted up everywhere.

Everyone had to report to the Judenrat building on Monday. The reason was clear. The Nazis wanted to know how many of us had survived. We did exactly as instructed – everyone did. It was far too risky to disobey such orders. When we arrived at the building that housed the Judenrat, an official told us it had been decreed that Bochnia would become a labor camp. A high-ranking Gestapo officer by the name of Schomburg had arrived to supervise the census and to issue identification cards.

We were still unregistered, a fact that so far had kept us from being taken to the labor camps or the day slave labor jobs. We had somehow gotten by with bartering our Judenrat rations. Whatever few possessions we still owned had already been used for this purpose. Our life now consisted wholly of the struggle to find something to eat and the continuing battle of wits with the authorities to avoid being picked up for labor or killed.

We lined up in front of a tiny window at the Judenrat. We noticed that the other ghetto residents who had survived the August Aktion seemed as depressed and defeated as we were.

"It is starting all over again," one weary woman said to me.

I thought she was ancient. I realize now she was probably only in her forties. Another woman said, "This is what they do. Today they will register only the ones they want to keep. They will take the rest of us away." She paused for a few seconds, and then said, "But you might as well know now that sooner rather than later they come back for everyone, whether you are registered or not. It is only a matter of time. This is a waiting game and they are the winners." Everyone in my family heard what the woman said. We were shaken by the specter of what would happen to us.

I was the first in the line for our family. I approached the window, which was little more than a slot. Looking through it I saw two Gestapo officers sitting inside. The older man was seated in the rear and the younger was attending to the window. He asked me for my name and place of birth. I stated my full legal name and my date of birth.

"I was born in Munkach, Czechoslovakia." The word *Munkach* came out louder than I had intended. I guess it was a memory I unconsciously needed to cling to in that moment. The older Gestapo agent came forward and asked me to state again my place of birth, and I did.

I watched him coming toward the window and I realized he must be Schomburg. He stared at me for a moment. He did not frighten me. He said to his deputy, "That girl does not get a Kennkarte." Still looking at me, he ordered two Jewish policemen to come over to the window. He said to them, "Bring this young girl to me tomorrow at 9:00 a.m."

I quickly stepped out of line. Mechel and the rest of my family had the wisdom to do the same. We moved swiftly out of the building in the hope that they did not apprehend the others. We went back to our quarters. Mechel and I were as agitated as we had been before the Aktion. Tattiko and Mammiko kept asking each other, "What does he want with her?" Mechel looked knowingly at them each time they asked the question. It was well known what high-ranking Nazi officers did with young and pretty Jewish girls and women. I did not let the family know that I too knew exactly what this meant. I assumed that the worst would be demanded of me. And I had already made up my mind that I would rather die than submit to a Nazi officer's demands.

Nobody slept that night. Before 9 a.m. two Jewish policemen picked me up to deliver me to Schomburg's temporary place of residence outside the ghetto. Mechel was told to stay behind. We all assumed that this meant that they were aware of how the situation would shape up – I would be "requested" to become a friend or companion to this high-ranking Nazi. What other reason was there for him to want to see me? Father ran after me and, putting his hands on my shoulders, whispered to me something that froze my blood, even though in my mind I was already prepared: "Remember Leiku, *Kiddush Hashem*! – It is better to die for the sake of Hashem than to allow the Nazis to molest you."

Tattiko was crying. Mammiko was crying. Mechel was paralyzed by his inability to protect me. Although Mechel knew I would never give in or surrender, he surmised what they were likely to do to me when I refused to cooperate. Mechel knew my strength of character and unshakable moral code from that dreadful night at Sommerglick's house in Krakow. Mechel also knew how I had kicked the Nazi soldier when they invaded our family's apartment. He feared that I would not come back at all if Schomburg wanted the usual favors from me. He was distraught he could do nothing to help me. Mechel and I could not force our eyes to meet. I asked the Jewish policemen if they would stay with me. They said they would, if permitted, and would do anything to help me that was in their power. But they had no power over such things and I could see they were also distressed.

As we set out, the people of the ghetto came over and wished me well. They were praying for me. Word spread overnight that I had been summoned to Schomburg's residence. He was occupying a confiscated house. We knocked on the door and the young Gestapo man from the day before escorted us inside. Schomburg appeared in the parlor. In elegant and refined German he asked me to sit down. His voice was gentle and soothing. This made me even more suspicious. I looked directly at him and saw he had a paternal expression on his face. He did not look at all like a predator.

"Tell me, were you really born in Czechoslovakia?"

I said yes, and I mentioned Munkach again. He asked if I spoke Hungarian...I nodded...and Czech...I nodded. He kept looking at my yellow armband with the Star of David. I spoke to him in Hungarian and then in

Czech. He complimented my language skills and also said that I spoke a particularly fine German. Mammiko had been right, after all, about learning German. For all the wrong reasons, my ease with his language was paying off for me. I knew it was the language of Goethe and Schiller, but German had also become the language of these killers. Schomburg knew many things about Hungary and Hungarian customs. Because of Mammiko's background I was fortunate in my knowledge of Hungarian. He was well acquainted with the Hungary of Mammiko's youth and not the Czechoslovakia of my childhood. It didn't matter. He asked if I liked Hungarian goulash, and certain Hungarian pastries. I knew all of these things, of course, and we chatted about them. He was completely at ease with me and I began to relax, although I never took my eyes off the swastikas on his uniform. He was acting in a kind and fatherly manner toward me but still, he was my mortal enemy. He asked me if I knew a certain Hungarian song and I did.

He pointed to the Star of David with contempt. "You should not wear this." His eyes suggested that he might actually be a decent man, although that sounds strange. Was he a righteous gentile? It is a claim I can't substantiate, but he was very gentle with me and I could see his intentions were honorable. Schomberg came a bit closer to me, and he tore the Star of David off my clothing and threw it away in disgust.

"You are a very lucky young lady," he said to my confusion. He asked his deputy to approach. "She should have an *Auslaender* (foreigner's) certificate." I wasn't sure exactly what that entailed, but I knew it signified that I was a foreigner, not a Pole, and that could only be good.

"This young woman need not wear identification as a Jew. She may move around and travel as she chooses from town to town. She does not need to live inside the ghetto."

He turned, "You are free, and you may leave this place with your new Auslaender papers."

Free? I was free to travel around Poland and I could leave the ghetto? What about my husband, my parents, my brothers, my sister-in-law Frieda? To leave them behind was not something I would do. His generosity and the accident of my birth would be worthless unless I was brave enough to take the next step. Before I lost all courage, I said, "I am not alone. I am married. I can't be free unless my husband can join me."

"You are married? How old are you?"

I made myself older. "I am twenty," I said. It was a fairly dumb lie because my age was on my birth certificate, but I was by now sure that he intended me no harm.

"Where is your husband now?"

"He is at home in the ghetto with the rest of our family. We are all from Munkach."

What a total lie that was! Mammiko and I were the only ones from Munkach, although Frieda was born in Slovakia and Mechel was officially of Czech birth. I dared not think of the repercussions if he found out the whole truth about everyone. I didn't know what we were going to do, but he said that we should all come back and get our papers and then we would all be free to leave the ghetto.

His deputy was confused, so Schomburg explained it to him. "Czechoslovakia is not under the control of the Reich. All Czech citizens in Poland are Auslaenders, aliens. They are, by law, exempt from the laws we have enacted here in Poland. They are not under any of the restrictions, including the ghetto and all the rest."

"All the rest" was the Aktionen and the murders and the bunkers and the filth and the squalor of the ghetto. It was the constant fear of death and torture and loss upon loss. I had been declared a Jewish foreigner out of the control of the treacherous arms of the Reich. I was overcome with gratitude and I kept saying thank you in German, "Danke schoen, danke schoen, danke schoen." I got up and I kissed his hand. I staggered to the door and the policemen helped me out. As we were leaving he reminded them, "Bring this young woman's relatives to the Judenrat tomorrow morning at 9 a.m."

The Jewish policemen and I approached the gate of the ghetto and saw people clustered around it awaiting my return. Mechel and my family reached my side first and we embraced and wept. Many had been praying and hoping for my safe return. One of the policemen made a statement to the crowd, which had grown rather sizable. He explained that I had not been harmed, that because of my birth, I was a Jewish foreigner and entitled to official certification as such. The Bobover Rebbe walked home with us. He stayed at my side and said to me, "The *Ribboino shel Oilam* [Ruler of the World] has chosen you to be a modern-day Queen Esther. Mechel told him my Hebrew name *was* Esther. It would turn out to be more prophetic than Mammiko and Tattiko could have known when I was born.

I didn't understand the reason for such joy on the Bobover Rebbe's face. I was not Esther. She had saved her entire nation. If we were lucky the next day, I would save my immediate family. However, later in the day, the Rebbe came back with his brother-in-law, who was the Limanover Rebbe. Again, they said, "You have been selected by Hashem to become a modern-day Queen Esther." I told them I appreciated their compliment but I was hardly on the level of Queen Esther. They explained why I was wrong. The Bobover Rebbe did most of the talking. One of his Chassidim was a young man who could carve letters into small rubber balls and make rubber stamps to use on inkpads to make false papers. With my new status, we would have a model to use to make counterfeit documents that the Nazis would believe were authentic. Without my knowing it, my conversation with Schomburg had opened the doors to liberation for many others.

We worked that night for hours. Together we produced thirteen false documents in one night. We only had two legitimate documents to copy – Mammiko's and mine. Mammiko's papers were truly Hungarian, and mine were Czech. Both Mammiko and I were multilingual so we inserted official-sounding phrases here and there on the other fake birth certificates. Mammiko was very clever at wrinkling them and pouring a little tea here and there to stain the papers so they looked old. We worked on through the night in the cellar with no concern about rest or sleep or food. As a high-ranking Judenrat official, the Bobover Rebbe had the use of a typewriter and a large supply of good-quality paper. We made Hungarian birth certificates for the older people including my father. We made Czech ones for younger people.

We also forged documents for members of the Bobover Rebbe's family. This is what the Rebbe had meant when he said I was a modern-day Queen Esther. I was helping to save part of the Bobover dynasty and others. I was humbled by the experience of the forged papers. From the hopelessness of the cemetery a few days before I had progressed to the miracle of my encounter with a Nazi officer named Schomburg. Mammiko was the final judge of what passed muster and what did not. Some of the papers looked pretty terrible, but Mammiko had an eye for this. She added little stains or smudges, and put extra fake stamps from the collection of rubber balls. She was a terrific forger. It was hardly a joyful time, but at last we felt we were gaining some control of our destiny. And so, yes, in a small way, we took some joy in what we were doing. Maybe these Nazis were not as smart as they thought they were.

Mammiko did not have to go to the Gestapo office the next day because she had her papers and now we knew that was all she needed. Everyone else went with their totally false and freshly produced Czech and Hungarian identity papers and gave them to the Gestapo agent in charge. They passed without comment or even a close inspection.

It turned out that my brother was the most gifted forger of all of us. He began by producing documents for his wife's family. They were so good and looked so authentic that the demand for his skills grew. He began to produce documents regularly. The Germans did not know how to check their origins or even read what was printed. In a short time, there seemed to be more Auslaenders in the ghetto than Polish Jews.

Since we could leave the ghetto legally that is what we did. Mechel and I rented a room in the home of a gentile family a short distance from the ghetto walls. In a few weeks, my parents and the Halberstams did the same thing. We did not wish to live too far from the ghetto. We now had more reason to fear the virulent anti-Semitism of the Poles than the Nazis. Poles who recognized Jews without Stars of David demanded to see documents. Many of them were illiterate and even those who weren't could only read Polish. Being accosted by Polish thugs on the streets or streetcars posed an enormous risk. It didn't take long for us to realize that our freedom to move around outside the ghetto was in reality restricted to the rooms we rented. Of course we knew we were not in danger of suffering another Aktion like those who couldn't get out of the ghetto. In our initial delight at being let out of the ghetto we had thought for a fleeting moment we were truly free. Of course, we were not. In order to keep from becoming unredeemably depressed, Mechel and I stayed in our room and made up games to play.

I think you would call what we did a form of the game of charades. We created "costumes" out of whatever clothing we had and put on disguises. Mechel loved to pretend to be different things and I would have to guess what he was. He changed his appearance drastically with only a few "props." We actually were able to laugh together. We were so much in love that rather than being bored with each other and with having to stay inside in such confined quarters, we grew closer. One day Mechel put on a truly ridiculous outfit and said, "Guess what I am." I couldn't guess.

"I am a monkey."

"You don't look like a monkey. You are standing too tall to be a monkey. You need to hunch over." Our bits of foolishness mitigated slightly the tragedy surrounding us.

We lived in every moment of each day. We had some books that had belonged to Baila. We read a great deal, and often read aloud to each other. I sketched portraits too, mostly of Mechel and of those we had lost. I made a few sketches based on my memories of the garden at Munkach. And I got the idea I could crochet and sell things, but there wasn't a market for fancy needlework of any kind. We were allowed to use the landlady's stove and ate only kosher foods, but of course a kosher kitchen was out of the question. One moment we were quite happy and played charades; the next we were very low and sad. We davened, knowing we did not possess the keys to the future or to the gates of life which might or might not be opened for us. Only Hashem had that knowledge.

Time had no meaning for us any longer. We did not keep a calendar. We knew when it was Shabbos each week and that was about as complicated as our date keeping went. One day, however, Mechel realized it was Purim. Purim was very important to us, now more than ever since the Bobover Rebbe had said I was a modern-day Queen Esther. "*Ta'anis Esther*," said Mechel, "the Fast of Esther is upon us." He sent someone to the ghetto to get a *Megillah*, which is the book that tells the Purim story, the story of Esther, and is traditionally read on Purim. The holiday fell on March 21 that year, and I made a special candied delicacy called "*noont*" made of honey and nuts, and I took it to the Bobover Rebbe, who lived two houses away. He received us with warmth and his eyes flowed with tears when he saw the traditional Purim gift I had made for him. Normal Jewish life and its cycle of holidays and observances had become so difficult that this small gesture was of enormous significance.

The plight of our rabbis had become increasingly difficult and tragic. Some of our people had lost their way, and the rabbis went to incredible ends and efforts to restore their faith. As public figures and as obvious Jews, they were always on the Nazi's list of the most wanted. The Bobover Rebbe remained brave and heroic, but he had a new vulnerability that pained me to see. He had shaved his beard and cut his peyos, which was a very intelligent thing to do. Yet it was difficult to see him this way, deprived of his public identity as a Jewish religious leader. His sister Gitche spent more and more time with us. She was afraid she might be apprehended when she was with her brother and sister-in-law.

Word circulated that another Aktion would occur soon in the ghetto. We knew only too well what it meant for those trapped behind the ghetto walls. The Bochnia Ghetto population had grown again and now reached 5,000. Those coming in were more desperate than the ones who had come before. Bochnia was now the only remaining ghetto in the region. Also, the word of Schomburg's kindness to Jews had spread. It would turn out that I was not the only one he had helped. We heard now that after the last Aktion the Nazis were turning the Bochnia Ghetto into a labor camp and dividing it into two areas: Ghetto A was for those with labor permits who could work; Ghetto B was for everyone else. The workers also wore another patch besides the ubiquitous yellow star: a white patch on their left arm for instant identification as workers. Husbands and wives and families were now separated from each other. Bartering had finally become impossible without risking your life. It was a dance of death. Ghetto A was being worked to death and Ghetto B was being starved to death.

Life on the outside was also becoming hazardous beyond belief. At every corner a Pole might scream out that there were Jews walking around without their yellow armbands. Gestapo men would rush over and demand papers. By now there were forged papers everywhere not just in Bochnia. The Gestapo had figured out our deceptions and were on the lookout for false papers. Sometimes Jews got away with it and sometimes not. Many were beaten and battered and left lying on the ground. Some died this way.

Mechel was far more adventurous than I. I didn't like him to do it, but he circulated around town to gather information. I would worry until he came back safely to our room, but I knew there wasn't any point in asking him not to leave. He was getting important information on the progress of the war. It did not seem that there would ever be any relief from the Nazi advances and what appeared to us at the time as victory after victory.

Mechel and his friends and acquaintances were tracking developments. The only place where it was still safe to go was into Slovakia from Poland, and then on into Hungary. You had to get to the Slovakian border by some form of vehicular transport. Then you were on your own to get to the Hungarian border. The issue was not only the danger of crossing borders. The hardest part was finding the money to pay someone to drive you to the Slovakian border without turning you in. The Nazis were offering twice the amount of money to inform as the Jews were being charged for transportation. Everywhere signs warned Poles that anyone found assisting Jews to escape would be killed. And these were serious threats; they murdered any Poles who were caught helping Jews get out.

One day Mechel came back from his rounds about town and said he had found "our man." The man was a coal hauler and was said to be very reliable. He had been tested before and was trustworthy. His truck had been outfitted especially to get Jews out of Poland.

"We will crawl on our bellies into the space between the fake truck bed and the real one," Mechel said. "He puts the false top on and covers it with his load of coal and wood. He drives us to a remote place in the woods, and then we have to cross the mountains on our own and on foot."

I didn't see how we could work this out. We didn't have enough money and we didn't know these mountains. But, as always, Mechel was a man with determination and a plan. There was no stopping Mechel, and I knew it was the right idea. What was the alternative? We had figured out by now that the Nazis were not just engaging in random acts of violence and killing. They had a precise plan of action. Every single Jew in Poland was to be murdered. The fact that we had survived to this point was a miracle. My parents, Moishe and Frieda, and my youngest brothers, Tuli and Ben, were with us in Bochnia. We needed to get everyone out with us.

Jews who had money were willing to part with every last coin they had to leave. There was no illusion that anyone would be spared. It took thousands of dollars per person to arrange an escape. This sum was real gold dollars, not paper money or zloty. Strange as it may seem, some Jews still had this kind of money, even after all they had been through. Some had found a way to keep or to hide a reserve of "hard" money. Savvy businessmen had sold their businesses for hard currency before the restrictions and the Aryanization began. Others had emptied their bank accounts and converted the money into gold before the Nazis seized accounts. Still others had enough valuable possessions and jewels hidden to turn into real money. Mechel and I had no money to spare, only barely enough for our room and meager food supplies. What we did have plenty of was time and the patience to plan the best method of escape and how to raise money. I was blessed with Mechel's unfailing ingenuity and optimism.

Rabbi Halberstam, the Bobover Rebbe, was still living practically next door to us and was part of the strategy sessions. He had made contact with a number of Poles working in the underground truck "business." These were freelance entrepreneurs who were also risking their lives; they set the fees and they had rules. They accepted only those who could be trusted to stay silent while hiding in the truck's false compartments, and all children had to be heavily sedated. At the border zone, passengers were to leave quickly and on foot. Some of these trucks, we were told, had the capacity to take fifteen people at a time.

The basic economics of supply and demand held true in these dealings as well. The haulers saw the demand and prepared to find those who were prepared to purchase their services. Polish brokers sprang up as the demand increased. Finding an honorable broker was as important, if not more important, than finding a trustworthy driver. Liaisons developed between Jews and Poles who formed human smuggling rings in which both sides profited. It was inevitable. There is no question that the Poles who undertook these trips were courageous beyond a simple desire for money. After all, they could turn anybody in and get twice as much from the Gestapo. And there were a few who did the work because they believed it was the moral Christian thing to do. In most cases, however, these relationships were based on a partnership of the cagey and the caged.

Our truck was not large enough to hold fifteen people. It would take seven, at most. Therefore we would have to go in shifts. We had learned that the smaller trucks were safer with less chance of betrayal. The sum we needed to pay the liaison brokers to arrange our escape was astronomical, even for those times. I despaired. Mechel felt that this driver was the only one we should use and I did not have reason to argue. After all, Mechel was the person doing the arranging, meeting in secret, and had already placed himself in a position of extreme vulnerability. Mechel was given a contact. They were wealthy Jews who wanted to escape with their families. In our private talks, Mechel and I called them the Millionaires.

We met. They were in their early fifties. This was an almost ancient age for the survival game. One of the men was as shell-shocked as an infantry soldier. His fear was palpable – evident in his expression, in his speech pattern, and even his breathing was that of someone in trauma. He was the representation of all the fears that Mechel and I had been able to repress – because of our youth and our love. We both worried about whether he had the psychological stamina to undertake the harrowing ride in the truck and the hike through the mountains, although his emotional state seemed more problematic than his physical condition. In any case, we did not have a series of people lined up and waiting to come along with us and pay the way for our entire family. We made our deal with them. They agreed to supply the money and we agreed to supply the strategic planning.

Mechel arranged all the details. The truck would go up into the High Tatras, about forty miles from Bochnia. It was the mountain range that separated southern Poland from northern Slovakia. Then we would get out of the truck and would be met by a mountain guide. It turned out to serve me well that I never paid any attention in my geography classes and did not know the facts. The highest peaks in Poland reached 8,000 feet in altitude. The passes into the Slovakian territory would be at about 5,000 feet. If I had known this I probably would have put a stop to the plan. Sometimes not all facts are friendly. Ignorance of all of this propelled me into the idea with a grim kind of "enthusiasm" to get the job done.

When we reached the top of the range, a woodsman who lived with his family in a mountain cottage would meet us. Under ordinary circumstances he earned his livelihood by hunting game. Now he had become a trusted mountain guide for fleeing Jews. Yet so much could go wrong. There were too many people involved. First of all, could we trust the Polish broker to deliver the agreed sum to the driver, or would we have a larger disaster than we had at our wedding? No money left and no truck! It would be far worse than no duck and no fish. Then, could we trust the driver? Would he take the money from the broker and go directly to the Gestapo and turn all of us in for double the money he'd received from the Millionaires? What about the woodsman – might he not be a secret Nazi agent?

Mechel came up with a plan. Our greatest concern was the broker. That was everyone's greatest concern. This is where the betrayals were most often reported. In order to take the measure of this man's integrity, Mechel gave our broker a test. He told him to send our driver on a dry run, with a full load of coal but without people hiding in the truck. Try as I might through the years, I have never been able to figure out exactly what "test" Mechel gave the driver. I only know that Mechel gave the driver a letter written in a form of code. Mechel was not forthcoming with the details. The liaison then had to present Mechel with a return letter, after the dry run, written in the same code. Mechel said his "test" was a success. It was as safe as it would ever be, and we decided to go forward. The Millionaires had provided a huge sum of money. We would need to provide a comparable amount in courage for all of us to remain calm and resolute and carry out the escape.

CHAPTER 13
Arrest and 'Ave Maria'

O ur plans for escape were now completed and in place. We no longer had to spend all of our time discussing various escape strategies. It had taken so much out of us that we were exhausted most of the time. We didn't read much any longer and we certainly no longer played our personal version of charades. We were taking a nap one afternoon in the hope of gathering some energy for the trip ahead when, without warning, we heard a commotion in the hallway. We knew instantly that it was a Gestapo raid. They barged into the room. My whole past flashed before my eyes: the image of the safe in our old Krakow apartment being opened and robbed of its silver in front of our eyes; of the Nazi throwing me on the bed and trying to abuse me; and the worst memory of all, of the infant the Nazi soldier murdered by slamming him against a door. Images I had consciously worked to suppress flooded my awareness. This was the end. There would be no truck. No mountains. No woodsman guiding us to liberty. There would be nothing now. It was over. And so I said the "*Shema*" (the basic Jewish prayer) over and over again in a whisper. Only my lips moved. When all hope is gone, a Jew recites the "Shema."

Wondrously, the Gestapo men did not harm us. They were rough and cruel, but they did not beat us or seem to want to shoot us. Instead, we were marched down the street in an aggressive fashion and taken into a building we recognized immediately. It was a jail. We were thrown into a cell with a dozen or so others, including my brother Moishe and his wife, Frieda. We knew almost everyone else in the cell. Many of them had been part of our false documents operation in the ghetto.

Ideas of all sorts crossed my mind. Had informers tipped off Schomburg? Had he figured it out himself? Or did he have nothing to do with our imprisonment? I didn't know then and I don't know now. What I suspected was that we had been too confident in our escape plans and we had been betrayed. Maybe our broker was responsible for this, Mechel's test letter notwithstanding. We expected the next step would be one of their infamous interrogation sessions. We assumed it would be about either the papers or our plans to leave. Then a terrible thought flashed through my mind. I had been the person responsible for the idea of forging documents. If our fellow prisoners, under the stress of Nazi interrogation, told the truth, I would be the one responsible. They could easily denounce me and set themselves free. I instantly disliked myself for such thinking. I had become paranoid because of the Nazis. Not everyone was a Moishe Schiller or worse. I took hold of my vivid imagination and looked around me. I saw that everyone in the cell was quietly trying to comfort one another. We were all captives. We waited and waited but the Nazis did not return. No one was dragged away for interrogation and beating.

The torture came in a different form. It was the *Schadenfreude* (the pleasure from another's misery) of the prisoners in a cell across from ours. They were all Polish women and none of them were upstanding citizens. Some were drunk and no doubt had been arrested for disorderly conduct in public. Others were part of a ring of petty thieves. Some were women of ill repute. There was a ringleader who appeared to be quite familiar with the jail and had a confidence the others lacked. She orchestrated the responses of the other women.

They chose to entertain themselves by humiliating us and deriding our faith with scorn. They screeched at us that we were going to Hell and we were going there quickly. They all joined in the game of making fun of us. You could feel the hatred and contempt dripping from their lips. It wasn't just what they said; it was the tone they used. Then the most upsetting part began. They started to sing (or scream) sacred hymns from their own religious liturgy, as derisively as they could in order to aggravate us. The others had no idea what they were singing, but I knew enough to know that they were Catholic chants. They ended with the "Ave Maria," one of their most

119

sacred songs, practically spitting out the words and then roaring with laughter. One of the older women in our cell just crouched down on the floor and cried. I will never know the reasons why she was crying. I now think that it was the sorrow of our situation coupled with the horror of observing the blasphemy coming at us from the cell across the hall.

The "Ave Maria" is a song of sacred love and prayerful pleading to their Virgin Mary. For them to use their most holy words and the music written by Schubert as a form of weapon was horrific to witness. They had lost their own faith in their hatred of all Jews. We were shocked and shaken.

At midnight we were still awake and awaiting execution. We had decided that there hadn't been an interrogation because they had decided to kill us and were just waiting for dawn. As if to foreshadow our fate, we heard gunfire just before sunrise. The ringleader of the women prisoners started up again, "You hear that don't you? You Jews better start to pray. And you better cross yourselves and believe in our God right now, because you are going to be murdered. Pray for your salvation. Get down on your knees and pray for your salvation."

We did not get down on our knees. We prayed. We all prayed together, reciting the ancient words of our faith in unison. The women became quiet and did not start up with us again. We prayed and prayed without pause, like Mordechai in Shushan.

Finally on the fourth day of our imprisonment, one of the men in the cell began to talk about what we needed to do. His name was apparently Lazer Landau. Landau was not a surname I felt good about, remembering with distaste the Kapo Landau in Krakow. However the others said this was a man with pull in the Gestapo who used it to help Jews. Maybe he was the same Landau and maybe not. In any event, he had bribe money and he paid off the Gestapo, and they let us out of jail. We were free.

This was not the end of the story, however, and the ending was not happy. Everyone was released except my brother Moishe. So obviously it must have been about the forging of documents. I think that Moishe had become overconfident in his power to save people and had become careless. People were frantic to get papers other than Polish ones. It would not have taken too many errors for Moishe, in an over-zealous frame of mind, to make big mistakes that would have led to him being fingered by someone. One too many Czech documents in the hands of people who didn't know a word of Czech or the names of any of the cities in that country could have spelled Moishe's doom. Then too he might have been turned in by someone for a large or even a small bribe.

Moishe was sent to Plaszow. I left the jail knowing I would never see my brother again. Frieda was released with us. Neither Mechel nor I said what we thought. We told her Moishe would be released after they interrogated him, and that we would be reunited. I am sure Frieda knew he would be murdered eventually, but we did not speak in these terms to one another. Moishe never returned. He was lost to us forever. Plaszow was a stop on the Nazi death route; it was where Jews were murdered systematically and in vast numbers. Our family was getting smaller and smaller. Once again, we had no time for the luxury of grief. One does not ordinarily think of bereavement as a luxury, but in this darkness it would have been that. Numbed and terrified, Mechel and I returned to our room to resurrect our escape plans.

꒰

PART FIVE:
A WAY OUT

꒱

CHAPTER 14

Escape

Mechel and I went over the escape plan. The truck driver would make three trips. The Millionaires, our bankers for this adventure, denied our request that our family leave together. We were the planners; we had found the liaison, the driver, the woodsman, but maybe they did not trust us fully. It was easy to imagine they might be leery of us. We had just returned from three days in jail, which hardly added to our credentials as trustworthy escorts. Maybe we were being watched still. Everywhere one looked someone was being turned in by somebody, or sometimes it was an accidental remark that led to arrest and deportation. We did not argue with our sponsors because after all, however brilliant our plans might have been, without their funds we would be stuck. Mechel and I thought that Mammiko and Tattiko should go first, as they were living with our financiers. My parents protested vehemently and we could not persuade them otherwise.

Late at night someone knocked at the door of our room. Standing in front of me was a young girl with blonde braids about fifteen years old. "Do you remember me, Lola? I am Rose Glazer of Niepolomice." I realized she was the daughter of the rabbi who had married us. She came into the room and told her story in a straightforward and truthful way. It was very difficult for Mechel and me to hear and to accept, although we had heard other similar stories by this time. In every region where there was a Nazi presence, the officers tried to rob girls of their purity. She and a girlfriend of hers had been victims of this form of persecution, which happened often, especially to

125

younger women. Rose was a perfect candidate for abuse as she was gentile in appearance, not at all "worldly," and heartbreakingly young. Those who resisted were often killed; a few did manage to evade the attacks and get away, but not everyone had the physical or emotional strength to fight or flee. For those of us who were spared these experiences, it is too easy to say what others should or should not have done. The atrocities perpetrated on Jewish women are individual tragedies inside the larger mayhem of the Shoah.

Rose was one of these victims. She had somehow learned of our escape plans, and this was the most alarming feature of her visit. Who told her? If she and her girlfriend were in the company were or captives of Nazis, should we assume that some Nazis knew? She assured us this was not the way she had found out. She said she had strong ties to the smuggling brokers. She was desperate to get away. Her girlhood had been sacrificed but not her good sense. She was determined to free herself of the mess in which she had landed. We could not judge her. I felt only sadness for the direction her life had taken. However, we had nothing to offer her. Mechel spoke softly to her. "Rose, there is no room for you. We are going to be lying squeezed together like wooden matches in a tiny box as it is. There isn't space for another person or even a tiny object. We will be crammed in there. I wish we could take you, but we just can't do it."

Rose's attitude changed dramatically. She became assertive and threatening. She demanded we take her along or she would see to it that our plan failed. It was sheer blackmail. She knew what she was talking about, though, and she regaled us with stories of failed escapes. Rose did not spare us the graphic details of what Germans did with those they captured trying to escape. I wondered if she had learned about these incidents from her German patrons or from the brokers and go-betweens. We just couldn't trust her because we didn't have a clue about her sources or how much she knew. She held us in the grip of her pathetic power. Mechel was enraged and told her it was extortion. I saw it somewhat differently. Yes, it was extortion, but of the most miserable sort. Rose, the daughter of a rabbi, couldn't see any other option to save herself and begin her life again. She had picked us because she thought we would take pity on her. She probably felt that because her father had taken a chance by marrying us during the restrictions in Niepolomice, we owed her this.

I took the initiative away from Mechel then. Rose could become a danger to us if her dispute with Mechel escalated. I realized that when I first opened our door to her, I hadn't been sure she was Jewish, so I thought she might be a useful human decoy. I told her to dress like a Polish peasant and wear a babushka on her head. I added that she should carry a basket of eggs and take a train to the border. Mechel told her how to get to the woodsman's cabin where she would meet us. By now she did understand that there wasn't room in the truck.

"If you can do this, then you can come with us," I told her. "We will go together through the mountains with the guide. It is the best we can offer you. Take it or leave it."

That was really false bravado on my part, because she had us cornered. I had also come to realize her native and fluent Polish might serve us very well in case of trouble. She was reluctant to agree to our terms. Rose wanted to be in the truck with us. She probably did not trust us. Perhaps she thought we had given her fake instructions and there was no cottage and no woodsman. After a few minutes she replied. "I agree, but my friend must come with us too."

I had to ask that awful question. It is one that many had to ask during those times. "Rose, does your girlfriend look like you or does she look Jewish?"

Rose paused and looked down at the floor. I could see her tough demeanor had been a façade. She was fighting back tears. Rose slowly shook her head no. We understood her non-verbal response: her girlfriend could not pass for a Polish peasant. She was saddened her friend would be left behind with the Nazis. Mechel ignored her. He was so angry he couldn't speak. I went over to her. "Rose, you know we cannot risk anyone else. We don't know your girlfriend. I am sorry but we can't take any more chances or we will all be lost. Time is short and soon the opportunities for these transports will end. It's too risky. We can't miss this opportunity."

Rose nodded and did not put up any further resistance or request anything else. When she left, Mechel insisted we discuss the entire "Rose affair." I could not do it and told him it was too painful for me as a woman to see what had happened to her. While I appreciated his rage, it was so different for me. I was overcome with the reality of what had become of the rabbi's daughter from Niepolomice. I was so grateful for my life and my personal circumstances.

"Mechel, you must hear me. Please. I can't talk about Rose. There is nothing to say and now there is nothing to be done except to meet her in the mountains."

Mechel protested further that we needed to talk about it. I would not continue with the conversation. I said something then that stopped him. I said that although she had behaved badly with us, she was trying to undo a sordid chapter of her life and to begin again. Her method was not admirable but she was trying to do the right and moral thing. Mechel understood, but of course we were both worried about the liability Rose might be.

It was time for us to go. There were seven of us: Mechel, the Millionaires, their friends, and I. We went to the agreed departure point, which was a vacant lot. It was pouring rain. Somehow, in the macabre world we were in, the storm seemed the right backdrop for our departure. The pouring rain made us even more wretched. In fact the bad weather might actually have kept us from being observed as so few people were out in it. The truck with its false wooden floor was waiting for us. We squeezed into the space between the real floor of the truck and the false bottom. We were lying on our stomachs. There wasn't an inch between us. It was very cold. The only air came up from the cracks in the floor of the truck but we could at least breathe. The smell of the wet roads was unpleasant and reminded me of things I did not want to remember. It was the smell of fresh dirt, and for me that was the smell of the cemetery after the Aktion. This truck would either be the means to our survival or a communal coffin on wheels.

More than an hour into the trip, the truck stopped so suddenly that we rolled on top of one another. We could see something through the slats but it wasn't clear where we were or what was happening. When we heard German voices, we knew that we had come across a Nazi checkpoint.

"Where are you heading?" we heard the guard ask the driver.

We could not hear the driver's response but did hear the rustle of his papers in the cabin of the truck. He was producing the bills of lading for the coal, which indicated he was on his way to a legitimate factory. The Nazi guards surrounded the truck. We heard a voice command him to "throw down this load of coal."

The driver began to shovel out the coal and he did so slowly. Presumably he did this to make sure we had enough warning and were silent. When all the coal was lying on the ground, a Nazi said, "And what's under here?" He hit the false floor with something that sounded sharp and heavy. We could hear it just above our heads. Mechel reached over and clamped his hand over my mouth in case I couldn't keep from crying out.

The driver was as calm as he could be. "There is nothing else in my truck," he said with a tone of indignation.

Suddenly, a metal pole plunged through the false floor of the truck in several places. If it had penetrated even an inch in a spot where one of us lay, a literal inch, the point of the rod would have impaled one of us. If we had been discovered, we would all have been killed, along with the driver. Death toll: eight. Miraculously, the point slipped between us. No one was touched and, just as miraculously, none of us lost nerve. By now our mutual resolve was harder than the steel rod that might have killed us.

One of the Nazis started to curse in vulgar German. Another guard said, "Forget it. He doesn't have anything except his coal. Let's go inside. It's raining again."

We heard the driver swiftly shoveling his coal over our heads, and then finally the truck lurched forward. It was such a close call that I worried about the consequences of shock to the older people. But they were strong and steadfast. A short time later the truck stopped again. The driver helped us out. He pointed to the closest mountain.

"Climb to the top and turn left. The cottage is there. They are expecting you." Then to prove he had delivered his load of coal, he dumped the fake cargo before he turned the truck around and drove back down the mountain.

Mechel and I were no longer physically fit and were not in shape for such a climb, but the older people were in much worse trouble. We needed to reach the woodsman's cottage. Not long into the climb, our primary financier said, "Please leave me here to die alone. I just can't make it. Go ahead. Save yourselves. Forget me. Leave me in peace," and he started to slide down the path. Mechel grabbed him and said, "We are a group and we go together. Stay with me and I will help you."

The truth was that everyone needed help. Every few feet, we would slide back a few inches because the pathway was slick from the rain. We kept skidding and sliding. Mechel and I quickly realized the only way to make it was to use our hands like animals' paws. We showed the older ones how to crawl up the trail on all fours to the woodsman's cottage. When we arrived, he and his family were quite friendly and their welcome seemed sincere. And there we found Rose Glazer who had arrived the previous night, according to our instructions. The hunter's wife had prepared a simple but nourishing meal. They had very little themselves and were generous in their offering. We couldn't eat everything they put out for us because there were things forbidden to us by the laws of *kashrus* (keeping kosher), but we made sure that they did not feel we were ungrateful.

After the meal we washed up and sat by the warm fire the hunter had built in his fireplace. We were relaxing in preparation for a predawn descent down the other side of the mountain. Our time for relaxation was not long. The hunter's wife began to shriek at the top of her lungs, as if she had been scalded with boiling water.

"Nobody move. You are not going anywhere. Someone has stolen my 2,000 dollars."

We looked at each other and turned pale with dismay. The money belonged to the Millionaires. It was part of the escape ransom they had paid. The 2,000 dollars was the hunter's share. Obviously, he had given it to his wife for safekeeping. The prime suspect was Rose. She had been there a day ahead of us.

I said to her quietly, "Rose, you need to give me the money if you took it. Please. No questions asked, just give it to me privately."

She became belligerent and even swore on her parents' graves she knew nothing about any money. I doubted she was telling the truth. Her oath on her parents' graves only served to indicate to me that her parents had perished, nothing more. Mechel came over and asked to speak with me.

"She has the money. I know she has the money. It can't be anyone else. Take her into the bedroom and pat her down."

I did what Mechel said, but I could not find any trace of money. Now we figured that the hunter's wife had made up the whole story to extort another 2,000 dollars from seven hapless Jews on their way to nowhere. I became quite insolent to the hunter's wife. "This is a rabbi's daughter. Maybe you want to look again in your home. Perhaps you misplaced the money."

She screamed back at me, "No. Don't you dare say such a thing to me! I have only one hiding place and my money is gone."

Mechel came over to me and Rose and said firmly to her, "Go back into the bedroom and either give Lola the money or she will undress you. If she has to do it, she will take every piece of clothing off your body."

These were extraordinary words for an Orthodox Jewish man to utter to a woman. We went back into the room. I was gentle and told her I knew she had seen enough humiliation in her life and that I did not want to be responsible for any further shame. She had to return the money to me. She began to cry. She had sewn the money into the hem of her under-slip. *Where had she found a needle and thread?* I wondered. She said she had taken the money only because she was afraid otherwise she would end up where she had been in Bochnia. All of her defenses were down. Having been compromised by the Nazis physically, she had now compromised herself morally by stealing. She had taken the two thousand dollars because she was so terrified that she might have to experience more awful things in order to survive. I could not judge her. I did not know the dimensions of degradation she had endured. I simply was relieved we had the money back.

Before leaving the room, I hugged Rose and told her I would figure out how to protect her. I took the hundred dollar bills back to Mechel and very discreetly spoke to him about how to handle the matter. I told him the whole story. He called all of us together and said he would speak for the group. He suggested that he tell the hunter and his wife that we had worked things out among us and that we would replace the money. Not everyone in our party felt as sympathetic to Rose as I. Some felt she should be exposed as a crook. Mechel and I explained that doing so might endanger the next truckload of escaping Jews. If Jews were found to be untrustworthy, it would hurt all the others trying to get out through the mountains. They finally agreed that Mechel would be our spokesman.

Mechel told the hunter and his wife that despite appearances, Rose had not taken the money. We did not know what happened to it, but we certainly did not want them to suffer any loss on our behalf. Mechel said we had all chipped in again. Then he gave the hunter's wife the same hundred dollar bills Rose had taken. Mechel, always thinking ahead, had crumpled them up and shuffled the order they were in. Possibly the hunter's wife would believe an intruder had come in and taken her money rather than one of us. She professed to believe Mechel's story and let it pass without further comment or drama.

Rose's escapade had eaten up the entire night. Nobody had slept and now it was almost too late to leave. There would be no breakfast. We had to depart immediately with the hunter guiding us down a treacherous trail. We followed behind cautiously, watching his every move and step. At some point, one of the older people stopped to rest and smoke a cigarette. He struck a match. In the flash of light from the one match, we saw that most of us were standing on the edge of a steep cliff. Some of us were within inches of plunging to our deaths. Our financier lost heart again and once more said almost the same words, "No, I can't go on with this. I want to die. Please leave me alone here. I want to die."

The hunter had absolutely no patience with the man. He was sick and tired of all of us. We were not worth his fee of 2,000 dollars. Although the light of the match had saved us from slipping into oblivion, Nazi sympathizers were always lurking around escape routes and might also have observed the light. And now there was the emotional outburst of a man wailing that he wanted to die. The hunter hissed angrily at the older man, "Shut up! We are almost there."

We reached a place the hunter said was safe. He directed us to a small pool of rainwater where we could wash up from the hike. We did so. I noticed how dirty all of our boots were. They were totally caked with mud. Mechel saw it as well. We looked exactly like what we were – an unlikely collection of Jews who had been slogging through forests and mountains running away from our captors. There was only one solution. I took off my boots and quietly licked the mud off the heels and the fronts. Everyone else did the same. What had we come to! I suppose it wasn't that shocking when you think of everything else we had experienced and so far survived.

Below us we saw the glow of daybreak and the checkpoint that signified the Polish border. The hunter told us how to cross without detection and avoid interrogation. We needed to speak Hungarian, not Polish, to each other. The uniformed men marched back and forth, two by two. They were Hungarians, dressed in the traditional Hussar costume, red jackets with ostrich feathers in their helmets.

Mechel and I went first, arm in arm, with Rose next to us. I chatted away furiously in Hungarian, as if we had just had a lovely hike and were glad to have a rest. Mechel did not speak Hungarian but he knew how to say yes. He took on a new disguise – that of a sweetly tolerant husband, encumbered by a chatterbox wife. Whatever I said, Mechel smiled, squeezed me close to him and said, "*Igen, igen, igen.*" It meant "Yes, yes, yes." I had figured out that if we were questioned we were going to say we were immigrants from Kosice, Czechoslovakia. People there would speak Hungarian, but not perfectly. The guards didn't bother to ask any questions or give us more than a passing glance.

I had tried to teach the financier, his wife, and his friends a few words of Hungarian. It wasn't so difficult, but by then they were just too weary to pay attention to the finer details of survival. Mechel, Rose, and I hid on the other side of the border and waited for their group to come across. They waited for the guards to turn their backs, but they must have timed it exactly wrong. Or perhaps they looked a little too Polish, or too Jewish, or maybe someone said a word in Polish. We will never know if all or any of these things caused their arrest. They were seized and sent back to the Polish side of the checkpoint. We watched as the guards used their field telephones to summon the authorities. They would be returned to the Germans. Their fate was sealed. Death in the mountains might not have been the cruelest end.

Mechel and I were crushed. Rose didn't show any concern at all. She was free and that was as far as she could think. And she wasn't beholden to the Millionaires, so she did not understand how Mechel and I felt. The couple that had made it possible for my entire family to escape had been lost in the enterprise. Their money had saved our lives. We made our way to Bardjov, Slovakia, where my Uncle Beri had relatives. Here we received another kind of shock to our systems.

Uncle Beri and his relatives had been living there for a year as part of the plan to help Jews get out of Poland. They took the three of us in and gave us a meal and fresh clothing. We told them everything we had experienced and all that was happening in Poland. They listened politely but they didn't ask any questions. They were skeptical about our stories. When forced to understand that we were not embellishing our struggles and the enormous losses, they took an even more upsetting stance with us.

"Such things as this will never happen to Hungarian Jews," one of them said.

We had not been exposed to this kind of thinking until then, but it would not be the last time our stories would be met with outright disbelief: we were *Poylishe Yidden*, Polish Jews, given to fanatical leanings. Who would be foolish enough to believe everything we said?

CHAPTER 15
Strange Interlude

We were in a state of suspended disbelief. We had actually crossed out of Poland and therefore escaped the Reich's territory. I wasn't Lola any longer. I was a person named Lola, who looked pretty much like Lola, but I was someone else. Mechel and I were both deeply fatigued yet we tried to repress our feelings of despair. We did not discuss our dreams, which were often nightmares. We had survived, but there were images in our heads, portraits of our dead. It was a slow-motion movie, unreeling itself day after day and night after night in our brains. We had seen too much: too much murder, too much betrayal, too much loss – loss of place, of self, of Jewish identity.

My love for Mechel had grown and deepened into a profound admiration and pride, more than the normal love of a wife for her husband. We were not just a devoted married couple; we had become true partners. He had maneuvered in a world of cunning and greed yet remained a moral and pure man. I had witnessed a few others who had done the same in our world; the Bobover Rebbe was one. Mechel wasn't fearless. Neither was I. Nobody was fearless. Our souls were riddled with holes where the fear had pierced through us. We had become practical, pragmatic, and resourceful in order to survive and to help others survive. To be aware that you are afraid, you have to remember a life that did not contain fear. Mechel and I no longer remembered a time when we were not afraid of "them."

Were we happy in our escape? Not really. We were not unhappy with each other, but happiness was not even a relevant concept. When we arrived in Kosice and were greeted by Mammiko's brother, my uncle Beri, we permitted ourselves an overt expression of relief. We took our first deep breaths in a long time. The family in Munkach had sent Beri to Kosice. He had arrived a year earlier to attempt to save family members. Word had not reached us that he was doing this work. He had left his own family behind in Munkach and moved to the border town to do what he could for our extended family as well as for others. He was part of a Jewish smuggling network, working against the fast clock of the Nazi extermination plan. It was a dangerous place for illegal immigrants. My uncle took care of us, although it was a risk for him to house us. He saw we needed rest and said we would make a decision later about what to do. Mechel and I would have to relocate, but we had no idea where we would go next.

My brothers Ben and Tuli had crossed safely and had been taken by my uncle to Munkach. I convinced my uncle and Mechel that we should stay in Kosice for a bit longer because I was waiting for the arrival of my parents. They did not come. We did not know what had happened. Mechel and my uncle had heard a rumor but neither of them shared it with me. Their kind "deception" allowed me to be a young woman for a brief time. I was not exuberant or joyful, but I did feel relatively young again. Whenever anxiety about my parents threatened to overwhelm me, Mechel or my uncle would say the same thing: "They are somewhere in Hungary and probably with the Bobover Rebbe."

I don't know if I really believed them. I needed to believe them, so I pushed skepticism to the side of my brain. Rose was still with us as she didn't have another place to stay. Mechel and my uncle had been discussing where we should head and their proposal was Budapest. Mechel initially thought it was too dangerous because he assumed we would have to cross the border from Czechoslovakia into Hungary. Bloated by the land-grabbing opportunities of war, Hungary was not as it had been. At this point it was an enormous country. We had been in Hungarian-controlled territory the moment we cleared the mountain checkpoint and gotten past the Hussar guards. There was no dangerous border to cross between Kosice in Slovakia and Budapest. We would not be Hungarian Jews, however, but "aliens" and therefore subject to deportation. However, after Bochnia, it seemed like an opportunity to live in an earthly paradise. Dear Uncle Beri escorted us and Rose to Budapest. He gave us all some money. Here Rose's life finally took a turn for the better. She met up with some friends who were going to Palestine and she decided to join them. I had known and been around Zionists my whole life and so her decision seemed like a sound one. I did not understand how difficult it would be to find safe passage to Palestine during the war. After much suffering and going through horrible ordeals, she arrived in Palestine safely and in one piece. She had suffered enough in her life. Her decision was a good one, but it would be a long time before we knew of her triumphs.

My uncle put us up in a lovely hotel in Budapest and notified distant cousins, who came to see us with fresh new clothing. It was the nicest place Mechel and I had ever been in as a couple, but it was far from a honeymoon. Although the setting was perfect, our mood was anything but romantic. We were still fraught by memories of the struggle and the ghostly whispers of voices we would never hear again. Now I was convinced my parents had perished, although I used all my energy to persuade myself they had crossed safely into Hungarian territory. This scenario seemed increasingly implausible, but I did not voice my suspicions about their fate. Nonetheless, Budapest was a most pleasant surprise. There was no ghetto into which Jews were herded. The anti-Jewish posters and placards that had been all over Krakow were not present in Budapest.

Things seemed a little too normal to believe. In fact, what we did not know was that the Allies had been holding secret meetings with the Kallay government, and the Hungarians had therefore toned down their anti-Jewish rhetoric. There was a Jewish Quarter, but it was not a hole of misery and plague of death as Bochnia had been. We took our meals at a kosher restaurant in the large home of a Jewish family in the quarter.

My uncle proposed a trip to us. He said, "Let's go to Munkach for Shabbos." I almost fainted. Back to the garden? Back to the gate that led to the delights of my youth and not a ghetto gate? He must be joking – but in those days there was no joking about anything. He was serious and we were going. Several days, although it seemed far longer, after escaping from Bochnia I would return to my true home. Because the war had intervened, Mechel had never been there. I was hoping against hope that it had not been spoiled and ruined by all that had ensued.

We arrived in Munkach to find my grandparents well and in rather robust shape for their age. Holding Goldie in my arms was a joy and comfort of unparalleled dimension. We both expressed our gratitude to Hashem, waves and waves of deepest appreciation that we should be together again. Ben and Tuli were indeed safe and living with my Uncle Hershel, who owned a textile business.

Mechel adored Munkach and my relatives whom he had just met. He was in his element. He was the old Mechel, charming, playful, always saying just the right thing. He brought the light of the Shabbos candles into everyone's heart. I gave him a tour of the house, which impressed and surprised him. He was probably thinking, "Well, my goodness, she hasn't made it all up, after all." He loved the garden. I showed him my favorite tree and how I used to climb it as a girl. I showed him the small cottage where the acrobat had lived. I took him into the gazebo, and through the orchard. I had come back! I really was in the garden behind the gate of my childhood dreams. And I really was showing it all to my husband.

Nevertheless things had changed tremendously and my joy was very brief. It was a strange interlude in my life. Once I had "come back to earth" I observed the reality of the situation. We tried to be happy, but underneath there was gnawing anxiety and realized grief. Moishe was in Plaszow or some other place just as bad. Mammiko and Tattiko had not been located. And I observed that Goldie, once her happiness at seeing me had abated, was an empty shell of a woman. She was severely depressed and looked ill. Mechel was very worried about her from the moment he met her. Everyone was always just a little bit in love with Goldie. She had been engaged to a distant cousin, also named Moishe, who was an ardent Zionist. He preceded her to Palestine. She was to remain in Munkach until he could send for her and provide proper visas for her entry into Palestine. In his absence, he asked his brother, Isaac, to keep an eye on her. This was a normal thing that was done in Jewish families. A brother was expected to keep his brother's fiancée safe. Dearest Goldie got busy preparing a beautiful trousseau for herself. At long last, Goldie who made things for everyone else was to have her own beautiful things for her new life as a married woman.

Her Moishe did in fact obtain all the visas needed and she was on her way to Palestine and to the forefront of the Zionist movement to create a Jewish state. The whole town of Munkach came to say farewell to Goldie

— who'd never made an enemy in her life. She would travel to the Romanian port town of Constanza and then take a ship to her destination. Much to her dismay, Isaac followed her and made such a fuss that Goldie did not know what to do.

Isaac claimed he had been secretly in love with her for years. If she left and married his brother, Moishe, Isaac said his life was not worth living. He would kill himself unless she would marry him. "I can't live without you." Unfortunately, Goldie was convinced he meant it and rather too obediently let him take her back to Munkach, to marry the wrong brother. The drama and stress of it was too much for Goldie and she fell quite ill back in Munkach. She was diagnosed with rheumatic fever. And then the worst trick of all was played on Goldie. Afraid that she was too fragile to be a proper wife and to bear children, the parents of Isaac (and of Moishe) forbade the marriage. Goldie, who wanted only one husband, had, without lifting a finger, acquired two suitors and ended up with no husband, no suitors, and no prospects. It filled me with anger and sorrow.

Mechel and I warned the family that trouble was ahead. Everyone in Munkach referred to what was happening as "IT" – as if by not naming the enemy, not saying words like Hitler, the Reich, the SS, the Gestapo, the Nazis, every danger would vanish. Much as Mechel tried, his powers of persuasion did not work. They simply refused to believe what we were saying. I couldn't believe that they didn't believe us. Only my uncle Jeno took what we said seriously and immediately put money into Swiss bank accounts. My grandfather was distracted by our conversation about crossing the border and began to digress about how my parents had met.

"It was in a border town. Just where you came from, I think. That is where they met. They had a one-day courtship. The wedding here was such an enormous affair that it lasted the full seven days of *sheva brachos* (festive meals during the week after the wedding)."

We all stared at him. Poor Grandfather! He had lost himself for a moment in a happy memory of the past before he realized he had inadvertently directed full focus on my parents. The "presence" of the absence of Mammiko and Tattiko was the largest thing in the room. We changed the subject. I looked at the faces of Uncle Beri and Mechel and Goldie and at that moment I think I did know the truth. Much later I was told what happened to Mammiko and Tattiko. Someone in Bochnia, a Polish child in the neighborhood perhaps, or perhaps Rose's girlfriend – someone saw them getting into the coal truck that was to leave after ours. It was reported immediately. The Nazis arrived before the truck could leave. They were pulled out of the truck, one by one, and murdered on the spot, along with the driver, and dumped into a mass grave.

Although I did not know this then, I was nonetheless filled with longing for Mammiko and Tattiko. I went into the kitchen to help Grandmother. She looked at me with tear-filled eyes, and in a gesture of acceptance and resignation took off her diamond ring. It was a beautiful ring that was always on her finger. It had a large diamond in the middle surrounded by smaller diamonds. It was a priceless and beautiful creation, for the smaller diamonds surrounding the large one were cut to look like flower petals. It was a ring with a diamond flower for the woman with the enchanted garden. This was the ring promised to me when I married.

"The time is now, Leiku."

Grandmother tried to place the ring on my finger but I hugged her so that she could not reach my finger. My heart was breaking and so was hers. We both knew this gift meant something else. She had heard what Mechel was saying. She did not know if there would be another opportunity to give me the ring. Perhaps she knew she would never see her daughter, my Mammiko, again. I refused the ring. I wanted to believe that if I did not take the ring, we would be reunited and whole again as a family.

"No. I want you to wear this ring until you are at least 120 years old," I said.

When Shabbos was over, we held a family meeting. I wanted to stay in Munkach and so did Mechel, but we were at a major disadvantage. We had papers that were Nazi in origin and had our real names on them. We were too close to the border to remain as "undocumented aliens." We would be under house arrest in the garden, which I thought was just fine, but it wasn't practical. We had to return to Budapest where problems of documents and identities could be "fixed." What a word to use I thought. Nothing could be fixed because everything in our lives was broken.

We said good-bye to my family. We were disappearing before their eyes and they knew it. I asked Goldie to come to Budapest with us. In fact, I begged her to come with us. Mechel implored her to come and stay with us. She declined. She would not say why but it was clear that even Mechel could not get his way this time. I believe she simply could not bear to leave our grandparents.

I looked back as we left and I saw my sister in profile standing at the garden gate in Munkach. She remained a portrait of beauty even though she was now pale, thin, and weakened. We waved to each other but there were no last-minute indications that all would be well as it had been when I had left for Krynica. I wanted to run back to her, but Mechel put his arm around my shoulders.

Goldie was taken while we were in Budapest. She was part of the deportations from Munkach in the spring of 1944. I do not know the exact date of my sister's death, only its certainty. She, like all the millions and all the individuals we lost, has no grave, no marker, no place to leave a stone that says I have been there. She lives on forever in memory in the glow of the garden in Munkach that last Shabbos we spent together.

My beautiful golden girl, my only sister.

PART SIX:
EVIL ESCALATES

CHAPTER 16
Nightmare on Pesach

I did not have time to indulge in nostalgic memories from my visit to Munkach when we returned to Budapest. Goldie was in my mind at all times and present in everything I did, but I knew I had to stop this indulgence if we were to continue to survive. Mechel and I had a major problem facing us. We needed documents and we needed them quickly. Obtaining false papers was a clandestine activity, although everybody knew how to do it. We were told there was a particular shoemaker's shop that also served as a gathering place for Polish exiles. When we got there we realized for the first time that Budapest had become a capital virtually dominated by a refugee population.

Not every refugee was a Jew. This was also somewhat of a surprise to us, because we had assumed that mostly Jews were running away. We learned that enormous numbers of Polish and German refugees in Budapest were gentiles who had either deserted from the army or escaped the German work camps. There was a smattering of Austrians as well, both Christian and Jews. For the most part Budapest had become the destination of choice for all Poles who were fleeing the war, for all the reasons you can imagine.

It surprised me to find so many gentile Polish intellectuals among the number of refugees. I asked Mechel why this was so as I didn't understand that the members of the intelligentsia were also on the Nazi death lists. Mechel explained the Reich had had spread a wide net. They had decided there were plenty of people who were not Jews but still not Aryan enough to be part of the pure German race of "superior" human beings. Consequently, what had been Poland was slated to become the location where "inferior" people would be moved forcibly and not permitted to leave. Slavic Poles were next on the list to be killed, after the Jews. Polish intellectuals threatened the Nazi master plan, and therefore they were hunted as well. Polish intellectuals were streaming into Hungary, just as we Jews were. Their lives were also at risk. Ordinarily they were not rounded up in large groups for mass murder, but many were included among the groups of Jews killed in the camps. We needed to become something other than Polish Jews, but nothing was a secure identity if you were a Pole.

Maybe it was due to my grief about my family, but I began to lose heart. Mechel had to bolster me and remind me that we must keep our wits. He argued that we had come so far, we must not allow ourselves to give in to feelings of defeat even though we were tired and grieving. I knew we had come a long way, but we had an eternity ahead of us before we would be truly free, if ever. I also wondered if we would survive at all. I no longer had much confidence in our longevity.

The underground movement in Budapest was organized and the document forgery business was an industry. It made our operation in the Bochnia Ghetto look like children's homework assignments. Here the documents were cheap and presumably as reliable as fake papers could be. The forgers did not charge excessively because they felt that we were all together in the same survival network and that we needed each other to go on living.

Mechel negotiated with the forgers. He easily convinced them that he was not an escaped political offender, a *politischegefangene*. They asked us to pick our new names, and in the stroke of the typewriter's keys we became new people. Introducing: Michael Nowakowski and Janka Nowakowska, a lovely Polish Catholic couple. The Polish part of the identity was not hard to prove, but our knowledge of the Catholic faith was all but nonexistent. I could perform a few rituals in public, if need be, like crossing myself at appropriate times, and we thought that between that and my gentile-looking features I could pull off the deception. Mechel's situation posed a far greater gamble. Everything about Mechel defined him as a Polish Jew. His essence, his very core, his speech and mannerisms, and his appearance made him far more vulnerable.

Incredibly, we were not consumed by terror and fear. Everyone in Budapest was a fake of one sort or another. All of us were living in denial and in disguise. We found a modest room in a pension that was something like a boarding house. After the events of the last months our life in Budapest seemed almost normal. Periodically, I would go into a deep depression about Mammiko and Tattiko. During these intervals Mechel would comfort me with extraordinary tenderness, but he no longer insisted they were safe and alive.

Because of my Hungarian heritage and my language facility, I made friends with some Hungarian Jews in Budapest. Mechel had difficulty because he did not speak any Hungarian. He also said he experienced condescension on the part of the Hungarians, which they showed toward all Poles, Jews and gentiles alike. It was petty silliness in the middle of such carnage, but perhaps anything that took your mind away from what was really happening in Europe was a tool for distraction.

I became friendly with an older Hungarian Jewish woman who lived alone, and she invited us for Shabbos. It meant more to me than to Mechel, although he was certainly glad to be in the company of another Jewish person on Shabbos. For me, it was a reminder of my grandparents and Mammiko and a life I would never know again. Another distraction for me was the Neolog (Reform) Synagogue where I met the *chazzan* (cantor) Bela Hershkovics and his wife. When I told the chazzan I was an artist, he warmly invited us to attend services. The synagogue itself was a grand Jewish architectural statement and not at all what we had experienced previously in our religious life. Mechel was uncomfortable there. The building was too ornate and the service was conducted in Hungarian and Hebrew. Nobody in the congregation spoke any Yiddish. My husband felt like an outsider there, so I didn't push it. Mechel said it was not a place to daven, but he thought it might be a nice place to attend the opera or a concert.

Although the pension where we were staying was modest, it was also expensive. It was a landlord's market as there were so many of us who needed immediate accommodations. All rental prices were exorbitant. We lived very carefully on the small amounts of money family members could send to us. There was another source of funds available to Jews in exile in Budapest through the administrative bureau of the kehillah, the Jewish community. These funds filtered in for Jews in need from sources in Switzerland. We did not want to tap that fund because there were many others who no longer had any family members left to assist them as we did. We did not want to press more requests on our own family either, because we believed they would have need of funds sooner than they realized.

We would have to move again. There was no other practical option. There was also no other moral option. We were young and able to move around in order to save money. We talked to other exiles and were told that Debrecen would be a fine place to live as Mr. and Mrs. Michael Nowakowski. It was 120 miles east of Budapest on what had been the border of Romania. I had some family connections there. My Uncle Bela's wife had come from Debrecen and members of her family, the Frankels, were still there. Another train ride, another unknown place, but at least this time we did not have to leave in the dark of night with layers of clothing piled on our weary bodies.

We got off the train and found the Frankel family without difficulty. We explained that we needed to find a decent, inexpensive place to rent. They said that was no problem. All we needed to do was look in the newspaper's classified ads for rooms available in our price range. Look in the newspaper to find a place to live? It was so routine and normal that we were a bit paralyzed by this information, but we did what they suggested. Armed with our false names and completely fake papers, we looked at a few of the listings. We decided on a room with a private bath, which was a luxury. The room was in an almost palatial residence called Piszperti Poloto. The sad twist of our fate was this: the owner was a Jewish widow named Mrs. Kuper. Mrs. Kuper could not know us as fellow Jews but as gentiles who had escaped from Poland. We said we had to leave because "Michael" did not want to fight in the army against the Reich. So there we were in Debrecen, the presumably pro-German, Polish Catholic tenants of a Jewish landlady.

There were so many deceptions going on at one time, it was a case of deceptions within deceptions. It was 1944. That Pesach we made a quiet Seder for the two of us. The rest of the time we didn't do much except play cards, especially gin rummy. We took walks in the park. I sketched more and more. Our relationship was undergoing a subtle but definite shift. Now I became the more independent one. My fluent Hungarian gave me a degree of freedom impossible for Mechel. My fair complexion and non-Jewish appearance gave me even further confidence to move around.

If I felt I was being observed, I crossed myself. When I needed to talk with the concierge of the building, I added a little Catholic expression or two, in a way that had become so natural to me it sent chills down my spine. I even hummed the tunes of the Catholic hymns I remembered from that awful night in prison. Mechel took up with the Polish expatriate crowd. They met in shul and exchanged news items as well as information about jobs that might be available for men. About a dozen Jewish refugee families were in the vicinity. My Uncle Yoshe Berger was there with his daughter, Toby, and her husband and also his daughter-in-law, Rosie, and her child, Micheline. Rosie had lost her husband, Moishe, in Krakow when he was identified as a Jew. It was quite a crowd, with an additional number of Mammiko's cousins from Budapest.

At this time a strange mood came over Mechel and he threw caution to the winds. He didn't bother to pose as a gentile in the street now. He walked to shul every single day carrying his tallis and tefillin in a briefcase. He made me so nervous I couldn't stand it another minute. He reproached me, "Why are you so afraid? There are no Germans here. We do not have to be ashamed to be Jewish here."

Taking on the identity of a Catholic was breaking Mechel's spirit and this was something I had not anticipated. He was in great distress and became careless in his defiance. One night we had an argument when I begged him to hide his tallis more carefully. I was moved and grateful that he went to shul to daven each day, but I recognized how reckless he had become. His next step really terrified me. Without consulting me, he became the leader of a committee of Orthodox refugees. I was aghast at this action. I was also surprised and hurt that he had not talked it over with me first. Our partnership wasn't over, but it was fraying around the edges. He was now openly associating with other Jews, yet he carried papers that said he was a Catholic. It was the perfect way to destroy our cover. Hungarians who were anti-Semitic were on the watch at all times for anyone who appeared to be Jewish. Mechel was courting disaster at every turn.

I could not reason with him. He would have none of it. "I have to be around our own people. Don't you understand? If we have to run to Romania or even to Switzerland, we must be prepared with a network in place to assist us."

With these words, the deep secret between us had been revealed. He wasn't any more confident than I was. In fact, Mechel was being his usual practical self, but this time it had a frantic edge to it. It turned out he had been working on yet another escape scheme from the very first days we had arrived in Debrecen.

March 19, 1944. The Germans invaded Hungary and our world began to collapse. The Germans marched right in and took over. Overnight,

Hungary became another Nazi puppet state with no autonomy whatsoever. Hungarian national identity was gone. Hungary was now another vassal in the new European entity that called itself the Empire of the Third Reich. We heard rumors that Britain might soon fall too. Hitler openly announced his intention to invade and conquer the United Kingdom and do away with all its Jews and intellectuals. Despite the fact that Debrecen was in the far eastern corner of Hungary, the Nazi forces arrived only a couple of days later.

It was the same horror we had faced before, yet it was different. Hitler's evil had escalated to new levels. The Germans bombed civilian Debrecen and enforced a 10 p.m.-to-dawn curfew. There was a strategic military reason for their violent aggression against Hungary, which we did not know then. The Nazis considered Hungary particularly untrustworthy because, after having allied themselves with the forces of evil, the Hungarians became weary of their alliance. It had cost them between 150,000 to 200,000 soldiers on the Russian front, and they realized too late that they were on the wrong side of the war. Word was out that Hungary had sent out peace feelers to the Allies. Moreover by March 1944 the Soviet Army was approaching the Carpathian Mountains. In Hungary, the Reich established its own brutal puppet government, which issued directives against the Jews. In order to make sure there was no misunderstanding about their power, they proceeded to intimidate Hungary further with devastating air raids.

It had taken the Nazis several months to hit upon the idea of locking the Jews up in ghettos in Poland, but now they had the techniques down pat. In Hungary they immediately herded the Jews into ghettos. The 7,000 registered Jews of Debrecen were pushed into the Jewish Quarter that they declared a ghetto in the blink of an eye. As Jews living clandestinely, we had to be particularly careful. For more than two weeks neither Mechel nor I left the second-floor room of Mrs. Kuper's home. When it was absolutely necessary to obtain food, I was the one who went out. Mechel was unusually quiet. I thought he had forgotten about his plans to escape. I speculated that there were no plans to escape because there wasn't any place left to go.

Pesach was approaching. This was our first Pesach in Hungary. It was a year when Pesach would fall on Shabbos. I debated about what to do. I didn't say anything to Mechel. Surely, we must not do anything. It was too dangerous and so we would just have to forfeit the observance of Pesach. Without any conversation about the past weeks, our partnership was reinforced and our bond renewed. We decided as a couple that we *would* celebrate Pesach. It was our duty and our desire to do so, *regardless of the consequences*. We would make a Seder. On Pesach Eve, Mechel davened the Ma'ariv prayers and I produced the matzos I had secretly obtained. We were not alone among the hidden Jews doing this. We had no wine, no festive meal, no ritual plate, and no guests. But we told the Passover story to each other.

I listened with tears in my eyes to Mechel reciting the account of our deliverance from Pharaoh in Egypt. We had a Pharaoh too: the Nazi forces that had nooses hanging over our heads. The words of the Pesach story had particular poignancy and meaning to us. We were not slaves, but we were most certainly captives. I saw tears in Mechel's eyes too, but he quietly continued the story we had been told and had recited since we were tiny children. "In each and every generation we will tell our children, that the Holy One, blessed be He, delivered us from the hand…"

At around midnight Mechel completed the entire Haggadah. We held each other and dried our tears and went to sleep. We were just about to doze off when we heard voices and banging on the front door of the house. Then the doorbell rang and rang. We heard the concierge of the building (who was not Jewish) engaging in a heated conversation with some men. I could tell they were Germans and I assumed they were from the Gestapo. I heard them scream that they wanted Michael Nowakowski. I heard our concierge tell them which door was ours. I heard their steps on the stairs and knew that Mechel was going to be killed. He ran into the bathroom and I tried to hide anything left from the Seder under the bed.

They pounded on the door and I opened it. I was in my nightgown and my robe. Several Germans stood in front of me. The head thug had a list. It was for the roundup of Polish political troublemakers and subversives. There were twelve on the list, all known to be living under false identities with fake documents. I looked over the top of the Nazi's list and read the names upside-down. Each and every name was a member of Mechel's committee and of course, Mechel was the ringleader. Obviously a local non-Jew had turned Mechel and his group in to the Gestapo. The entire room smelled like matzos to me – the aroma of Pesach. I thought for sure they knew that smell too. The smell of Jewish food was not unfamiliar to our killers.

I forced myself to become an actress again. I was very polite and very much the lady. "I am sorry but my husband Michael is not here with me. I am all alone."

An officer standing right behind the one with the list asked me, "Is your husband a Jew?"

I blanched white in melodramatic horror and disgust. "You must be kidding me? My husband is the grandson of a very famous Polish railroad engineer named Nowakowski. He ran from the Polish army because he had no intention of fighting against Germans. I have no idea where he is or what has happened to him."

My acting did not support the evidence in front of their eyes. Mechel's clothing was right next to the bed where he had taken it off to get into his pajamas.

"Really?"

One Gestapo officer went over and picked up the clothing and looked at me in a menacing way.

I had to think of something to say to save myself, or surely they would just shoot me. "Well, he was here, but we had a bad fight and he left."

The head Gestapo officer was done with me. He knew I was lying. Apparently I was of no interest to him, which was a relief, but I knew that Mechel was now in mortal danger. He might be living the last minutes of his life on earth. The Gestapo men talked to each other. One said that the concierge had said that nobody had left the building during the evening.

"He is in this building somewhere." They said to each other. They moved around our tiny quarters, and ended up in the bathroom. I waited for the inevitable, but Mechel was not in the bathroom. I couldn't imagine how he managed to escape. Just as I was about to thank Hashem, one of them stood on the toilet and looked out the tiny window.

"There he is. Look, he's down here. He jumped out of the window."

There was a deep ravine between our house and the next building. Mechel was down in the ravine with an injured leg. The concierge led the Nazis right over to Mechel and I watched as they stormed down the stairs and hauled my husband away. Now it was over. Everyone was gone. Not only would I never see my parents again, or any of all the others I'd lost, but now Mechel, the only one I had left in the world, was torn from me. Without him there was no point in fighting on against these creatures from Hell. I had neither reason nor wish to survive. I instantly knew what I wanted. I did not have to think about it for even a minute. I flew down the stairs in my nightgown and robe.

"Take me along with him. I am also a Jew."

A man's voice pierced the night. "No, she is not. Don't believe her. She just wants to be with her husband. I can assure you, this woman is not a Jew."

It was the concierge. He restrained me by putting his hand firmly on my shoulder. I wanted to hit him. As far as I was concerned he had helped the Gestapo arrest my husband. He was saving my life but I did not think of him as a good man. After leading the Nazis to Mechel, why did he suddenly care what happened to me? Then it dawned on me. Maybe he believed my story. He really did think I was a Catholic woman married to a Jew. Or maybe it was his way of helping me. I will never know. I pulled away from the concierge and went back into our rooms, which smelled of Pesach and of Mechel. The Nazis had taken away my brave, now injured husband. They would kill him. It was the end of everything for me. My entire life had vanished on a Pesach Shabbos.

A forbidding, gated wall went up swiftly around the Debrecen Ghetto. Even if Mechel were somehow released or could escape from the prison in Budapest, he would know better than to return to Debrecen. I sensed this and so I told Rosie I had to go to Budapest to try to get him out of prison. She said she would come too, and her friend offered to drive us. However, it was a small car and with Rosie and Micheline there wasn't room for me. I opted to take the train. Since all the Jews of Budapest were now in a ghetto with a Judenrat in place, we decided the easiest thing was to meet at the Judenrat headquarters. As in the other places, Rosie and I presumed the Judenrat would be easy to identify once we were inside the ghetto's walls.

I was filled with apprehension on the train. Perhaps Mechel wasn't really imprisoned in the place they said he was? Maybe he was in a less dreadful prison, but how could I learn where he was? Budapest was a large city, and even with my gentile appearance and my fake papers, asking too many questions about an imprisoned husband was risky. Anything I did put me in harm's way. I was a Jew moving about illegally as a Christian outside the ghetto. In the ghetto I would be a Jew, but one with false Christian papers. I heard the Jewish police inside the Budapest Ghetto often were lenient about letting gentiles bring food in for Jews. I figured my best chance was to continue to remain under cover with my false identity as Janka Nowakowska.

The train pulled into the Budapest station at 9:50 p.m., just ten minutes before the curfew would close the ghetto's gates. My heart raced as I rushed toward the old Jewish Quarter, correct in my assumption that it would be where the Nazis had located the ghetto. I slipped in just before curfew. The guards did not acknowledge me. I had no idea where the Judenrat was however, and I could not see any obvious sign or posting of directions. It was past curfew and doors were being shut and locked everywhere. I wandered around, but there was nobody to ask and I had no place to stay.

I saw one door that was still open and dashed for it. Inside, I headed down the basement stairs. I thought it was the least likely place to be discovered. I sat on the stairs about halfway down, tired and terror-stricken. A few minutes later I heard the janitor making his rounds. He locked the front door and went upstairs. I had no idea what sort of building I was in or what I would do in the morning. I could not sleep so I decided to venture upstairs to see what I could determine regarding my whereabouts, but after a few steps I lost my nerve and returned to my spooky seat on the stairs, which had been transformed in my mind into a shelter.

About an hour or so later, I heard a door above me open and then close. I heard footsteps. Then there was silence and I detected the odor of a cigarette being lit and smoked. I heard a muffled cough that sounded like a man's, but how could one be sure from only a cough? I crept farther down the stairs almost into the basement. I stayed there for at least another hour, too petrified to move. Finally, I decided to creep back up the stairs because the building had become silent again. I climbed a few stairs, trying to do it quietly, but the stairs were old and made of wood, and filled with cracks from wear that creaked under even my slight body weight.

"Who is there?" It was a man's voice.

"Nobody...I mean...I'm sorry...I missed the curfew and I am sitting here until the morning. I mean no offense to anyone." I barely stammered out the last few words.

A man with glasses started down the stairs toward me. He walked normally and without aggression or threat in his steps. I saw that he was balding, of fair complexion, and had a pleasant expression on his face. He was probably in his forties, of average height, and a little chubby. When he got closer to me I could tell that he was a Jew.

"Are you Hungarian?"

"Yes, yes, I am Hungarian."

"Well, I have to ask you then, where is your armband?"

That was the one question I had forgotten about. I was so "assimilated" in my role and used to being accepted as a gentile woman, I had forgotten about the armband issue. Of course! There I was in the ghetto, and what would a gentile be doing in the ghetto after curfew? My lies and deceptions could no longer be maintained. I was too tired to keep all the lies organized coherently and I ached for Mechel's return. I took a long look at the man and decided to tell him the truth. There was something about him that made me feel comfortable enough to blurt it out.

"I am a Jew, but I have false papers."

He nodded nonjudgmentally and did not criticize me. His voice was soft and he asked me what I was doing there and what was wrong with me. I told him about Mechel's imprisonment and told him I was trying to reach the Judenrat for help.

"Well, you don't have to look any further. I am the Judenrat – I am the head of it. You have come to the right place. I can't offer you a room here, however, because I have just given my own quarters to a woman with a small child."

I had miraculously ended up where I needed to be, but I wondered why there was someone else that needed a room in the Judenrat headquarters. An absolutely crazy idea entered my head. A woman and a child? *It couldn't be,* I reasoned with myself. But then I thought, *Well, I think it must be so because so many things have happened that cannot be explained.* It began to register that it probably was Rosie and Micheline who had preceded me to Budapest by car. I was about to ask him what they looked like, but he continued talking.

"She said she and her daughter had to have privacy and so I said I would be happy to let them stay. I would sleep in the basement for the night. That's where I was headed, when I found you."

"May I please ask you what this woman and her child look like?"

He described them exactly – even their clothing.

"That's my cousin and her daughter."

We both looked at each other in disbelief. I began to cry. He told me I had no reason to be so upset. He told me he had a great deal of power and would find out where Mechel was. He introduced himself. He said his name was Kasztner.

"Please, don't worry. This is not as hopeless and dire as you may think. However, in order to help you, I must get more information."

He took out a small notebook and I told him everything I knew. He wrote it all down carefully. When I was done he looked over his notes. He then asked me to fill in certain details I had skipped over in my rush to remember. He said that we would meet again in the morning. He told me I should stay where I was, as it was a safe refuge.

The last thing he said to me was I should try to get some sleep, or at least try to close my eyes. After he walked away I was overcome by what had just occurred. Had I just been duped? Was I in the presence of another Moishe Schiller? Was he actually an informant who would now go find Mechel and have him killed and then come back for me and Rosie and Micheline? I could not believe my lack of caution. What would Mechel think of this behavior? Yet somehow I felt this man was not an informer or a Kapo. I believed he would help me find Mechel. I thought the fact that he had given his room to Rosie indicated he was a good person with a generous heart.

Just after daybreak Mr. Kasztner returned and told me to meet him in the park later in the day. He said it was best to discuss these matters outdoors where there was no chance of being overheard by informers. Now, of course, I was ashamed of myself for having distrusted him as a potential traitor to his fellow Jews. I made a note in my mind of the precise directions he gave me to the park.

"Would you like to go upstairs to your cousins now?"

Helplessly, I let him lead me upstairs to what he referred to as his apartment but was only a dingy, dark room. There, still asleep, were Rosie and Micheline. I ran to Rosie and woke her up, and could not stop weeping and clinging to her. Rosie was calm and little Micheline patted my back. Kasztner was quiet and did not intrude on our family reunion. When I calmed down he told us we should stay together in the room until he found a place for us to live. Then he left. I thought it most unusual that Rosie did not say good-bye to our benefactor. Nor did she thank him. I thought it was rudeness but wrote it off as exhaustion.

After I had rested, Rosie told me things were not as they appeared with Mr. Kasztner. He had made "approaches" and she'd had to make a scene to get him to leave her alone. She'd threatened that if he did not she would scream at the top of her lungs. That is why he had gone downstairs where he found me hiding. He was not an informer, apparently, but sadly, neither was he a gentleman. Beyond the fact that he was a cad, we knew we could not stay in the Budapest Ghetto. We had fake Christian papers and no armbands. In any event, there was no reason to believe anyone in the ghetto would be willing to share sparse accommodations with strangers. And even if he allowed us to remain in his room, the building concierge would turn us in to the authorities promptly because we did not wear our Jewish stars.

We stayed inside all day. I didn't think I should go to the park to meet him, but Rosie and I both reasoned there was nothing else to do. We did not have another avenue to pursue. I left for the park reluctantly at the appointed hour in the afternoon. When I reached the exact location he described, I was confronted with a scene I will never forget. There was a large line of distraught women begging him for information. He stood at the front of the line with the women lined up, crying out for his help. He spoke to them in turn, one by one, and just as he had done for me, he wrote down everything they knew about what had happened to their husbands and when it had happened. The cries were in different voices but they were all the same desperate plea.

"Please, Mr. Kasztner, help us… My son is gone and my husband… My children and I are alone… My husband, my husband… my husband…" The same cry of alarm and sorrow echoed from each of them, and it reverberated through me as well. Nobody was alone in this misery. I stood quietly to the side and he nodded, indicating that he had seen me. However, he did not approach me. He kept taking notes as each woman spoke, but as the day progressed the line of women grew longer and longer.

So he was not an informer. I thought perhaps he was the head of the Judenrat. Whatever his position, he was clearly the man to see if you wanted help in getting your loved one out of the grip of the Gestapo. I could see he was treated not only as someone with power, but as a kind of ghetto personality, if not a celebrity. He was almost holding court. It is hard to explain how he behaved and how the women responded to him. There was something theatrical about the whole setting. The "park" as he had called it wasn't grand; it was a large lawn with a few benches – that was really all it was. It might well have been something quite lovely before the horrors. It was adjacent to the ghetto but not fenced in; people came and went freely.

Sunset was not far off, and as darkness fell I did not know what to do. Kasztner finally spoke to the last woman in the line for that day. He told those he had not spoken with when to come the next day. Then he came over to where I had been standing the entire day, just waiting. He was charming and kind to me and apologized for the long wait. He said he never knew how many people would come on any given day. I told him I understood and was grateful for any help he could give me.

"You know I am a yeshiva man," he said. "I have no idea where my wife is now, but I fear she is in Auschwitz. Nothing is normal any longer."

I felt a fleeting tenderness for him as a man who had lost his wife and possibly the rest of his family. However, I also knew how badly he had behaved with Rosie and so I was guarded. This turned out to be the correct stance. He tried to put his arm around my shoulders. I moved away gently without saying anything or making a fuss.

"Please," he urged. "These are not times when God judges us for being human. See, just across the way there is a fine hotel and I am known there. I am allowed to stay as a guest. Come with me. Let's get away from the ghetto and our sorrows and worries for one night."

I burst into tears rather than fight back like a tiger. I was so thoroughly offended that my outrage boiled inside me without finding a verbal outlet. *That a Jewish man should ask this of me? After all I have been through with the Nazis? Now, one of my own asks me to do this?*

"No, you misunderstand. I do not mean you harm. It will be good for both of us and God forgives these things now."

"Not my God. He does not forgive such things. If I am to ask for His help in finding my husband it will not be found in this manner."

"And just where do you think you will stay tonight then?"

"Don't worry about that. I've been through more things than you can possibly imagine. Your offer does not tempt me in the least. I will find a place to stay."

I walked away from him and did not look back to see his expression. My gait was steady. I made sure my posture told him I was a dignified married Jewish woman who did not compromise her fidelity. Only after I got back to his room, where Rosie and Micheline were, did I express my anger. I told Rosie everything and she was not surprised. Mostly she was horrified that he kept me waiting the entire day for nothing. I said that as Kasztner had stopped bothering her, she and Micheline might as well stay in his room for another night until we figured out what to do. During the day of waiting, a kind woman had left the line and come over to me to see if she could help. She had given me her address in the ghetto. I went to her place and was welcomed.

Later that very night, the Gestapo went to the hotel where Kasztner was staying and arrested him. I detested what he had done to me, but I was horrified that the head of the Judenrat could be rounded up like everyone else and thrown into prison. Within days we learned of his release. The Nazi officials said it was an unfortunate case of mistaken identity. After his release I had no better idea than to appear before him during the day in his office to see what he had learned about Mechel. He greeted me with caution but not complete hostility.

"When I was in prison I met your husband."

I blanched, wondering if he had lied to Mechel about our encounter in the park.

"I told him he had the most amazing wife in Europe. 'Never, ever, have I seen or met such a wife as yours,' is what I told your husband." He wanted to continue telling me how he had praised me to Mechel, but I gave him a very harsh stare, which he did not appreciate. His feelings toward me quickly turned to contempt.

"Here is the truth. It is next to impossible, if not totally impossible, to do anything for him. You will never see your husband again. They are not going to release anyone from that place."

He said it somberly, without a trace of sympathy. I had not played by his rules and I was going to be punished because of it. He would do nothing to secure any favors for Mechel because I had dared to refuse him. I left without saying good-bye. Mr. Kasztner and I were finished pretending with each other. He held me in contempt but I held him the same. However, I had gotten one very valuable thing out of the meeting. I knew exactly where Mechel was.

I never saw Kasztner again, and had no wish to ever see or hear about him. Oddly enough, his name came to my attention again in the 1950s. He remains a mysterious figure in Holocaust history. Some said he was responsible for saving thousands of Jews. He was not the head of the Judenrat – that was a lie. However, he was indeed a powerful man. He was the deputy chairman of the Hungarian Zionist Organization. The Zionist Organization in Hungary completed major operations in the successful rescue of Polish and Slovakian Jews like Mechel and me. Kasztner was linked to the aborted "Blood for Goods" plot to save Jews in exchange for war materiel – especially trucks. The larger plan fell apart, but Kasztner did arrange a transport that delivered more than one thousand Jews safely to Switzerland, including the Satmar Rebbe, Rabbi Joel Teitelbaum. Others insist that Kasztner was responsible for halting a mass murder of Jews in Auschwitz in late 1944.

After the war, he made his life in Israel and resumed his original career as a journalist and political activist. In 1953 Malkiel Gruenwald, the publisher of a newspaper based in Jerusalem, accused him of having been a Nazi collaborator. In Gruenwald's allegations, Kasztner was accused of hastening the death of thousands of Hungarian Jews. Kasztner was by then an Israeli government official and the Israel Attorney General's Office successfully defended him. Gruenwald was then indicted for libel. On appeal, however, the court held on June 22, 1955, that Gruenwald's accusations were true and Kasztner had been a Nazi collaborator. The Israeli government appealed again, insisting that Kasztner was completely innocent. On January 17, 1958, the Israel Supreme Court overturned the lower court's decision and cleared Kasztner's name completely. It would not change the course of his life though, because Kasztner was already dead. He had died the year before on March 12, 1957, at the hands of an assassin on a street in Tel Aviv. Even his first name was buried in a cloud of confusion and obfuscation. The newspaper article that reported the assassination said he was known as Rudolf a.k.a. Reszo a.k.a. Israel Kasztner.

CHAPTER 18
Appointment with the Devil

Rosie and I wanted to get out of the Budapest Ghetto. The distasteful Kasztner experience lingered as long as we stayed in the ghetto where he was lurking around. And we couldn't find a suitable place for the three of us to live. We might have reclaimed our Jewish identities, but the Nazis were liquidating ghettos at breakneck speed. We didn't know that the Reich was under extreme pressure then and that their last-ditch strategy was to get rid of Jews in large numbers as quickly as possible. The Allied Forces were finally closing in on Nazi Germany.

We moved as far from the ghetto as we could and retained our Christian identities. We rented a room, but our shared life had become even more difficult because we were now four. We had taken another little girl into our care. Besides Micheline, Rosie's niece Blanka was now part of our family. The Jewish underground's news "grapevine" had contacted Rosie and informed her that Blanka's father had disappeared. The child's mother, like many Jewish parents, had placed Blanka in an orphanage. Jews who had become despondent and expected the worst for themselves took their children to orphanages in the belief that it was the only chance for the next generation. Blanka was one of these children, and like so many others, she had been moved from one orphanage to another. When Blanka ended up in an orphanage in Budapest, somebody knew how to contact Rosie. We didn't confer about what we should do about the child. Rosie was Blanka's "Auntie"; there was nothing to discuss. It complicated our lives economically and heaped an additional burden on our already fragile existence. However, it was a tangible favor I could do for Rosie, who had been so kindhearted and generous to me.

We could not tell the landlady in our new residence that somehow we had mysteriously acquired a second child. That had all the markings of Jews on the run and masquerading as Christians. Any landlord found harboring Jews would be punished or killed; if someone looked even the least bit suspicious, the landlords called the authorities to investigate. We had no choice but to take Blanka into our room; likewise, we had no choice but to hide her under the bed or in a closet when anyone came in. We took some blankets and turned them into a makeshift cot. It was a terrible ordeal for a little child. There was, however, at least the possibility that with us she would avoid arrest and deportation to the camps. When we took her outside for air and exercise, one of us would distract the landlady with Micheline and the other scurried outside with Blanka half-hidden by an extra coat. We did the same thing on the way back into the building, but in reverse. One of us engaged the landlady in mindless conversation while the other whisked Blanka back into the room.

Rosie was our manager of finances and practical matters. She told me I had only one job to do – "find the leads" to free Mechel. This was my assignment. It was also the sole reason for my continued existence. I had to get my husband out of prison and save him. Rosie sold her precious engagement ring, which Moishe had given her, to raise substantial funds for me to use as bribes to "friendly" informers and members of networks working to help Jews. I often returned to our room dejected and cheated. Once again, both gentiles and Jews were quick to take our money but slow to deliver information, if they delivered it at all.

All too often, once the money was paid they simply disappeared into the interstices of the underground of operatives and informers where they could never be traced. It was the same form of betrayal we had experienced trying to arrange our wedding dinner only worse. This time, I was trying to get my husband out of a death cell; it was much more than a mere inconvenience like not finding a duck or a fish. I continued to steam with anger at Kasztner's behavior, and it became clear to me that he had plenty of power. He could have helped me but would only do so on his terms.

I prepared myself every night to learn the next day that Mechel was already in a mass grave somewhere, or was being tortured in the prison.

Nonetheless I got up each morning and kept searching for any clue I could find. I wasn't waiting for crumbs of rumor or information tidbits to drop from the tables of those who knew things – no. I was crawling around on the ground, as it were, looking for anything that could lead me to someone who could help. In order to do this, I had to circulate around Budapest appearing as if I did not have a care in the world.

Budapest, like other European cities under siege, was filled with exhausted people. Everywhere we looked we saw similar expressions on peoples' faces – people whose entire beings had been shot through with horror. All that was left of them were their grief-stricken faces and eyes. It was a monolithic gray wall of dazed humanity. Thousands of people were walking around as if half-dead themselves but still attempting, usually without luck, to get information about lost or missing family members.

There was only one way to beat the system. I had to stand out as someone and something totally different. I had to present a bright, pretty young face, be a well-dressed and perfectly groomed figure in the crowd of monotone grief. When I put on this visual disguise, doors began to open for me. I was not what they were used to seeing. I was a puzzle, a mystery, and a curiosity. I had created a character on the outside that was far different from the one living on the inside.

Rosie made it possible for me to retain a shred of hope for Mechel's release. I moved around Budapest that spring in fashionable Italian high-heeled shoes and silk stockings, which Rosie insisted I wear and continued to supply me. Jews were not allowed to wear fur, so we thought I should wear a Persian lamb coat we'd found in a flea market that was in fairly good shape. Sometimes I wore another coat with a large fur collar on it. Everything was an act in a studied performance. There wasn't a moment of pleasure in dressing up for these meetings or referrals to people who might know what I should do. I had weekly manicures and wore light makeup – lipstick and powder, just enough to appear classy and not something else. I couldn't take any more bad behavior from men. I acted a bit aloof and felt anything but alluring, but I was elegantly attired and serious in my manner. I say serious to distinguish my manner from the despair I felt inside and which was common in others. It took a tremendous amount of self-control to maintain this façade, which fell apart the instant I returned "home" to Rosie and the girls.

One night Rosie became agitated, which was unlike her. While I was out following leads, she had become the eyes and ears of our operation, not just the banker. She'd just heard something that worried her. Someone had come into the house and spoken to the landlady in words Rosie couldn't quite make out but was convinced it concerned us. We moved immediately.

Another rented room, the same deceptions, and then another room and another and another. We didn't stay in any one room for more than a couple of weeks, or one month at the most. All Rosie needed to hear was one person questioning a landlady or a concierge about us. Had our papers been checked? Where were we from? Why didn't we have husbands with us? Was there any chance that we were really Jews? Although the concierges never asked too many questions when we rented the rooms, we no longer trusted a living soul, except one another. We would take no chances of any kind.

Rosie's nerves were now unsteady. The constant struggle to get us money was also wearing her down. The bribes were too costly and they were not producing results. Every move we made took us further into the world of victimization and that is, of course, a world ruled by sheer panic. That was our state at this time. It seemed we spent more time moving than anything else. We packed at night and smuggled the girls and our two decent suitcases out as quietly as we could so that nobody heard us leaving. We had been confident of our gentile appearance, but now we began to wonder who we were kidding. One night in yet another of our shabby rented rooms, I said to Rosie, "Look at us. All four of us – just look at us! We look like what we are, Rosie. We are Jews on the run from Hitler and his gang of murderers. I don't think we can get away with this much longer."

I could tell from the sad look in Rosie's eyes that she'd been thinking the same thing. She obviously had the same fears or we would not be moving to a new room at the mere suggestion of a doubt or a half-question. During the next few days, as I became more and more fearful of being apprehended when I was outside, I also became far more observant. I looked deeply into the eyes of everyone who passed by. And here is what I saw: an entire city of people worn out by the oppression of war and bombs and death and deprivation. Every person – young and old – revealed a look of terror and had the telltale wrinkles of internal turmoil etched on their faces. That included Hungarians who did not have one drop of Jewish blood. We all looked exactly the same. The Reich thought Jews all looked the same.

Well, now the cosmic irony was that Hitler had made everyone a victim, so we all truly did look similar, and distinguishing a Jew from a gentile was becoming very difficult, if not almost impossible. It was Hashem's subtle but effective way of protecting us from discovery.

I had devised a trick that seemed to be working. When we signed up for a new room, I would, in the most casual and conversational way, ask the landlady what her faith was. If she was a Protestant, I said I was a Catholic, if she was a Catholic, I became an instant Protestant. And then, I would ask appropriately, "Could you tell me where the closest Catholic church is and do you know what time Mass is said?" or alternatively, "Would, you by any chance, happen to know where the nearest Protestant church is and when the services are held?" Whether posing as a Catholic or a Protestant, I made it clear that I was a devout Christian woman. On Sunday, I would walk toward the church I had asked about and enter it. Sometimes I walked in the front and right out the side door, but if I thought there was a chance I had been followed – I stayed for the entire service.

It was easier for me to pose as a Catholic because I had absorbed a few songs and chants from my prison experience. It was May 1944 and the Mass said at that time of year had a routine to it that was easier for me to memorize and follow than the more varied services in different Protestant congregations. It was more of an annoyance than a danger, and perhaps I need not have been so concerned, but I felt anything that cemented further my identity as Christian helped all of us. In the Catholic churches I became very proficient at kneeling and crossing myself, as if I had been doing it from earliest childhood. After all, besides saving myself so I could get Mechel out, I needed to be a protective human decoy for Rosie and the two girls.

The shoemaker's shop was still the front for passing forged documents and linking up with the underground networks. Obviously I had to visit it as part of my routine, but I did not go there frequently because it was too dangerous. It was there that I was able to stay in touch with the eleven other wives from Debrecen. Either they had moved to Budapest as well, or they sent messages to us from elsewhere, which we received at the shoemaker's establishment. Every other week we were permitted to send parcels to our husbands, but they were not supposed to include any notes or letters. I found a way to hollow out a paprika, a Hungarian pepper, conceal a note in it, and put the top back on the vegetable. The men would smuggle out letters to us with only bits of information, but almost all the letters advised the women to see to their own survival and run away. Nothing had changed for the men or their messages.

Mechel hadn't changed either. His words were always a variation of what he had said to me that day at the fence. I had to get him out before he was killed. One letter said, "You must remember that only if we are together is there a future. I can't live without you." When I read those words I had renewed energy. It forced me to work harder and to become more selfless. Rosie, still grieving for Moishe, had a different interpretation of Mechel's pleadings. She was completely supportive of what I was doing but she said his words were selfish. In her opinion Mechel should suggest that I too run for my life, even if he prayed I would not.

"It's not good for you to read these messages from Mechel. Of course you are trying to save him, but he is asking you to go into the lion's mouth. Why doesn't he tell you to be careful and not endanger yourself any longer?"

I understood Rosie's feelings. She no longer had a husband for whom she could sacrifice her life. But I also knew that Mechel could not live without me, and he knew that without him I would lose all will to live. He was right. If we could not be together in the future, there would be no future. Writing the words other husbands wrote in such circumstances would have been hypocritical, and Mechel was always honest and authentic. The fact that prison had not changed his basic character or his tenacious personality gave me new resolve. After all, Rosie had Micheline; if Mechel were lost to me, I would be utterly abandoned. Nevertheless Rosie felt better when I explained that even though the other wives got messages that said, "Save yourself and forget about me," all of them were engaged in actions and meetings to help their husbands escape. They were not abandoning their husbands, and why would I want to do that? Especially when our love was so deep and our connection almost mystical.

I should add that Rosie was always on the hunt for clues herself. She did not leave everything to me. She was much more at ease with gentiles than I was and continued to treat them as friends, and that could provide the key to Mechel's freedom. A friend of Rosie's had learned there was a Gestapo officer who lived in a resort area, with a home on Lake Balaton. He was known for being able to secure the release of Jews for a bribe and had been watched to see if he would betray them in the end. He was thought to be fairly trustworthy, or at least not bloodthirsty. He could be influenced or persuaded with money, apparently. A Christian man Rosie knew offered to drive us to Lake Balaton. He looked gentile, but now I wonder if he really was. The times were so strange; perhaps he too was a Jew posing as a gentile, but I don't think so. I am sure that he had no idea Rosie and I were Jewish.

We went to the officer's home and learned he was away for the day. Since we were already there, and to keep up the disguise, we rented a paddleboat and circled the lake. Our escort-driver soon grew tired of the lake and our company and handed me the paddles. "I need to take a nap now. You look strong. You can take the oars." I was doing just fine until an enormous boat came speeding up to us and I had no idea of how to turn our tiny boat out of the way. Rosie and I screamed at our driver to wake him up. I think Rosie gave him a sharp poke in the ribs. He was of no help. At the very last moment, the big boat saw us and swerved aside, but its wake all but submerged us. We were still afloat but our little tub was half-filled with water.

I would have laughed in relief if I had still known how to laugh. The Reich was bearing down harder and harder on Jews; Rosie's Moishe was dead; everyone else in my life was dead, and maybe Mechel was too; yet there we were on a lake waiting to see a Gestapo man and we were almost killed in a paddleboat. It sounds outrageous to say now, but perhaps this was Hashem's way of reminding me we were in His protection at all times. Perhaps it was a lesson to me that common accidents could occur in the most evil and uncommon times. I had to remember that caution was required at all times, not just in connection with the Nazis.

We headed for the shore and returned the rental boat to the concession stand. Somehow we dried off and cleaned up and felt as if we looked presentable. Our escort treated us to a drink, and we pretended we were on a day-vacation retreat. As always, the sleight of hand we performed was this: despite the war, we were not in mortal danger because we did not appear to be poor, despised, and hunted Jews. It was the only magic we had to use, and we had to employ it everywhere except in our room.

We went back to the officer's house after sunset and he was at home. However, his "staff" said that he was unavailable because he had a guest. We knew that meant he had a woman with him. I wrote him a letter in my perfect German, once again thinking of Mammiko and her insistence on learning perfectly a language I had grown to detest. I thanked her silently again. Without my skill in the German language, there would have been fewer opportunities for me to work for Mechel. In a fluent and grammatically correct letter, I explained to the Gestapo officer that I needed a favor and asked if I could call again at a more convenient time. I explained the lie in simple and natural language. My husband, Michael Nowakowski, was completely innocent of any wrongdoing but had been imprisoned. He had been wrongly accused and arrested for political misdeeds. We were Polish Christians who had fled to Hungary rather than fight against Germany and the Reich. There it was in black and white…in my own writing, the whole fragile tissue of lies and deceit.

Rosie and I went back to Budapest and waited for a reply from the Gestapo officer who lived by the lake. I didn't have to wait too long. I received the reply through the man who had driven us out there. The Gestapo officer was unable to do anything to help me.

I felt the cold arms of fear closing around me, especially at night before I went, or tried to go, to sleep. Time was running out and it seemed to me I should adopt more aggressive tactics. I had not been clever enough until now. Rosie agreed with me; we were not any further along than we had been, but we were losing time and money at a rapid rate. I procured the services of a woman named Marika. I suppose I could use the word *hired* but she was the kind of woman whose services were "procured" for a high fee. She used to "entertain" Nazis until they were so drunk she could extract information from them. It was an exceedingly unsavory business. She enjoyed having me as a client of hers, although she had many in similar straits. She could smell my frustration and the predicament we were in and she took advantage. Marika asked for more money each time she provided a scrap of information and also extracted some mink fur from us to put on her coat collar. In exchange she did get parcels to Mechel that contained hidden notes asking him for as much information as possible. And she did indeed get his communications back to me so that I had a better notion of what was going on and his exact whereabouts in the prison.

One night I went to leave a parcel for Mechel at her apartment as planned. I knocked on the door and a high-ranking German officer answered. "I am sorry, I will come back later. I was just coming by to see Marika." I stammered out my words in Hungarian, but the officer gave me a look I knew by now foreshadowed a problem. He pulled me into the apartment and asked me to join them. Marika was making a dinner party for a group of Nazis. There they sat, shoving stuffed cabbage into their faces. And they were all drunk by then and singing popular cabaret tunes. It was a decadent and debauched scene. The officer who had opened the door kept me close to him and led me to the table. "Sit down with us. Marika has cooked this herself. You must taste it."

He took a fork loaded with food (of "unknown origin" as far as I was concerned) and pushed it into my mouth. Of course I knew better than to refuse him. I held it in my mouth and took a napkin and tried to spit it out without anyone seeing me. I asked to be excused and went to the bathroom, where I got rid of the cabbage and left the parcel for Marika in a place she would know to look. All I wanted to do was leave so I slipped out of the house without anyone noticing my departure.

Marika never forgave me for the way I left her drunken Nazi dinner party. She felt that I had been rude and offended her "guests." She was not the most kindly person to begin with, but in those dishonorable circles she was among the better specimens. Marika punished me by not sending the parcel to Mechel, and in a nasty way told me to leave her alone. She did not know we were Jews, and if she had been discovered helping us she likely would have been killed. It was possible she suspected we were Jews but did not push the matter to a conclusion. Much as I disliked her methods, I had gone to her for help. She had not sought me out, and so I thought it would be best to try to make up with her for she might well have been denounced because of me. So I did try to patch it up with her, still thinking that Marika, through her Nazi acquaintances, would be the most likely to accomplish something. It was no use. She refused to talk to me again. I did not want to make Marika my enemy but now she was, and there was nothing I could do to change that.

My dejection turned into the deepest depression. I was returning to the same place I had been Pesach night when they had taken Mechel away. I was living in a personal abyss and I couldn't scratch my way to the top of it. I had let Mechel down and I had used Rosie's money, all for nothing. One day when I was probably at my lowest point, one of the people I trusted in the "shoemaker's" circle of confidants said something that caught my attention.

One of the most important members of the Reich had been dispatched to Buda (the nicer half of Budapest) and had set up a command headquarters.

He was said to be one of the most powerful and most evil of all of Hitler's close advisors and accomplices. His name was Adolf Eichmann. Everybody knew he had taken over a palatial villa in Buda, but nobody knew exactly where he himself was. It is likely that nobody wanted to know where he was; his name was synonymous with death.

Eichmann was the Devil on earth. He was the logician and tactician behind the Final Solution. He had engineered the efficient transfer of millions of Jews in trainloads to their end. He was proud of his work and boasted about it. In two years of committed, zealous hatred, five million people had been transported to their deaths in a complicated railroad operation run according to Eichmann's plan and design. Hitler had now sent him to Hungary to carry out the efficient deportation of Hungary's remaining Jews to Auschwitz. Without Eichmann Hitler might not have achieved his horrific feats to such an extent. He was more than Hitler's loyal comrade in arms – he was a part of Hitler's very brain.

With great difficulty, I was able to find out exactly where Eichmann was staying and headed there. I had gentile papers and could speak a superb German. There was nothing Rosie could do to stop me; I would seek and obtain an appointment with one of the major devils of the Reich. Dressed beautifully, I arrived at Eichmann's headquarters in Buda and gave my name and said without hesitation that I already had an appointment. Was I afraid? I do not think I knew any longer what fear felt like. I was always afraid, so this sense of being in peril or danger had become a part of me. The main thing was that I was not paralyzed and that is what counted.

While everyone else was trying to stay as far away from Eichmann as possible, I marched into his path. The soldier on guard took me at my word and escorted me upstairs. I heard the soldier say to Eichmann's assistant, "A Miss Nowakowska is here and says she has an appointment."

I waited only a few minutes when the soldier returned and said, "Please come this way," and he took me into Eichmann's private office. A surreal, calm confidence came over me. My heart was not racing; I was totally at peace with my decision to speak to Eichmann himself. Eichmann was standing on the terrace outside his villa office. He was smoking a cigarette and motioned to me, as if I might well have had an appointment with him. I looked at him and nodded. Eichmann was elegant, tall, and handsome, dressed in a formal SS uniform. He gave no outward sign that he was responsible for the mass murder of an entire population and culture of

Europe. In a civilian suit, he would have been mistaken for an upper class European gentleman of fine breeding.

A young officer was seated at a desk inside. Eichmann stayed on the terrace, standing with his profile toward me, smoking a cigarette, and looking out over the city he would soon decimate. The officer functioning as Eichmann's private secretary told me to give him the details of what brought me to see his commander. He took out a fresh pad of paper and opened his expensive fountain pen. I mentally reviewed the "facts" I was about to present to the Devil's private secretary.

"My husband is Michael Nowakowski and he is being held on suspicion of having engaged in political agitation in Debrecen. This is not true." When I said those words I said them emphatically and with emphasis, enough so that Eichmann looked right at me from his perch on the terrace. "He was swept up in a dragnet, but he is not a subversive. Michael is an intellectual who did not want to fight against the Reich." I knew the Nazis hated all intellectuals, and suspected them all, but I had to come up with some plausible reason why Mechel might have been arrested. Certainly it was better for Eichmann to think he was a Polish intellectual in jail with other gentile agitators rather than another piece of Jewish "rubbish." My reasoning was that if Michael were not a Jew, and I made the case he had not been a political agitator against Hitler, perhaps he would not be killed. Perhaps my courage to plead his case before Eichmann would soften him enough to release this Christian Pole with the loyal and beautifully attired wife.

The private secretary's face was impassive. I could not read his thoughts. Eichmann remained glued to his spot on the terrace. I thought I had made no impression on either of them, so I went for a dramatic flourish. I looked down, straightened my skirt, and touched my face as though I were about to cry.

"I am just so bewildered because I don't understand what has happened to my husband." I used my little-girl voice and whimpered slightly, "Why? Why would a man not mixed up in any of this...this politics between countries be taken away as a criminal? It's just so *unfair*."

My voice cracked with emotion at the word *unfair*. I stopped speaking because I had nothing left to say and because I had stepped over a line. How had I, an insignificant and lowly woman, dared accuse Eichmann of being unfair? It was not part of my original mental script and now I was going to be hauled away too. He heard the word *unfair* and stepped inside. Perhaps even the Devil wants to be considered fair.

"What exactly is going on?" He did not have a sharp tone to his voice and he sized me up with his piercing eyes. I have often reflected on the fact that I was face to face with this monster but he did not look like the personification of malevolent wickedness. He looked normal. It was a lesson I have never forgotten.

The private secretary gave him the summary of the details I had recited in monotone, short sentences. I was fairly sure Eichmann had already heard much of what I had said, and it seemed as if they were putting on a performance for my benefit. The private secretary concluded in a dry and remote tone, "The woman is here to seek information about her husband."

I looked directly into Adolf Eichmann's face. "My father-in-law was an important conductor with the Polish railroad. My husband, Michael, was never in the Polish army. We escaped here, to Hungary, and we are refugees, but we are not mixed up in anything, not in anything at all."

Eichmann listened and nodded, and when I finished he invited me to sit down. I said, "Thank you, sir." However, as he turned to walk out onto the terrace with the secretary I remained standing. The secretary returned from the terrace with a list in his hand. Eichmann had given him instructions. Eichmann resumed his original stance; he took out another cigarette, lit it, and looked into the near distance. One could only imagine what he was plotting for the ghetto and its Jews. The secretary started making phone calls. He must have been on the phone for half an hour, maybe less, but for me the time hung suspended like heavy lead and I felt years passing in front of me.

My knees knocked against one another but I willed them to stop. The secretary finished his call, and when he looked at me I knew my game was over. He had reached someone in charge of the prison. I read his eyes as if he were shouting at me: "You dirty Jew with the Jew-husband. Get out of here." But I stood my ground, silent and still. The secretary went to the terrace and put his head close to Eichmann, who now looked at me with eyes that betrayed the true man he was and raised his voice just enough for me to hear him speak to his secretary.

"Well, *that* is a fact that is very easy to find out."

Then Eichmann's face returned to an expressionless mask. Mechel had been identified as a Jewish prisoner in the phone call. It was thus likely that just as I had lied about my husband's heritage, I had been deceiving them about my own. I had failed totally. Perhaps I would and I might not even reach the front door of the villa without a group of Gestapo thugs waiting to escort me out for immediate deportation. I put on my coat extremely slowly, and with a gracious soft voice, I thanked the secretary for all his efforts. I even nodded good bye to Adolf Eichmann. I walked down the stairs assuming that I had just arranged the dual executions of a wife and her husband. However, I left the building without anyone saying a word to me. All the way back to our room I thanked Hashem for saving my life. For days and days I could think only about how close I had come to arrest.

Rosie and I went over everything in minute detail. When I finished we were aghast at what had transpired. I had failed in my mission and I had exposed my husband as a Jew in prison to none other than the Devil in charge of Budapest.

We assumed that the report of my visit to Adolf Eichmann would be used against Mechel in the prison. The guards there would not believe that the wife of a prisoner would come up with the idea to appear before Eichmann on her own. Surely they would assume that Mechel had given me a smuggled or clandestine command to attempt such an audacious stunt.

Mechel was punished severely. My deceptions and fanciful tales in the Devil's inner sanctum had reached the ears of the guards in charge of Mechel's group of inmates. My husband was beaten – almost to death – as a return favor for my afternoon "appointment" with Adolf Eichmann.

CHAPTER 19
Mechel's 'Madness'

Even as I was spinning fictional stories for Eichmann and his henchman, all of Hungarian Jewry was being sucked into the gas chambers and then the crematoria. I did not know it at the time, but by the late spring of 1944, Hungary was almost totally "sanitized" of Jews. An ethnic cleansing of monumental scope and brutal efficiency had been accomplished. Much of this was due to the decision to place Eichmann in Budapest, which picked up the pace of death.

The Munkach I had known had vanished by then. It was a place so identified as Jewish that it was called in Hebrew, "Ir va'em beYisroel" (literally: "A city and a mother in Israel" but loosely translated: an important Jewish heritage city). Everyone's mother and mother's mother and the children and the husbands and fathers and brothers and sisters were gone. The brick factory had been used as the deportation point. There was no need for an elaborate system of Judenrat or the apparatus associated with running a ghetto because the Jews were not detained long enough to require any of this. By the Festival of Shavuos in the Hebrew year 5704 (on the secular calendar May 28, 1944), 14,000 or more Jews had been deported from Munkach. This of course included all of my family who had remained in Munkach and all those dear to me. And in Munkach all the Jews were dear to me.

Had I known of these events, I am quite certain I would not have been able to function. I would have died internally, become a statue of grief and longing. Since I did not know the fate of the rest of Hungary or of my beloved town, I could continue with my plots and schemes to get Mechel out of jail. However, Rosie and I were running out of everything. Money, energy, ideas, sources of information, and most important, we were losing hope. We saw what was happening in Budapest. Inside the ghetto the Jews were hanging by a hair, not even a thread. We were told the next major convoy would take all the Budapest Ghetto residents.

Even so, the myth of Nazi invulnerability was beginning to weaken and crack. To the northeast the Soviet army was on the march and to the west the Allies were breaking through. In the northwest, however, the Reich was preparing to make a last bloody stand. In Hungary collaborators were beginning to fear the future if the Allies were victorious. For this reason alone, certainly not for any humanitarian one, they ordered a halt to the deportations of Jews on July 7, 1944.

I picked up these few facts and rumors about Allied victories and a possibility of the demise of the Reich from the network of other fugitives and resistance workers. The shoemaker's shop was filled with news and rumors, and it was never easy to know what was really happening or which source was reliable. The most tangible sign that I personally observed was the Soviet air bombardment of Budapest. It encouraged all of us to hold on for yet another day, but it was not the answer to my prayers. My prayers were constantly for Mechel. Rosie was involved in the daily dream of the war ending, and talked of nothing else. In my fog of pain and obsession about my husband, I noticed something was amiss and then realized belatedly that Blanka was missing.

Rosie wasn't home when I discovered that Blanka was gone. I had hours to engage in paranoid delusions. I was sure that Blanka would never have run away from us. I assumed she had been kidnapped and was being held somewhere, or that she had been identified as a Jew and murdered and therefore we would be next. Rosie returned and reassured me. She was sorry I had such a dreadful time worrying about Blanka. Rosie had sensed the turnaround in the war and intelligently returned Blanka to the orphanage. She was right to think it the likely place a parent would look for a child. (Blanka's father did survive, returned to Budapest eventually, and indeed found and claimed little Blanka at the orphanage.)

I was sad Blanka was back in the orphanage but it was good for her future, and truthfully it made our lives easier. We were back to a small family of three and no longer had to smuggle Blanka in and out under our coats, or sneak outside through back doors. About the same time Blanka left our household, a man contacted me through a source in the Jewish activist network. He said he knew Mechel was safe and could be rescued. He seemed very credible. Rosie and I decided to trust him and meet his demands.

He was a prison worker and had access at all hours. He explained how he came and went freely without being questioned. Once again Rosie reached out to people sympathetic to my situation and raised some money. He demanded a large bribe but insisted we refer to it as his "fee." We gave him all he demanded and were told to meet him the next day at noon. We were to bring a set of men's clothing so that Mechel would not walk out of the prison in his jail attire. We were given an exact location for our meeting. We did as we were told. He took the clothing and drove off in his car, telling us not to worry. He would see us as planned and then I would be reunited with my husband. Rosie and I concluded anybody who was driving a car in Budapest in 1944 must have considerable power and influence. We were confident.

Rosie, Micheline, and I arrived at the designated place quite early. The address was that of a still decent outdoor garden with a bar and café.

"Let's celebrate," said Rosie, with a lightness in her voice I had not heard for years. I was certainly ready to celebrate. At last, we had found the lead that would produce results. Rosie explained to Micheline, "We will have Uncle Mechel back with us in no time at all." We ordered drinks. She ordered a soda of some sort for Micheline and seltzer for herself. I was so relieved I wanted something stronger to relax and also to mark the happy occasion. The waiter brought me a sweet mint-flavored cocktail called "Unicum," which is a kind of crème de menthe. After only a few sips, I was silly and a bit tipsy. Rosie tried to shut me up because we were making a spectacle of ourselves. We were two women alone in war-torn Budapest with a small girl in our care. It was too suspicious to go unnoticed for very long. Rosie sobered me up by telling me that I was about to jeopardize everything we had worked for so long to attain. I quieted down and sobered up quickly.

Time passed. Hours went by. The man did not come with Mechel, nor did Mechel come to us alone. Yet I refused to believe the man with the car and the nice clothing who acted like such a gentleman was just another con man. I sat stubbornly and made Rosie and Micheline wait with me. It was only after an inordinate length of time, maybe the entire day, that

Rosie convinced me we had been tricked – again. We left the garden café-bar with Rosie supporting me. She had to help me walk, but not because I was drunk. I was sobbing uncontrollably and unable to walk without her assistance. There were no more possibilities to explore. I did not tell her that I didn't believe I would ever see Mechel again – alive or dead.

A few days later, much to my surprise, Marika sent someone to see me. I had not spoken to her since the stuffed cabbage episode. Now, through one of her contacts, for another bribe of course, I was given the name and address of a Hungarian doctor who worked in the hospital section of the prison. Without paying attention to the date, I went to the address one evening around supper time, assuming he would be home with his family. He was definitely home and having his Christmas Eve dinner! I was mortified to have barged in on him and his family while they were sharing their Christmas feast, and apologized and wept. As I moved toward the door, his kindly wife stopped me. "Don't leave, please, wait a moment. Let me get my husband for you."

I heard her go into the room and above the laughter of a happy family at Christmas, even during the war; I could hear her voice. "You must help this young woman in the hallway. Something is very wrong. Take care of her. It's Christmas Eve."

The words the wife said made me cry even more. I tried to compose myself before the doctor appeared. I immediately asked his forgiveness for interrupting his holiday but he was gracious and kind. He took me into a private room and talked to me for several minutes. The prison hospital was reserved for those who were either insane or had a contagious disease. The Germans were particularly worried about people with bad rashes, for example. He told me to go to the drug store and get a pill that caused a terrible rash in healthy people. He did not give me a prescription because that would have been the end of him. However he did give me all the information I needed to know. He had sized me up quickly as someone intelligent and with a good memory. He took me to the door and wished me good luck. The last words he said to me that night were these: "Remember, if you want to see your husband again, make sure that he gets transferred to the prison hospital. Once he is there, it might be possible for you to visit him."

I left in wonderment and gratitude to the doctor and to his willingness to adhere to the Christmas spirit in times of such hatred and un-Christian behavior. After Christmas I went to the drugstore he recommended and asked for the pill with great assurance in my voice. It was quite a show because I had total lack of confidence in my mind. I waited for the druggist to ask for a prescription, but he did not. He came out from behind his drug counter with one capsule, which he put into a small paper envelope. I paid him and left.

I had to face an enormous challenge. How would I be able to tell Mechel what to do with one mysterious pill? Getting parcels to him was not an impossibility, but I couldn't imagine how to tell him what to do or how to hide the pill. It took me days to figure out the best way to disguise the pill. Finally, it came to me. I would put it into a wooden box that had a cloth lining. I had such a box for some reason, and I realized it was the perfect camouflage for a red Hungarian pepper. I slipped a tiny piece of paper into the pepper with the word "Look" written on it with an arrow. The arrow pointed to the lining of the box, where I made a slit in which I put the pill. I also was able to put in a small nailbrush with very stiff bristles, in addition to some clothing and some food.

Writing in as many languages as Mechel could more or less read or piece together the meaning, I instructed him. "Take the pill, then use the brush to scratch your face and make it bleed. Then act sick and as insane as possible. I was sure Mechel's innate intelligence and strategic thinking ability would enable him to unscramble my code. I was right. He followed my instructions to the letter. He took the pill and injured his face with the brush. The Hungarian doctor I had gone to on Christmas Eve came to the hospital when the jailers notified him that there was a contagious prisoner who needed to be moved to the hospital. The doctor came and said that he had contracted a contagious disease and should be put in isolation immediately.

In cases that required transfer to the prison hospital, a second doctor had to certify the Hungarian doctor's diagnosis. The second opinion, of course, was from a Nazi doctor. By the time the Nazi arrived, the magical pill's effects had disappeared. Mechel's face showed no trace of a rash and his self-inflicted wounds from the brush were not convincing. He appeared to be in normal health. The Hungarian doctor got word to me that the plan had failed and I also learned that Mechel had been beaten for "playing tricks."

Once again, my own "escape tricks" had brought brutality to my husband. Rosie kept things going in our life while I slipped back into a state of serious emotional decline. Rosie reminded me that all was not lost with

Mechel. She made me think things through and would not permit me to continue to wallow in misery. After all, she said, I included many "clues" in my notes that if the rash didn't work he should act like a crazy person. Rosie would not let me give up on the dream that Mechel would be free and come to me. And she also made me concentrate on how clever Mechel was and that he would not sit around waiting to be shipped off to another prison or to his death. He was a fighter and so was I. Thanks to Rosie's strong encouragement, I listened to my inner conscience and counted on the power of faith and love. Mechel was far too smart to attempt to act crazy within days of having a false rash. He would wait it out, and he would do it properly. I had to be patient and I had to have more faith.

While I was waiting for some word about his fate, Mechel was making mental notes for his next move. Each day as I recited the morning prayers I prayed also that Mechel was working on the plan as I had described it to him. I believed his "madness" would be his salvation. In fact, that is exactly what happened. After waiting for suspicion to dissipate after his fake rash, he began to roam the large cell at night. He touched inmates gently, woke them up and chattered in meaningless words. The rest of the night he prayed compulsively and loudly. This became his standard routine – he was either bothering other prisoners or chanting in Hebrew. He became known as the Crazy Rabbi. Mechel wisely did nothing to dispel the mythology that he was an ordained rabbi, nor did he confirm it.

A group of prisoners announced he was a saint or a prophet who was receiving visions from above. He became so well known as the Crazy Rabbi that when there was a quarrel between the men, they called him over to mediate the disagreement. He did so, but in a half-insane manner. He never stepped out of his newly created character. His performance was perfect and continuous. After babbling incoherently or praying loudly, he would fall absolutely silent for hours, refusing to acknowledge anyone's presence or communicate. During these long silences, he was eavesdropping on the prisoners' conversations with one another. By doing this and keeping everything in order in his mind, he learned very private things. His technique was so skilled that none of the men knew he had overheard their secrets.

Mechel took his act of madness to the next level. He roamed at night, as usual, but instead of crazy chattering, he gave prophecies about their families and what was happening to them. They could not figure out how he knew so many details, names, and locations. He became not only the

Crazy Rabbi and the Saint, now he was the Mad Genius. Finally he reached the goal he had desired from the beginning. All the others wanted Mechel out of the prison. They had become afraid of him.

"He's crazy. We don't know what he's going to do next."

"Get rid of this lunatic. We can't get any sleep."

Their complaints went on like this for a few weeks. The prisoners were close to revolt. Even his former committee members believed he was insane and posed a threat to all of them. The jailers became convinced as well. Mechel's dramatic performance had worked. Once again, our benefactor, the Hungarian doctor was ordered to come in for a thorough examination. Knowing full well what was really going on, he arrived at the hospital totally prepared. He said Mechel was incurably insane and must be moved to the hospital. Once again, the Nazi supervising doctor was called in for the final approval.

Obviously dubious, the Nazi put Mechel through his paces and Mechel responded as an authentically mentally ill person. The doctor had a final test. He looked into Mechel's eyes and instructed Mechel to follow the doctor's finger with his eyes. Instead, Mechel grabbed the cigarette out of the doctor's mouth. Mechel began taking puffs of the doctor's cigarette with rapid jerking motions at the same time he made a noise deep in his throat. The doctor was convinced and disgusted. Mechel was moved immediately into the hospital. When the guards came to move him, however, they found the orders were that he should be taken to the hospital inside the ghetto and not the prison hospital.

I knew nothing of what had been going on with Mechel. The night he was transferred to the ghetto hospital I went to sleep, as I did each night, with prayers and with tears streaming down my face. In the middle of the night I had a nightmare. This was not unusual; I had them most nights. This nightmare was extremely peculiar because I heard Mechel talking to me. His voice was so distinct and clear that I was sure he had gotten out of jail and come to our room. I jumped out of bed and searched for him, but he was not there. I looked out the window. Perhaps he was outside calling to me? Again, there was no sign of him.

I went back to sleep. Within a short period I was awakened again by Mechel's voice, and this time his words were specific. When I was fully conscious I remembered that his words were the same in both dreams: "Lolishe, come to the ghetto!" I shook Rosie out of a sound sleep and told her that I had to go to the ghetto immediately at daybreak. I asked her if she would wake me. I did not want to oversleep. I told her I had business inside the ghetto. Rosie sat up in bed, rubbing her eyes.

"Lola, what is the matter with you? We are not going into the ghetto. There isn't anyone in the ghetto for us to worry about now. No one we know is in the ghetto. You've had some bad dreams again. Go back to sleep."

I wouldn't let her go to sleep without promising me she would wake me up at dawn.

"What is wrong with you? Tell me, what are you thinking?"

I knew better than to confess that Mechel had spoken to me in my sleep, so I said, "I need to go to a restaurant that is still in the ghetto... I have to meet someone there."

"Yes, yes, fine, I'll wake you in the morning, but there are no restaurants in the ghetto now where you can meet people. You are just not fully awake, Lola, it's part of some dream you had. There's nothing and nobody for us in the ghetto."

"No, you are wrong. I know I have to go to the ghetto. There is either a letter or some sort of message about Mechel waiting for me there."

"Lola, stop it. You are blithering now. Do you think for one minute I am going to let you go into the ghetto now? It's a trap. You will be caught, with or without papers, Jewish or gentile. The ghetto means death and I will not permit you to go there. Stop this and get back to sleep. You are overwrought and overtired."

So I knew Rosie would not assist me. It was the only time she had ever refused to help me, but I understood her reasoning. However I knew that I was right. Mechel had spoken to me. I stayed awake the rest of the night and slipped out of the room before the sun had fully risen. We had not been near the ghetto since we left after our disagreeable encounters with Kasztner. I walked through the gates at an illegal hour without anyone seeing me. I affixed my yellow star to my clothing. There were no police watching me and I walked around without being noticed.

Admittance hours were now very strictly enforced. If you were caught coming into the ghetto at the wrong time, the Jewish policemen who were still there were now all collaborators and would turn you in to the Nazis to earn favors or perhaps money. For some compelling reason, I made up my mind to act out my own fib about the restaurant and went to the place where a restaurant had been before the Nazis clamped down totally. There was no restaurant in the ghetto any longer; the building was just another residence with families that hadn't yet been deported.

The ghetto was wrapped in a ghostly silence even though it was still early morning. It was *too* quiet. It felt as if the noose was tightening around the communal neck of the entire Budapest Ghetto. I stood in front of the building that had once housed a restaurant on the ground floor. I did not know what to do next. From a few feet away, I heard a woman calling my name. She rushed to my side.

"Are you Janka Nowakowska? We have been looking for you. We had no idea where you were."

She was a stranger to me. She was a young Jewish woman who seemed to know me, but I had no recollection of ever meeting her.

"You are looking for me?"

I did not tell her I had come looking for anyone or anything.

"I have a letter from your husband." At that, she handed me an envelope and disappeared before I could thank her or ask for her name. It was a letter from Mechel and it read: "Lolishe, come to me now. I am inside the ghetto hospital. Please, hurry, get me out of here."

I ran to the hospital. It was all but deserted of patients and there were no doctors or nurses making the rounds yet. There was Mechel, lying on a cot alone in a room. He had the blanket pulled up to his neck to hide his prison outfit. He looked terrible – pale, thin, and gray. I had no time for reunion kisses or questions.

"How did you get here?" I whispered.

"I did what you told me to do in the clues you sent. I was an entirely credible crazy man."

I told him that I had to get Rosie and some clothing and he must not let anyone discover him in jail clothes. The trolley ride back to our room felt like it would never end. Rosie was relieved to see me, having figured out I had gone on a fool's errand into the ghetto. If she had not been so afraid for herself and Micheline she might well have come to find me. Thank God she did not. Instantly, she sprang into action with me. We knew time was not with us. The Jewish police could send Mechel back to the prison immediately if they discovered him.

We threw some of Mechel's clothing into a plain bag and hurried to the ghetto. The hospital was open for visiting hours now and I was worried we would come into an empty room. But Mechel was waiting for us, still covered up to his chin. We gave him the clothes, and he went into a bathroom, changed, and stuffed his prison uniform into the pillowcase. We put the pillowcase behind a door. He told me when he had written the letter to me. It was almost exactly the hour in the night that I'd heard his voice telling me to come to the ghetto.

Fortunately the doctors and nurses had not begun their rounds. He had not yet been registered officially and therefore there was no chart or name tag hanging on the foot of his bed. We walked out of the hospital building, pretending we had been visiting someone. Again, I employed my Hungarian and kept a steady stream of conversation about our dear elderly woman friend who seemed so ill, so emaciated. I continued to say it would appear she would be an invalid for life now and would never walk again. Rosie and Mechel just nodded, and I finished with a flourish. "We must come back during the afternoon or evening hours and see how she is doing."

We walked through the ghetto gate again without attracting notice or questions and ran to catch the trolley. The conductor had already started the car but, amazingly, stopped it, possibly because he saw Rosie struggling with Micheline to board the car. Mechel's hat was pulled down to cover most of his face, and his scarf was wrapped around his neck and up to his lips. He was so obviously pale and worn from prison that he would have been picked up for that alone, if not because his features always announced his Jewish identity. He was therefore in double jeopardy of being stopped and taken away. By concealing his face, he hoped he would not be noticed as either a fugitive from prison or as a Jew.

Our next hurdle was to get past our landlady. Sneaking Blanka past landlords was hard enough, but how would we accomplish this with a grown man in a hat and coat and scarf? I looked at what we had accomplished together – there was the living presence of Mechel, holding Micheline's hand as we got off the trolley. The rest was going to be easy! Rosie and Micheline went into the building first and Rosie asked the landlady if she could talk to her privately. They went into the kitchen where Rosie made up a problem of some sort that she claimed concerned her. While Rosie and Micheline were in the kitchen talking to the landlady, Mechel and I walked past quietly and entered our room.

We were together. I didn't touch Mechel. I was still in a state of disbelief. Maybe I was looking at an apparition I had made up and it wasn't really my husband. Then Mechel smiled and opened wide his arms, and I was whole again. Rosie and I wanted to cry for joy, and to celebrate, but we had work still to do.

Mechel slept the entire day. It was probably for the best that we did not learn everything he had gone through. I had to obtain new clothing for him, which was not too difficult. The big issue was the matter of his documents and there was no question that was going to be tricky. Michael Nowakowski, the Polish Catholic intellectual conscientious objector, needed to disappear without a trace. I made my way to the shoemaker's shop, my unofficial "headquarters," once again to seek their help. As I turned the corner and was a few feet from the door two men approached me. They were Jewish policeman from the ghetto. My heart stopped. Someone had betrayed us! Here were the traitorous informers who had come to torture me until I told them where Mechel was hiding.

"Aren't you Janka Nowakowska?" one of them asked me.

"Yes, that is my name, and why do you ask?"

"Do you have a husband who is in the hospital?"

"No, I have a husband in jail."

"No, you do not. You are a liar. You have a husband in the hospital in the ghetto and he is looking for you."

"No, I am sorry, but my husband is most definitely in prison."

"He is in the hospital and misses you. He wants to see you. Come with us and we will escort you there."

"He's not in jail? Wonderful! Of course I'll go with you, but first, allow me to stop in this shop. I have something to pick up."

"Yes, but we must accompany you."

I reached the door to the shoemaker's shop a few steps ahead of them and ran inside and said in Polish, "*Ratuj cze mie. Ratuj cze mie!* – Save me, save me!"

The Polish men in the shop confronted the Jewish police. "What do you want with her? Leave her alone."

"Her husband wants her. He is asking for her."

"That is not your business," said one of the Polish men who knew me fairly well. "Why are you bothering her?"

These Jewish policemen were not expecting resistance, and they began to argue among themselves. Two of the men in the shoemaker's shop surrounded me and got me to the door. "Run. Run," they screamed at me as I raced down the street. The policemen ran after me. One of them blew his whistle and another reached me and grabbed me. The men from the shoemaker's shop were in hot pursuit and they caught up with the policemen and started an all-out brawl.

I ran frantically. I jumped onto a moving trolley, clutching onto the back railing of the car as it went down the tracks. While the streetcar took me away from the skirmish, the fight continued. I could hear the echoes of the Polish men screaming, "Leave that young woman alone!"

I returned to my room exhausted and unable to speak. I could not catch my breath. We had come once again too close to the razor's edge of extinction. I finally told Rosie and Mechel what had happened. Mechel said, "My papers will wait for another day. Hashem has given me back my life, and saved you just now. With or without new documents, our life can resume."

It took some days before I had the will to venture out again. When I did I learned something of great importance about goodness in a time of rampant evil. My friends inside the Jewish underground had learned the details of Mechel's release from prison. The German doctor had approved his transfer based on a confirmed case of incurable insanity. However, the Nazi instructions were that he be taken to the prison hospital. The Hungarian doctor "accidentally" ordered the guards to take him to the ghetto hospital.

Returning to the prison, the guards were asked where they had been. When they told the authorities what they had done with Mechel they were ordered to go back to the ghetto and bring the prisoner back to the prison hospital. The Germans said they would hold the ghetto hospital responsible for his return; that is why the Jewish policemen pursued me. I do not know the reason why the Hungarian doctor was willing to take such a chance, but his decision saved my husband. In those times, individual acts of bravery and disobedience saved lives. These actions are not recorded in a systematic way. Many of the names of these heroes are lost to us, but those of us who were rescued will never forget those personal triumphs of courage and morality.

CHAPTER 20

Terror Continues

Autumn 1944. Hungary was overrun, and full surrender to the Soviet Union was imminent. Having chosen the wrong side, the Hungarians now beseeched the Russians to save them. The loss of Hungary was a devastating blow to the Reich. With Hungary's collapse, there was no way to stop the allied invasion into Austria, and inevitably, Germany itself. Hungarians still committed to the cause of fascism and anti-Semitism did not, however, fold up their battle maps and quietly go away. In a desperate move they staged a coup on October 15, 1944. Admiral Milos Horthy, the regent of Hungary, was engaged in final surrender negotiations with the Soviet commanders when he was arrested. The renegade fascist government under party leader Ferenc Szalasi made a last pathetic stand to keep Hungary for the Reich. The Hungarian National Socialist Party (Hungarian Nazis) was called the Arrow Cross and its army was under Szalasi's command.

It was a last-ditch effort that could only fail, but it enabled the reign of terror to continue. Despite the encroachment of the Soviet Red Army, Szalasi gave the order to seal off the ghetto completely. It was absolutely déjà vu for us. We were not in the ghetto but the images we saw and heard about were replicas of the Bochnia Ghetto in its last phase. Mechel and I continued to live outside the ghetto but we were in a terribly precarious situation.

Arrow Cross thugs raided the ghetto on a regular basis, murdering people by the hundreds. Those who survived between raids were made to work in labor so arduous that many died while working. Their last act of atrocity

189

happened just as winter approached and the Budapest air was turning chilly. The boundaries of the ghetto were drawn even tighter. In an area of less than one-tenth of a square mile, which is the equivalent of a few city blocks, 70,000 Jews were crammed together in appalling conditions.

In November and December several thousand Jews were evacuated on foot. It was another of the infamous Death Marches the Nazi minions were carrying out throughout Eastern Europe. The Hungarian guards led the residents of the Budapest Ghetto on foot in the direction of Austria, presumably to work in labor camps. Stragglers were shot on the way, and most of the rest perished in one manner or another.

The Arrow Cross had turned into marauding mobs of street gangs. Their raids were nothing like the systematic horror of the SS troops we had seen in the early days of the war. These thugs grabbed people randomly and either tortured or killed them outright. They were not accountable to a commanding hierarchy and were beyond immorality – they were totally amoral. These roving gangs stopped people, asked for documents and if they thought your papers were not legal or if they didn't like your looks, you were doomed. Chaos and anarchy fueled by vehement anti-Semitism set the tone. We had entered a time with no rule of law whatever, because these outlaws had suspended even the rules of the Reich. Anyone not associated with the Arrow Cross was in danger.

Mechel remained undocumented. I was not in a position to return to the forgery operation at the shoemaker's. It was too close to the ghetto, and now that I was well known I could endanger those working in the underground. We had reached a major fork in our road. We had to do something. Keeping Mechel in our room without papers threatened all of us including our landladies. Moving from room to room was no longer a safe option either, as Mechel was such an easy target for the Arrow Cross.

Rosie said she would go and get forged documents for Mechel. There was simply no other option. I told her it was my responsibility. She argued that me going was an impossibility. I pleaded with her and so did Mechel. We were overcome with alarm by her insistence. What would happen to Micheline if Rosie did not return? It was not discussed, but we understood the terms of our family connection and love. If the worst happened, of course Micheline would become our child and we would care for her, but it troubled us. The child had not known her father and now her mother was risking her life to get Mechel papers. Rosie, ever rational and pragmatic, spoke the essential truth: We were all at risk as long as Mechel remained undocumented.

One day without forewarning she left, saying she would be back as soon as possible. Mechel and I knew what she was going to do. She returned very late in the day as white as a ghost. She did not tell us anything – what she had accomplished must have been so fraught with danger she dare not speak of it. In her purse were the precious forged documents. We did not ask how she had obtained them, but knew that she had endured a fearful experience. Nothing more needed to be said. Mechel remained Michael Nowakowski on his new false papers. As I was still Janka Nowakowska; the people who had prepared Mechel's documents said it was the only feasible plan.

Once again we were posing as Polish refugees. Although we understood the rationale behind the decision, it was surreal. Mechel was still a fugitive with the same false identity that had landed him in prison. Budapest was being bombed regularly by the Soviets. We needed to think about where to go next. It was now 1945 and I thought about our lives together since 1939. I don't believe we had ever stayed in any one location for more than four or five months. It felt like we had stayed in some places for decades, for example in the Bochnia Ghetto, but we had been on the run for almost six years. Despite my inadequate grasp of geography, Mechel and I discussed our limited options.

Debrecen drifted in and out of the discussions. I was totally opposed to returning to that place. Even the name chilled me, but Mechel felt it might be a smart move. We spoke of Bucharest but didn't really know what we were talking about. We were trapped animals cowering in fear. Either the Arrow Cross would get us or we would be killed by a Soviet bomb aimed at our enemies. We were in the crossfire during the anarchy of the last days of the war. This is the way wars usually come to an end, with people scrambling about in terror, not knowing who or what might kill you. It was ironic that the Soviet bombardments were bringing Hitler to his knees but placing us in constant peril.

With Mechel's papers in hand, Rosie resumed her role as our "real estate" agent. It was unsafe for us to stay anywhere. We were back to moving from room to room with only the whisper of a chance we would not be caught eventually. The city was awash with refugees from Romania and elsewhere. Mechel was afraid to go outside because he could so easily be identified as a Jew, even without beard or armband and with his false Christian papers. When he did leave the room, he covered half his face with his scarf and kept his hat low on his forehead.

One evening, Rosie got word that the Arrow Cross was closing in on our particular neighborhood, conducting house-to-house searches. We evacuated our room without a moment's hesitation even though we had no other place to stay. We moved so fast, I had no idea what we left behind. We didn't care. We felt victorious because we had beaten the thugs to the house, although we had no way of knowing if they actually came. Rumors fueled more rumors. We had learned it was best to assume the worst.

With no place to go and without secure leads to a room, we passed a couple of days riding the trolleys. Budapest had one streetcar line that ran back and forth across town until 4 a.m. We rode for one fare all day and into the night. The conductors didn't seem to mind or even to notice. There were so many bedraggled refugees that we didn't stand out from the others. The cars were heated, which was a great blessing. One night when the others were asleep I noticed a distressed looking young woman sitting directly across from me. She was clearly in dire poverty but had the look of someone who knew how to survive.

I followed my hunch and asked her where she slept after the streetcar stopped operating. She was friendly and offered to show us. We got off with her and went into a questionable neighborhood and entered a disreputable apartment building. Beds were for rent, but they were really just cots and blankets priced by the hour. We understood what we were doing but needed to stretch out, and so we rented one cot and took turns resting. When not resting, we served as security guards for each other, mostly watching for thieves, not the Arrow Cross. By morning we decided the streetcar was like a furnished apartment. We vowed that no matter what happened, we would not return to that flophouse.

We couldn't find a place to rent, but as happened to us again and again, a seemingly random event changed the course of our lives. We saw two sisters of the Bobover Rebbe, Rabbi Shloime Halberstam, on the street. We had not seen them since Bochnia. We could not believe our eyes, but there they were in Budapest. When they found out we were homeless or room-less, they took us to their apartment outside the ghetto. They opened their home to us and refused to hear our arguments about their own safety. They were taking an enormous risk, but our family histories were forever intimately intertwined. We accepted with gratitude to the One Above – and astonishment that we had found one another.

The Halberstam sisters had their own horror stories to tell us. The Rebbe, Reb Shloime, had escaped from Bochina with the help of his brother, Reb Chaskel Duvid, who had hired smugglers from a town outside Bochina. The rest of the story was quite similar to ours. Their group included his two sisters, Gitche and Chumche, and Chumche's two children. The ages of the group ranged from seven to seventy. Their journey had been harrowing, much of it on foot, just as ours and as so many others' had been. Once inside Czechoslovakia, they were urged by Jews there to move swiftly into Hungary. Again on foot and in darkness they proceeded to Budapest, with the knowledge that members of their extended family had already been murdered. In Budapest they obtained false papers and so lived in the shadow of the law just as we did.

In Budapest Rabbi Halberstam worked hard to rescue Jews still trapped in Poland, using the same method that had saved us from arrest and death. The coal trucks with false bottoms were much in demand in those years. During one fateful mission there was a grave accident that led to the death of all those in the truck and ruled out any further coal-truck rescue trips. After the Nazi incursion into Hungary, the Halberstam family went as far underground as they could, which wasn't far because of their religious visibility and fame. Some friends of theirs went to Bucharest, Romania, where they set up an escape route. Part of the Halberstam family began this journey in May 1944 with disastrous consequences. Everyone in the group except Rabbi Halberstam, his youngest son Naftuli, and a friend were killed, captured, or sent on convoys to Auschwitz. The remaining three were able to bribe their way to the Romanian border and settle in Bucharest.

As we listened to their story, Mechel and I grew quiet. I thought about my lost family, and particularly in that moment about my brother Moishe who had been so involved in our Bochnia forgery operations. Mechel became somber and silent. I knew that he too was recalling the Bochnia Ghetto and the awful night of the Aktion and the morning burial and all those we had lost there. How strange our world was that now a safety net was to be found in Bucharest when just a few years earlier Romanian Jews had fled to Hungary to avoid slaughter.

We sat with the Rebbe's sisters and all of us were lost in the memory of the time when the Bobover Rebbe himself had come up with the typewriter, the good quality paper, and the young man who could carve a stamp out of a rubber ball. My mother had supervised the final documents. My brother Moishe had been an integral part of it all. Inadvertently, by the accident of my Hungarian birth, I had started the process in motion that morning at the Judenrat when I said I was born in Munkach. Now, the Rebbe's sisters were offering us refuge. The circle was complete.

Rosie felt that she and Micheline should not stay, for the safety of all of us. We were not without feelings and emotions during this time, but survival and the protection of those we cared about and loved was paramount. There was no room for sentimentality and sad farewells. When Rosie said she felt it would be best if we parted, we acknowledged she was making the right choice. It was a hard parting for me as she was the last tie to my own family. In the tireless efforts we had both made to achieve Mechel's release, Rosie and I had become like sisters. And with no children of my own, Micheline was very dear to me. Nonetheless, we supported her departure and she was happy we had found a home with the Halberstam women.

Now, in a "real" apartment, we began to establish a routine. It wasn't a normal life, and we were still far from free, but there were pleasures, however small. I could cook for our new "family" and help them with other chores. We were always aware of the catastrophic breakdown of everything outside our doors, but we were able to establish a feeling of domestic stability that had not been possible in the endless succession of rented rooms. The Halberstam sisters welcomed our presence and we were very happy in their company, and in our shared traditions.

The war was winding down and yet the atmosphere was more toxic and lethal than ever. As Hitler lost more and more ground, his leadership decisions spun further out of control. We wanted the defeat of the Reich but were unprepared for the devastation and disorder that would accompany his exit from the world's stage. The stench of death was part of each day's reality. Neither Mechel nor I talked about what to do or where to go any longer.

We thought we might end our days in Budapest with the Halberstams. As the bombs dropped from the sky we put ourselves on automatic pilot. We went about our routine tasks, said our prayers, kept a Jewish home, and waited for any scrap of news that would make us believe in Mechel's words, "There will be a world after this."

CHAPTER 21
The Winter of 1944-1945

Elegant Budapest was coming apart at its architectural seams and so were its human inhabitants. Buildings crashed, turning into powdered stacks of rubble within moments of the bomb strikes. We were on alert for the unmistakable wails of the air raid sirens that signaled another air offensive. Everyone scampered like lemmings, not to the sea, but to the closest basement or shelter. We waited under buildings and in tunnels to get the all-clear siren. Leaving the shelters we never knew what we would find on the ground. Sometimes there was no damage in our area; other times there was total destruction. The Germans were no longer transporting Jews, but we were moments from a tragic ending of a different kind.

A political war was in full swing about which we knew nothing at all. The fight between two future enemies was under way – the clash between what would become known as the "free world" and the world behind the "Iron Curtain" had begun. We did not know that a future we would refer to as the Cold War would become the status quo. In Budapest in the winter of 1944–1945 we were still in a white-hot and noisy war. The bombing schedule was impossible to figure out, even for those of us who prided ourselves on being canny. The Soviets and the Western Allies coordinated the timing of their advances against the Reich. The Germans were in retreat, but there were already significant plans in place about how to divide up the spoils of war between the Soviets and the democratic nations of Europe. In Hungary, the internal political maneuvering of the two forces fighting Hitler gave the

Arrow Cross and the remaining Nazis plenty of elbow room to continue their "work." In the last year of the war, or perhaps even the last six months of the war, tens of thousands of Jews were murdered in Hungary.

It was never safe to venture outside, but I had to do it and so did the Halberstam sisters in order to find food. We bartered or we badgered someone until they let go of a tidbit of something for a ridiculous price. At times people helped each other with generosity but not too often. It was a time of such deprivation that most people reverted to primal concern for only their immediate families or themselves. We learned how to scavenge for edible food. It was a skill everyone picked up quickly. It was either that or die of starvation rather than from a bomb. On lucky outings I found a store open that had a few miserable tins of food or wilted vegetables left. We rarely came across a peddler with fresh food. Those were joyous events, even to see a peddler with a cart.

This was our life. We engaged in two major forms of activity: dodging bombs and searching frenetically for food. There wasn't time for anything else. In a manner of speaking, it made life easier. We were down to the basics of survival. The streets were littered with corpses both human and animal – mules and horses. At first, the horror of the scene overpowered our senses and our emotions, but after a short time, we did not stop to look.

The terror of that winter was so extreme that the "playing field" between Jews and non-Jews had become somewhat more level. Everyone was in peril of being a victim of the next bombardment. Therefore there was less and less time to inspect the person standing on line to buy a carrot or the person in the shelter. Distinguishing the Jew from the non-Jew was not worth most people's efforts any longer. The exception was the Arrow Cross, ever vigilant to find the last Jews in Budapest and shovel them into the convoys to Auschwitz.

My Uncle Yoshe Berger and his family had escaped into Budapest from Poland, but had not managed to get out of the ghetto. They were swept up in one of the last Aktionen in the ghetto. Crossing into Slovakia, Yoshe jumped off the train, but his wife, Rushe, and their daughter, Toby, and their grandchild, ten-year-old Halinka, ended up in Auschwitz. They survived only because the Nazis were so afraid of the Russian invasion that they stopped operating the gas chambers. After liberation, Uncle Yoshe's family was reunited and returned to Krakow, but their story does not have a happy ending. One night the doorbell rang, and my Aunt Rushe answered the door. Anti-Semitic Poles, knowing it was a Jewish family, shot her dead standing in her own front hallway. My Uncle Yoshe fell to the ground as if he had also been killed. The surviving members of the family fled Krakow forever.

Our time with the Halberstams ended naturally. Most of us were functioning with an internal clock that designated the appointed time to move on, to protect our benefactors and ourselves. We would be safer alone rather than with a well-known Jewish family, and the Halberstams would be better off without two permanent houseguests. Also Mechel and I were very uneasy about remaining so close to the ghetto.

We walked around town on an unusually quiet day without air-raid sirens and looked at streets and neighborhoods. Budapest was a crumbling mess of a city. We went into one of the best sections. Why not? What was there to lose? We found a house on what had been one of the finest streets in the city and rented a room two floors up. The landlord seemed happy to have extra income and apologized for the distance between our room and the safety of the basement. We were young and still in fairly good shape, despite everything we had been through. Dashing down two flights of stairs did not intimidate us and we took the room immediately. The concierge told us it was best to take some bedding to the basement before the next bombing. We did that, establishing ourselves in a corner with a blanket, pillows, and some provisions.

One day I decided to explore the neighborhood, taking my chances that my foray outdoors would not coincide with firepower from the sky. I sensed that I knew the neighborhood when we first rented our room but wasn't sure why. When I was alone on the streets, the flash of recollection became a true memory. My Aunt Hendi and Uncle Nandor lived on Andraszy Utca, which was a few streets over from our room. They had been part of our extended family in Munkach. I found their house and learned that they had continued to manage with gentile papers as we had. Their daughters, my beautiful cousins Mimi and Katy, had been close friends of mine when we were girls. Now we were all in Budapest and settled in for the duration, and we speculated about the length of time that might be. They were in much better shape than we were, having been protected by truly righteous gentiles.

By early January things turned from impossible to unbearable. Ghastly sirens screamed, often without interruption. We were in the basement more than we were anywhere else. The basement shelter had at least fifty other occupants by January 1945. In mid-winter, the house took a direct hit. The shaking was so intense and lasted so long, that I was sure it was the end of us, indeed the end of the world. *So this is the way the entire world ends and it is happening now*, I thought. Finally, the house stopped tilting and the noise ceased and the basement filled with such thick dust we could not see across to the other side. There was the stinging odor of explosives and our eyes hurt and our throats closed. When the dust settled and the air cleared somewhat, the men investigated the damage.

The walls of the basement had not cracked. The perimeter foundation was solid and firm. The house, however, had toppled over on an angle and blocked the basement entrance. There was no way to ascend the stairs. The fallen bricks and stones of the house blocked the small basement windows. We would all suffocate if we did not make an air passage quickly. We immediately began to clear one window. Everyone worked. We got some air quickly, but it would take a few more days to create a sizable opening.

Once the opening was large enough, Mechel and I climbed out and ran away. We did not want to go back there. The house was demolished and it gave us the chills to think about going back to a place where we had yet again cheated death by inches. We saw a building that was still intact and had an open basement door. Sirens wailed again as we ran into the strange basement. In this cellar were two large rooms, packed with people. We had nothing with us, not a blanket, not a scarf, not a pillow. We assessed the place and figured this was our best chance of surviving. Rumbles started, the latest air attack was underway. We took a place at the back of one of the rooms with about twenty other people, all lying side by side like sardines. We found some newspapers to cover us and settled into our corner.

The concept of charity toward others had given way to the basic impulse to survive. Nobody was going to share their food with us, if food is what I should call what they had. Nevertheless they had something and we had nothing at all. Mechel could sustain himself for long periods with virtually nothing to eat. I was unable to do this. I begged some people who were cooking on a small burner to give me just the water left over from their noodles or rice. They obliged me. Mechel and I "ate" the broth of the water with some starch left in it from their "dinner." Mechel was holding on, but I was so hungry that I was hallucinating and was faint from starvation. I went upstairs and into the backyard and went over to the shattered remains of a shack, which must have been a chicken coop before the war.

I saw a stone next to the rubble in the yard, but for some reason I picked it up. I realized it was a piece of bread. It must have been intended for the now-dead chickens. I scraped at it and determined that it was in fact a heel of hard bread. It was emerald green from mold. And, it was winter so it was frozen solid as well. I brought it back to the cellar and presented it to Mechel as if it were a fine piece of chicken or beef. I continued to claw at the mold with my fingernails. Mechel tried to take it away from me, but I fought him. I was crazy from hunger, like the old man I had met the morning after we buried Mechel's family. Now I knew what it meant to beg for a piece of bread.

"Don't you dare eat this thing! Give it to me. Lola, you must listen to reason. If you eat this you will become very ill."

It was no use. I kept scraping away at the mold. Mechel was so weak that he just stared at me in disbelief and horror. He knew what was going to happen to me but he was powerless to stop me. I finally found the bit of bread underneath the mold. It was no larger than a fingernail, but I ate it. It stank of mold and rancid yeast. It was only a bite but I gobbled it down. Then I begged everyone in the cellar for a sip of hot water, but I was ignored. The pipes were frozen. There was no source of fresh water. Those who had water in canisters were not going to part with what they had for a strange, half-starved crazy person.

Mechel had gone to sleep underneath the newspapers. I could not stand it. I could not endure it another minute. All around me people were shivering and moaning. I made up my mind I would go to my aunt and uncle and bring some provisions back for Mechel and for me. I made my way to the door of the basement and asked a woman who camped out there if she would tell my husband where I had gone. I pointed out where he was and said that he was sleeping, but insisted forcefully that when he woke up, she must tell him where I was. She said she would.

I had not been outside for days. Budapest was at the end of its civilization by then. The streets were craters filled with corpses and body parts, a head here, an arm there, torso after torso piled up on each other, and horses were also strewn around, many of them decapitated. I lost my nerve and thought that I couldn't bear to see any more. Knowing there would be even worse ahead, I turned back to go into the cellar. I would vomit up what was left of my stomach if I saw any more of the abomination on the streets. I picked my way over the corpses and the rest of the grotesque remains of what had been life, human and animal, and stopped. Somehow I had to go to Andraszy Utca if Mechel and I were to survive. Even Mechel was not a camel. He would die of starvation and thirst; it was only a matter of time.

Bravery took over and I turned around again and continued on my way. I jumped over the corpses as whistling bombs landed and exploded before my eyes. I saw buildings topple and windows shatter. I realized just in time that the buildings were the targets, not the streets, so I ran down the middle of the road. I was an unstoppable force. I was a child of the winds. The worst Nazis or Arrow Cross thugs would not have been able to catch me. At the very moment I turned onto the street with my aunt and uncle's home, a bomb struck it. I stood just feet away and waited for the house to fall, but it did not. The rocket or cannon shell had hit the building at an angle, causing only a portion of the house to crumble. The basement side had been untouched. I rushed into the basement calling out the names of my aunt and uncle and their family.

There they were, safe and with plenty of provisions that they must have been storing for months. I sank to the floor in exhaustion and in relief that they were not harmed and that I had made it without being hit by a bomb or flying pieces of debris. Now I could save Mechel and myself from starvation. Hendi *neini*, Aunt Hendi, let me rest and then gave me soup she had made with a boiled potato in it. She tucked a sack of rice, potatoes, and a warm blanket into a sack she had. "Take these to Mechel."

It was starting to get dark and my family urged me to leave before Mechel became too worried. I wanted to go while it was still light because I would not be able to navigate the obstacle course of destruction in the dark. The sirens continued and I heard explosions in another section of Budapest. I ran as fast as I could and prayed, "Please if I am to die, may I do so next to my husband."

There had been more casualties while I had been with my family in their basement. The street scene was even more grisly than it had been earlier. There would be no way to identify any of the corpses, or to have proper burials for any faith. It was a nightmare of the greatest magnitude and of a proportion that can never be expressed adequately in words...or even in pictures.

I was steps away from our basement bunker when a fragment of a bomb whizzed by my side and hit the street, ricocheted and struck my sack, tearing open the bag of rice. Rice poured out like water. I stood there weeping and dropped the sack of potatoes and tried to scoop the rice up with my hands. I put what I could back into the rice sack and ran, forgetting the potato sack. I could barely recognize where I was as the light was so dim. I was hopeful the woman I spoke to had informed Mechel where I had gone.

Unfortunately, she had not. Perhaps she did not understand what I said, or she might simply have forgotten. When I returned I found Mechel hysterical with worry. He couldn't believe I would venture out and not tell him, or venture out at all. I held up my sack to show him I had rice and potatoes for us to eat. There was nothing left, a tattered bag that had held the rice and only the story of the forgotten potato sack. The only thing I had to show for my foolhardy escapade was a blanket. Of course I had eaten, but Mechel had not. Just as I settled down in our corner with our blanket of newspapers, my troubles began.

It was the revenge of the moldy bread, just as Mechel had warned me. I was convulsed with intense pain. My stomach was tied in knots and I was doubled over as if knives were sticking into me. I moaned and groaned and my stomach performed loudly as well. I clutched my tummy, holding it tightly, hoping to muffle the sounds. Everyone looked in my direction. I was a mess. I had survived the Bochnia Ghetto, had survived a ride in a false-bottomed coal truck, forged documents, and a meeting with Eichmann, rescued my husband from prison and now I would die from eating rotten bread that acted like poison. Mechel comforted me and somehow got me through the night of agony.

The next morning we heard footsteps; they were the heavy steps of large men wearing boots. We were terrified. The Nazis must be back. The cellar door opened with a loud bang and there stood an enormous Russian, his beard caked with ice. He came in and looked around at us, and I wonder now what he thought. The Russians were not strangers to suffering during the war.

"Does anyone speak Russian?"

I piped right up, "I do." I spoke enough words and sentences to communicate in an elementary way with him. I had begun to learn Ukrainian in the Czechoslovakian school I attended, and it was close enough to Russian so that I could fake it. I was lucky that my ability with languages did not mirror my geography skills. I appeared to be the only person in the cellar who spoke Russian, although Mechel spoke a little too.

"You are liberated," he exclaimed.

I turned to our cellar-mates and said without any feeling. "We are liberated. It means we are free."

He had a large container and gave us hot tea to drink, and he left the container with us and departed. We all sat where we had been before our "liberation." Everyone was in too much shock to know what to do, and frankly, none of us were terribly excited about going out into the urban killing grounds. A woman turned to me and said, "You really must see a doctor for your stomach. There is one across the street. Now you can go there, just cut across diagonally and get some medicine."

Well, the Russian had said we were liberated. Liberated people are free to move around and to go to a doctor, if one could be located. I told Mechel what he would see if we went outside. He said to me, "We are free now. We can't help the dead ones, and we have to get you some medicine before you get sicker."

He picked up the blanket and without a word started to leave the cellar. I followed him. I knew he meant business. He was kind enough not to scold me by saying, "I told you not to eat the bread," as many other husbands might have done, for which I was grateful. We moved across the mountains of corpses, which had not been taken away. Mechel showed no expression when he encountered the first barricade of bodies. He said, "I wonder just which building the woman meant the doctor is in – do you know?"

At that moment, we heard Russians at our backs, and they screamed, "Halt!"

The commander said, "Where are you going?"

In Russian I explained that I was ill and that we were going to a doctor we had been told lived across the street and then I dramatically clutched my stomach, pointing to it.

He looked us over and said to his comrades, "These are Nazi spies."

I kept telling him we were going to a doctor and we were not spies. The men stole our watches from us but somehow did not take my mother's ring off my finger, which I still wear. The leader gave his men a command and they raised their rifles and pointed them at us. They would shoot us there, on the spot. I screamed at them the word *Evrei, Evrei* (Jews) but they forced us against a wall in an alley. I looked into the entrance of a basement right next to the wall and I could see it was filled with the corpses of Nazi soldiers, heads down and feet up. They were going to shoot us as they had shot them and throw us into the basement with the dead Nazis. They were liberating Budapest by killing Germans street by street. We were going to be added to the collection. We would die with bizarre false identity papers and become a forgotten historical footnote.

Our faces were to the wall. The commander was giving his men instructions about how to shoot us. They were Special Forces of the Red Army. Our life as a liberated married Jewish couple was going to last about five minutes. Mechel said to me in very harsh tones, "Say 'Shema Yisroel' – *now*."

I couldn't imagine what help it would be. He commanded me loudly. "Say the 'Shema'!"

We started to wail in the loudest voices we could summon: *Shema Yisroel! Hashem Elokeynu, Hashem Echod!*

A Russian coming from down the street jumped over bodies and screamed, "Stop. Stop. Don't shoot them. Don't kill them! They are Evrei."

"We are Jews!" we said. "But the leader of the firing squad insisted that we are spies on our way to see the Germans.

"No, they are really Evrei," The Russian said.

The rifles were lowered and they stood down. The man who had heard our chanting of the "Shema" asked us, "What are you doing outside? It is not safe. Get into that basement."

We slid into the nearby basement, falling over dead German soldiers. This was our third basement, and this was the absolute worst. Now the Soviets controlled the streets and were capturing the buildings one by one. A few other live people were also stuck in the basement with the dead Germans. Mechel and I still had our blanket. We found a corner and held each other. There we were between the living and the dead, between Hell and the hope of life. All of this commotion and near death by Russian firing squad had scared my stomach into behaving.

At the front of the cellar were two beautiful young sisters who had survived the war. They were now alone and clinging to each other. I spoke to them briefly. They too were Jews, surviving with false papers. One was

18 and the other 20; they were more frightened than we were. I tried to tell them that the plague of war was almost over and to just hold onto each other and to have faith. They were polite but not reassured by what I said.

As the night progressed, I understood why they found no solace in my words. Russian soldiers returned to the basement quite drunk and saying obscene things. They grabbed at the girls and started to take them away. I screamed to the Russians to leave them alone. "Then, you come upstairs with us instead," one of them barked at me. The girls were already being dragged to their fate – one cried out for her mother. "Mama, Mama." It broke our hearts. Their Mama was undoubtedly lost to them forever and now they would endure the abuse of the liberators. They were returned to the cellar before daybreak, weeping and distraught. I did not approach them and neither did the other women. We could not help them and they needed their privacy. At least they still had one another. It was one of the most hideous events I observed, because the Russians supposedly had been on the side of the good.

In the morning, more Russian soldiers came into the basement. They were sober, at least, and fairly well behaved. "Who speaks Russian?" one asked of us. Mechel was not about to let me be endangered as the young sisters were, he spoke loudly, "We do."

"Then, both of you come with us."

They told us to get into a truck. We had no idea what was going to happen to us; perhaps we were going to be questioned…or worse? The truck was falling to bits from overuse and lurched forward on the ruined streets, attempting to swerve around the corpses.

One of the Russians asked Mechel, "Find out where the banks are located."

They wanted to loot banks, not shoot us. We were with would-be bank robbers in war-ravaged Budapest. They wanted someone who spoke Hungarian who could translate back to them in Russian. We found some people who told us a few bank addresses.

"We will share the money with you," one of them said and offered us candy and those disgusting Russian cigarettes.

We arrived at the first bank. They smashed into the building, found the safe, and shot at it but nothing happened. One of them took a grenade and blew up the safe. It was completely empty. We moved from bank to bank, and in each case the money had been cleared out of the safes. They came away empty. They didn't seem that bothered.

"Well, let's get some vodka instead."

Now Mechel and I had to obtain the addresses of bars and restaurants. At the first location, we found a full bar. The place had been bombed, but the owners had boarded up the windows before the attack, and so the Russians pried the boards away and went inside to get their vodka.

I was utterly sick of the whole miserable mess of Budapest and disgusted by these Russians. Mechel tried to pull me back, for he was still wary of them, but I boldly asked, "May we please leave now that you have found the bar?" One of them looked at us, and motioned that we were free to go and we left quickly before they changed their minds.

It was the middle of the winter, 1945. We were free, but we had no destination – no home. I told Mechel that the best thing to do was to make our way to my relatives on Andraszy Utca. By now their street had been cleared and cleaned. The Soviet forces controlled the entire area. We found their house in shambles but it was still standing and they were alive and safe. They had been through a great deal and had much more knowledge than we did. They became our news source. Budapest was still in the throes of a blood-soaked struggle whose outcome was uncertain.

Some thought the German retreat was a trick or a clever tactic and the Germans would be back. Others thought the Soviets would take over and the Germans had lost the war. If the Germans came back, all the remaining Jews would be killed, but if the Soviets controlled the region, the Jews would suffer anyway. Mechel and I were confused. Then we learned about the meaning of being Jewish under Soviet rule. It meant not being Jewish if you wanted to survive. Mechel was disbelieving at first.

"But they were our Allies against the Reich," he said.

"Yes, but…" Nandor *bacsi*, Uncle Nandor said, using his hands to gesture that it still spelled danger for us. "We all need to get out of Budapest as soon as possible. The city is surrounded. We are going east."

Their goal was truly east, because they wanted to live in Palestine, so for them, heading into Romania meant a possible route to Eretz Yisroel. Mechel and I did not want to go to Palestine, but we surely wanted to get out of Budapest. If there had been a chance of rebuilding a Jewish community in

Budapest we would have considered risking it, but it was clearly an impossible fantasy. Furthermore, Budapest was not yet fully liberated. In January 1945 the Soviets and Hungary reached an armistice, but it was for the Pest section of the city. It was not until February that the Buda section was freed. And it would be early spring (April) before the last Nazis and their collaborators, the Arrow Cross, had been driven out or slaughtered.

Hungary did not hold much appeal for Mechel, even without the bloodshed and political intrigue. He was not Hungarian and did not speak the language. He was a proud Polish Jew. We were unaware of the total obliteration of Polish Jewish life at that point. We knew the death toll had to be enormous, but it would be much later that we learned the numbers. We stayed on with my relatives and I tried to figure out how to survive until we decided what to do and until they left for Palestine.

There were a few produce markets beginning to open and I frequented them, for food was very scarce. At one of the stalls I ran into an acquaintance who told me about a safer place in a nearby suburb. The woman informed me that the Rebbetzins Chumche Stempel, with her two children, and Rivche Halberstam, and two other sisters of the Bobover Rebbe were living in that suburb. We immediately sought them out, and they welcomed us again and asked us to live with them. They were in a relatively calm neighborhood and had more food and provisions than we had seen in five years. We met other survivors and their families. Many of them had escaped Bochnia with forged papers and made the border runs as we had. The older women were very kind to me, but I did not connect to them as friends. Mechel established a small network of acquaintances, but still he felt as lonely as I.

One night he said to me, "I have an idea, Lola. Let's go back to Debrecen."

Why on earth would he come up with that notion? It made no sense to me, but I saw that he meant it, and I was worried about the reason. "What about Mammiko and Tattiko? They will never look for us in Debrecen. Look at the survivors we have met recently. And we have survived, and so perhaps have they, and my brothers too and maybe our family and friends from Munkach."

Mechel knew better. He knew what had happened to everyone, but he kept his own counsel. I knew better too, and had for a long time, but I would not let go of that thread of hope that our family would be reunited.

"We can't go back to Poland yet, Lola. We need to give it more time. Things are not normal yet."

Although Mechel was far more informed than I was about living conditions for Jews in what remained of Europe, I listened but wasn't persuaded. It was true that the Arrow Cross was finished, but their virulent anti-Semitism had fueled the engines of a hatred that was still present in ordinary people. Mechel reminded me that the Bobover Rebbe himself was living in Bucharest and did not intend to go back to Poland to try to find his family because it was still too dangerous. It was still so hazardous to look Jewish that even the Rebbe had not regrown his beard. If life was this risky in Hungary and Romania, Poland was sure to be even worse.

We were arguing for the first time in our marriage. As far as Mechel was concerned Debrecen had been a friendly town to us. I asked him how he could talk like that when that was where he had been arrested on Pesach night. He said that if he had not been arrested we would have stayed there. I had to admit (but not to him) that he had a point. And I was starting to relent a bit when I remembered that Rosie's father-in-law, my uncle, was still there, so we had some family connections.

Mechel won. I agreed on condition that we not make it our permanent home. I did not understand that he already knew we would never go back to live in Poland. We were packing up our few things and getting ready to go to Debrecen. I wasn't happy, but it was not a time to persist in petty domestic squabbles, above all when we had been so blessed to survive. We were all ready to leave and were about to make our grateful farewell to our hosts, when a letter arrived for us. I saw it was in Yiddish and I gave it to Mechel.

His face brightened. "You won't believe this, Lola. It's from the Bobover Rav. He has asked us to come to Bucharest immediately and to celebrate Pesach with him, and to help him with the Seders."

Winter was really over. Spring had at long last broken through. We were so happy to accept the Rebbe's request and change our plans. On second thought, Mechel and I looked at each other and understood the deeper meaning of the letter. It meant that the Bobover Rav was alone for Pesach, and that perhaps we were the closest acquaintances of his who had survived. We acknowledged the loss and the sorrow, but we also thanked Hashem that this would be a Pesach we would enjoy without an arrest and with our Rebbe. While there was so very much to grieve for that we could not yet comprehend the magnitude of our losses, this was a blessing to take in with full appreciation and joy. We headed to Bucharest, to the Bobover Rebbe, and to a Pesach without the constant fear of extinction. It was, after all, the beginning of spring and our new world together.

PART SEVEN:
SPRING AT LAST

CHAPTER 22
Bucharest 1945

We left for Bucharest with hearts half-alight in hope and half-shadowed in darkness. My relatives gave us some cash for our trip as we were without any resources. We had the clothes on our backs and one fresh change for each. With nothing to burden us the trip was made easier. No more layers of clothing on our bodies or swaying carts dangerously overweight with household belongings. We had each other and a profound sense of gratitude. Danger remained with us as our now-constant companion. There was still the risk of air raids in Budapest and we were advised to clear the city limits as swiftly as we could.

We walked for hours toward a railroad junction we had been told was our safest choice. On the way we encountered hundreds of refugees; many could barely walk because of what they had endured, yet they were still clinging to bundles of possessions. We understood this feeling. We had experienced it in earlier phases of our journey to survival. We were surprised to see refugees fleeing Budapest in horse-drawn carts and with proper suitcases and crates loaded in the back. Not everyone had suffered the same deprivation in the war, quite obviously. Occasionally we heard the echo of explosions, and I shuddered with the all-too-recent memory of what we had seen and experienced. I had no particular feeling about Bucharest, but I wanted to get out of Budapest.

We finally came to the railroad junction and saw several trains waiting there. We asked other refugees who were milling around if these were cars that would take us toward Bucharest. They all said we were in the right place. They were cattle cars, although this meant nothing to me at this point. I was blind to the irony and meaning of the form of transport we were going to take. I would learn later that these were the cars that had been used to take Jews to slaughter. All I could think of was that I did not have to pretend to be someone I wasn't and I no longer had the fear of being asked for papers. We were no longer afraid of deportation, railroad conductors, or SS officers. There were no conductors on these cars in any event. And there were no tickets. We climbed aboard with a group of peasants, a few remaining Gypsies who had not been murdered, and some Hungarian soldiers, along with masses of refugees of assorted nationalities and ethnicities.

The clothing worn by the traditional peasants fascinated me. They all dressed in the same style. The men wore jackets with embroidery on their sleeves and lapels. The women were in long dresses, and all wore scarves. They sang songs with lovely melodies constantly, probably to calm their nerves. I picked up the tunes and sang along with them. The car we had boarded had two kinds of "accommodations" – one end of the car had straw on the floor and the other did not; it was standing room only. Mechel jokingly referred to it as "first- and second-class" sections. We found room in the straw area and lay down.

The ride was uncomfortable in many ways, but there were no complaints from us. The train stopped for the night just outside a town called Koloshvar, which was in Romania. (Today it is Cluj-Napoca. In my childhood, I'd heard it referred to by its Yiddish name, Kloizenburg, and it was noteworthy in our world because it was the home of the Kloizenburg Rebbe, Rabbi Yekusiel Halberstam, a cousin of the Bobover Rebbe.) We got off the train and found a family to take us in for the night. It was a Jewish family and there was much gaiety in their home. I don't remember the rest of the family, but the young daughter impressed me. Her name was Gabi and she was pretty and sophisticated.

She was excited because it was the evening of a major wedding in town. The Satmar Rebbe's daughter was going to be married. Gabi asked me to help her get ready for the wedding. I helped Gabi and she loaned me a few pretty things as well. It was the first moment of true happiness I had in all those years. We were invited to the wedding and were delighted to be included. Naturally it brought back thoughts of my own miserable wedding, but it did not detract from my ability to share the joy that filled the air. The wedding was held in the Rebbe's backyard on a beautiful night with a sky filled with stars. There was a fine tablecloth on the table, well-cooked and delicious food, and gifts! And there was not a whisper of fear about gunfire or arrest, or an impending Aktion. What a beginning to our stay in Bucharest; I happily anticipated good days ahead.

When we returned to the railroad tracks the next day, as we had been instructed by the other travelers, we found a different cattle train waiting there. The passengers were roaming around in the fields, some congregating in groups talking to one another, others just too weak to continue the trip. We boarded. The cattle cars swayed precariously from side to side. We rode on for another 300 miles to Bucharest, crossing the Carpathian Mountains on the way. At some point toward the end of our journey I met a young man called David Horn. He was from Upper Silesia near Katowice. He made a most favorable impression on me and I thought about the wedding we'd just attended, and how Gabi would make a fine bride and he, a fine bridegroom. I contacted her parents once we were in Bucharest, and sure enough, I made a *shidduch* (a match). I've made others since, but this one was very special for me because it affirmed that I was alive, and it restored to me my own womanhood.

The train slowly entered the center of Bucharest. I was startled because I liked what I saw, and of course my eyes saw things differently now. I looked out at Bucharest with the eyes of a person beginning a new life, not as a terrified Jew waiting to be caught in the Nazi net. The city did not appear to have been bombed. Bucharest had been liberated about six months before Budapest, so conditions were far more settled. As we left the train, we saw it was market day. All around the central square, we observed the peasant farmers selling corn flour, a staple in Romania, and huge chunks of sheep cheese.

I shared with Mechel my first impressions of Bucharest. Mechel was chilled by my remarks, for he knew what I did not: that its recent history was one of horror and death. More than 760,000 Jews had lived in Greater Romania before the war. Romania joined the Nazi alliance in late 1940. Jews by the thousands had been immediately mobilized for slave labor. Romania was a fascist dictatorship run by local Nazis who were supported by the Germans. By 1941 there were 330,000 German troops, Wehrmacht Army divisions, inside the country. The Romanian fascist movement and its police enforcers started the seizure of Jewish homes and businesses as early as the winter of 1940–1941.

In June 1941 Romania fought along with Germany to invade the Soviet Union. In return, Romania regained territory it had lost to the Soviets and a bit of the Ukraine known as Transnistria. The Romanians deported 150,000 Jews into this zone, and by the time they were forced to relinquish it, 90,000 of them were dead.

I was much sobered as we walked through Bucharest. It was beginning to infiltrate my brain that the war against the Jews had been thorough, country-by-country extermination, and almost successful, but for those of us still alive who defied by our existence the Final Solution. The next weeks would further my education, not as a Jewish woman but as a survivor. Bucharest was my first postwar, hard lesson. I had not imagined the dimensions of the reality until this moment. The Reich, aided by its enthusiastic supporters within the nations it overran, had ravaged Europe. European Jewry was in shreds. The tapestry of centuries of our life as a people had been ripped apart beyond recognition – but hopefully not beyond its ability to be rewoven.

We wandered around and asked for directions to the address the Bobover Rebbe had mentioned in his letter. When we reached the right neighborhood we were puzzled. It was a strange collection of buildings and dwellings. It was as if someone had thrown together spare sets and props from a large theatrical production. It made no sense to us. On one corner there was a mansion, on another a hut with a thatched roof. And the old royal castle was still standing, making it all too bizarre to take in at first. We saw a man riding a horse and someone on the street said, "There's the king's son." We were confused and bewildered, but with great relief arrived at a beautiful building that was the address the Rebbe had given us.

The building was close to the royal palace. The Rebbe was living in a small apartment with his son. They had a bathroom – an absolute luxury! – and the extra bedroom served as the Rebbe's study. The living room did not have a couch in it, but the dining room had an enormously long table. There was one chaise lounge on which to sit. The foyer was large but empty. There were two cots folded up and waiting there, so we understood this was to be our bedroom by night. I looked around and realized there was no kitchen. I was crippled with anxiety. How could I begin to make a Seder for the Bobover Rebbe without kitchen facilities? I asked and was told that indeed there was not a kitchen available.

Mechel and I noticed that the apartment was packed with sefarim, which had been saved from burning or rescued from trash bins. I wondered how the Rebbe had managed to retrieve so many and how he had hidden them during the times of peril. I did not ask, however. I saw that the apartment was overflowing with medical textbooks as well. The Rebbe was not only a Torah scholar but also had a serious interest in medicine.

We were there to make Pesach and I was not going to be defeated by the lack of a little item like a stove! Or a kitchen! I discussed with Mechel my idea of how to turn the bathroom into a kitchen and he agreed. We found wooden planks at the lumberyard, and laid them over the bathtub, which produced an instant kitchen countertop. We purchased a small gas tank with two burners.

Always confident in languages, now I had reached a place where I could not communicate. I did not know a word of Romanian. How could I negotiate at the market and with the butcher? The Rebbe taught me a few basic words, and how to count, which was the most important. The Vizhnitz community had a *shochet* (a ritual slaughterer) but he did not *kasher* (salt and soak) the chickens after slaughtering them as required by Jewish law. I had to do this in the bathtub. The Vizhnitzer Rebbe had wine and matzos, which he made available to us too. I bought some prunes and some fish. It was so simple to perform difficult domestic tasks because I now knew what mattered and what did not. Without any commotion or drama, I was ready with our Seder meal. It was March 28, 1945, a Wednesday; in the Hebrew calendar it was 14 Nissan 5705.

This was the most unforgettable Seder of my life, unsurpassed until today. When we began to recite the Haggadah, we all wept. We did not need to add extra discussion linking us to the Israelites' departure from Egypt and the miracles they experienced. We were a remnant, a mere fragment of a vibrant and huge population of Jews. We represented all that was lost as much as we represented the reality of survival. We were not telling the story of the ancient deliverance that night but were living the contemporary recital of our own survival and the continuation of our people. It was a Seder of joy and tears. The wine we spilled from the glasses to signify the Ten Plagues could also represent the losses we had only recently suffered. The Bobover Rebbe did not know what had happened to his family any more than I knew about mine, yet we both knew. His face and mine were mirror images of one another. Our nightmares and fears were as yet not specific in detail but were nonetheless present in our hearts that night.

We knew there had been nothing random about Bochnia or Krakow or Niepolomice or any of the other emptied out cities and villages of Europe. It had all been a part of a systematic plan to arrest, torture, murder, assassinate, bludgeon, gas, and burn millions of Jews. Seated around that Seder table in Bucharest, we understood without articulating it that our parents, grandparents, and their children were undoubtedly lost forever, yet the Jewish hope for continuity and belief in our ancient covenant with Hashem was alive that night. Maybe, just maybe some members of our families and those dear to us had escaped and survived. We did talk about how it *could* have happened. We had no answers. There are still no answers, none that really work at any rate. There are explanations for the Shoah, but those are not answers.

The Rebbe began to sing a song, but I heard it as a prayer. I always will.

Di Mamme hot gehaissen, nisselach fun boim oopraissen
Oy, vi niderik zenen di kinderlach
Zei konnen nisht dergreichin
Mother told us to pick nuts from the tree
Oh! How high the branches are!
Oh! How low the children are!
They can't reach them.

We cried and sang and ate, but mostly we cried. It was a Seder of longing and grief, but together we made it through to the end of the Haggadah, and it established a lasting bond between us.

We stayed with the Rebbe after Pesach. In the days and weeks that followed, we all remained glued to the radio. We learned too that the Rebbe had turned his Bucharest apartment into an unofficial relief center. Jews from all circles, friends, relatives, and strangers came to him to search for lost family members, to find out how to emigrate, to get married, and for guidance in performing other Jewish rituals. The Bobover Rebbe did not return to Poland, perhaps because he was afraid of what he would find there, but I think he stayed in Bucharest doing what he did as his way of offering thanks to Hashem for having been spared. He viewed his work in Bucharest as a blessing. Our numbers were so decimated that his decisions were enormously important to our future; he became the very oxygen of religious life for many of us.

CHAPTER 23

Liberation

May 7, 1945. Mechel and I happened to be outside taking a walk. We spent much time inside with the Rebbe, either listening to the radio or helping him in whatever ways we could. It wasn't the usual time for us to be out walking, but on the spur of the moment we had decided to take some air. Suddenly crowds were shouting for joy, screams of jubilation engulfed us. We did not have to speak the language to understand what had happened. Strangers grabbed one another on the street and embraced. Others kissed and hugged each other. Some burst into spontaneous song.

It was, at long last, over.

Berlin had fallen.

We did not know it, but similar celebrations were erupting throughout the free world. The United States and the United Kingdom had suffered great losses and they were also celebrating. The day became known in the English-speaking world as V-E Day – Victory in Europe. Mechel and I began to cry openly on the streets of Bucharest as we watched everyone else doing the same. Hitler and his devil forces had been vanquished. We had prevailed. Later we would learn the price the Allies had paid to ensure this day. At that moment in Bucharest our focus was on ourselves. In fact, it was very much on our marriage.

During the Shoah we had done everything we could to keep our customs and continue our observances. We were unable to carry out each commandment exactly as we should because of the situation, but we never gave up because we thought it was too much work. We never said, "We'll go back to all this after the persecution is finished." Quite the opposite, and often at the risk of starving or being exposed as Jews, we continued to practice Judaism. We chose consciously to disobey one commandment, however. That was the commandment to be fruitful and multiply. We felt that to have a baby would be a source of mortal danger for the infant and ourselves. That day in Bucharest, V-E Day elsewhere, we knew the time for new beginnings had come at last. We were liberated. Spring truly had arrived.

Hashem was good to us, and our prayers were answered almost immediately. It was as if we had just married and were expecting a baby. The pregnancy helped both of us heal and although we were still struck quiet at times by the absence of our loved ones, we began to do normal things. I went for a swim. I had not been swimming in so many years that I forgot my condition and took a dive into the water. My diving technique was still good, but my internal state was very shaky. Diving and expecting a child do not mix well together. I was so sick when I got to the edge of the pool that I had to be pulled out of the water by some other women. I murmured the Shema believing I had accidentally killed myself. The women calmed me down and explained a few "facts of life" to me about having babies. I gave up on my need for extreme physical exercise and we engaged in less strenuous activities. We continued to spend a lot of time with the Bobover Rebbe.

We were so involved in our personal happiness and our plans for a family that at first we didn't notice how Bucharest was changing weekly. Jews were leaving in large numbers. Some groups headed southeast to the ports on the Mediterranean in order to sail to Palestine. Another large mass of people moved toward the west, going back into Hungary, Austria, and even into Germany. Those going west were either looking for lost relatives or trying to move quickly before the Communists took over Eastern Europe, especially Romania. All the borders were open then and many saw it as an opportunity to get away before the Soviets clamped down on people living within its jurisdiction. Winston Churchill had yet to use the phrase "Iron Curtain" to describe life in Soviet-controlled regions, but it would not be long before his phrase was recognized everywhere as a valid description.

We learned from those around the Rebbe that in Austria and in Germany the Americans had established "displaced persons" (DP) camps where it was possible to get a visa to emigrate to the *goldene medina* (the golden country) in other words, the United States. We thought this was where we too should try to go eventually, but we were not in a hurry. Even the small foyer in the Rebbe's apartment seemed like home to us. No more trains or hikes or hiding. We were content to stay in Bucharest and recuperate and put our lives back together. We gathered more news with each passing week. Finally we began to write letters to contacts in America.

Mechel's cousin, Moishe Lieber, lived in the States and was associated with the chocolate company of the same name. I had an uncle there as well, Rabbi Dovid Nussen Leser, who was my father's brother. The relatives we had in America lived in Brooklyn. We had heard that it was not easy to be an observant, Orthodox Jew in America. Our heads had been filled with stories that we would not be accepted, and that America was only for secular Jews. The cliché went "even the stones in the United States are *treyf* (not kosher)." Our relatives responded that there were many exceptions and that it was an unfair characterization of Jewish life in America. The point of America, they explained, is that one is free to practice one's faith whatever it is, in freedom and with dignity. From our relatives in America we learned something about the rest of our family members. That news was mostly what we had dreaded we would hear.

We became complacent about leaving Bucharest. I was expecting, we were with the Bobover Rebbe, and I felt secure and comforted by the presence of other Jewish women. Mechel said he thought we should wait until things returned to normal in Bucharest and then we would proceed to either Austria or Germany to seek visas to the United States. We did not see what was coming. Fortunately for us, our relatives in Brooklyn *did* see what was coming because they were living in a "real" world and not inside our cocoon of false safety. When their letters took on an urgent tone we paid attention. They told us that if we remained much longer we would be living under a brutal, totalitarian regime. We would be under the control of a Communist government, run in the Soviet style.

We knew better than to play the odds. We had had our own experience in Budapest with Soviet soldiers. We got the picture. We left Bucharest in August 1945, and we were not alone. Many Jews in Bucharest left when we did. Once again we climbed into cattle cars and headed back to Budapest, and from there, we hoped, to a destination in the west and to complete freedom. Most of the refugees streaming out of Bucharest were not native to Romania, and most of us heading toward Budapest were not native to that city either. Both cities were temporary safe havens for Jews who hoped to start their lives again in a new place and a new country.

We were astounded when we got to Budapest to see so much repair work had already been accomplished. There was still evidence of the war and the bombings, but it was not the same city we had left. There were still Jews in the old ghetto, or some who had returned. We found survivors from Poland who had come to seek family or learn the truth and mourn. It felt to me like there were masses of Polish Jews, but then Mechel and I did our arithmetic. There was no such thing as masses of Polish Jews, or masses of any other kind of Jews anywhere in Europe. And those of us who had survived were all in transit to somewhere else, or to an unfulfilled dream of finding even one family member who had survived. It was a ghastly and ghostly experience. We moved into a refugee center in Budapest and there we "interviewed" everyone upon arrival. Mechel made sure we wrote down everyone's contact information. Again, nothing we heard gave us any reason for optimism. Mechel was more realistic than I and questioned the refugees about the procedures for gaining entry into America.

One day at the center, I saw Rosie and Micheline. It was a reunion filled with raw emotion and unfinished sentences. Rosie and Micheline had spent many months with my Uncle Yoshe Berger, her father-in-law, in Debrecen. Rosie and Micheline had just arrived in Budapest with Uncle Yoshe's daughter, Toby, and her husband, Itche Pflancer. Only six years had gone by since I helped my aunt Raizel, Toby's mother, in her corset and lingerie shop in order to prepare for Toby's wedding. It was at that wedding where I met Mechel. Only six years before? It could not be! Or could it? I had a hard time remembering if it were even in my own lifetime that these events had occurred. So much was blurred by what we had gone through, but the Bergers and the Pflancers had endured transports and concentrations camps and we had not. Rosie said they were all headed back to Krakow. Without any need for elaboration, we understood that they wished to return to their old lives in Poland. We told them we were hoping to go to America. As I said good-bye to Rosie I did not tell her how much I wished she would not go back to Poland, nor did she disclose to me what she must have felt about us moving to America.

Mechel and I were not convinced that America was the answer, but we did not have a better idea. We received information from incoming refugees about Munkach. We learned that anyone deported in 1944 had gone to Auschwitz and that meant my remaining siblings, Tuli, Ben, and of course, Goldie. We had assumed that Moishe had been killed earlier because of his forgery involvement. We were wrong about Moishe. He did not survive, but the circumstances of his death were a terrible blow to us. He had somehow managed to survive both the Auschwitz and the Death March, and then was struck by an Allied bomb and instantly killed.

Goldie had endured a little while, because despite her pale complexion and weakened heart they thought she was able-bodied. She was worked to death. We were told she died in my aunt's arms, but we don't know when. I wanted some confirmation of my sister's fate, yet at the same time I blocked it from my mind. I needed to maintain that last image of her in Munkach, not only for the sake of my sanity but as a memorial to my entire family and to a place I would never see again. We heard that Mechel's brother Yoel had gone to Italy. He sent us parcels in Budapest, and then we lost touch with him, which was not uncommon in a time of such upheaval. The time we spent in the refugee center in Budapest was depressing us. We both recognized it was not a healthy environment for me. The stories were of death and the technical details of how the Nazis had killed so many of us were not the best setting for a pregnant woman.

We went to see my Nandor baci and Hendi neini, who were still in their Budapest apartment where we had left them when we went to Bucharest. They were still planning to go to Palestine but were wisely waiting until the situation there was more stable. My aunt was so happy to see me pregnant that she really spoiled me. She ordered a beautiful maternity dress for me, and purchased a full layette for the baby, including a *kishele*, a soft bassinet feather pillow with a special lace cover. She had several embroidered baby shirts made of the finest cotton. Mechel was given a tailor-made coat with a Persian lamb collar.

As autumn progressed the Jews in Budapest fell into one of two groups. The largest consisted of those of us using Budapest as a way station to move on to the next destination and, hopefully, ultimate home. But the Hungarian Jews of Budapest were determined to reestablish themselves and the Jewish community. It would not be long before many of them would chafe under the yoke of Communist domination and intolerance and flee Hungary for America.

We encountered the Bobover Rebbe again, but this time completely unexpectedly. He did not leave Bucharest when we did, so we were surprised to see him in Budapest. He was on his way to England with surviving members of his family. When we saw him in Budapest he had good news. They had obtained visas and were free to go. He would go on to make a life in an environment quite unlike anything we had known in our years together.

Getting to America was not easy. Immigration visas were hard to come by. American citizens had to sponsor you and assure the United States that they would support you. We were most fortunate that Moishe Lieber, Mechel's cousin and my Uncle Yoshe's nephew, Moishe Berger, were our sponsors. The responsibilities of sponsorship could be time-consuming and draining for those willing to help. An affidavit was only the beginning of the process. After that, your sponsors had to fill out an application for a visa and wait to see if it was accepted or rejected. If rejected, the sponsor had to wait six months to apply again.

The United States immigration policy had quotas by country. Mechel and I did not have birth certificates, which made it more involved for our sponsors. Despite the cooperation of our relatives in America, Mechel remained dubious about our prospects. He thought that America did not want more immigrants, and especially not Jews from Eastern Europe. There was peace but there was also chaos. Bricha, the Zionist organization, was working to arrange the movement of as many people as possible to Palestine, which was under British blockade at the time. Their plan had people going to Romania, or later on into Italy, but they were soon overloaded with people. Bricha thought it best to redirect the flow of refugees toward the American occupied zones in Austria and Germany in the hope that if enough Jews clamored for admission to Palestine, the British would buckle under the pressure and remove the blockade.

Mechel and I were not Zionists and so were not involved with the Bricha, but we knew that the best place for us at that time was probably the vile and blood-soaked land of Germany. It was simply the best way to get into an American-controlled zone. After two months in Budapest, we moved west. By then it was late autumn 1945 and the fluidity of the borders had ended. We could no longer hop a railroad car and go where we wished but would have to sneak across the mountains into Austria. To me it seemed a depressing replay of the life we had lived under Hitler, and Mechel had to remind me that it was not the same at all.

We joined a small group of people and hired a guide. We layered our clothes once again, but I had to admit it was quite different. The guide did not charge us much and we rode to the mountains in a jeep, not in the false bed of a coal truck. We did have to hike through treacherous mountain passes to cross the Austrian Alps, however, and I was by now six months pregnant. If we were caught, indeed we might go to a detention camp for a time, but we would not be killed. We were not unafraid during this border crossing, but we were nonetheless filled with exhilaration. Somehow we knew that it was going to be fine for us and for our baby. Naturally we prayed to Hashem to give us the strength to go forward in this last stage of our liberation.

We left on the scheduled day and after about 100 miles the jeep stopped. We got out and followed our guide as we began our climb. It was a chilly Alpine evening but at least it was not raining. The ground was wet and muddy but it was far too early for snow. I was no longer a young mountain goat and I had trouble keeping up with the group because of the weight of the pregnancy. I kept pushing myself when I fell behind, but my excitement had turned into fatigue. I was the only pregnant woman, but I wasn't the only one panting and scrambling. We shuffled forward, one foot in front of the other. No thoughts were in my mind except to keep moving. I kept my head down to watch for any slippery patches on the trail. I walked into the person in front of me only to realize the group had stopped. We were finished with the climb; we were on level ground. Our guide pointed to something a short distance from where we standing.

This time there were no Hussar border guards awaiting us and we needed no instructions on how to sneak through the crossing. There was not going to be a communal bootlicking ceremony this time before we passed into Austria. What was waiting for us was – a bus.

A regular, nondescript bus! We were in Austria. Our guide took us to the bus and helped us climb aboard. We were told that we were only fifty miles from Vienna and would arrive there around midnight. We would be taken to the Rothschild Hospital where other Jewish refugees were staying.

I remember the scene before my eyes when we arrived at the Rothschild Hospital. It was a movie, not my life. There were Jews – families and single people – everywhere you looked, and everyone there was determined to emigrate. I found a place to rest and fell asleep. Mechel was invigorated by the activity in the hospital and moved around, talking to everyone, learning where people were going and gleaning tips about how to achieve our goal. He came back to me and said, "Listen, Lola, things here are very well organized. The Bricha commanders are in charge and know what they're doing. Tomorrow night we will go to Germany by train. Everyone here is headed either for Palestine or the United States."

What he meant was that we all had a dream to end up in America or Palestine, though it seemed a distant vision to me at that moment. However, I was encouraged and bolstered by Mechel's attitude. He no longer had the appearance of a trapped man. He was in his favorite mode of action – figuring out a plan and following it to a successful completion. His renewed self-confidence reassured me. I ventured to suggest something for myself.

"I want to see Vienna, Mechel. For Munkachers, even the gentiles, Vienna is the city of culture. This is where Mammiko and Babbiko used to come to replenish their wardrobes. Don't you think we could see a tiny bit of Vienna? We may never come back to Europe."

At first he may have thought my request frivolous. Go sightseeing when you are yet trying to shake the memory of the still-smoking ovens of Hitler's Reich? But then he probably saw the old light coming back in my eyes, and he was reassured that the former Lola had returned.

"Why not? Let's do it, but we don't have time to see much."

Off we went. We did see the Opera House and the Schoenberg Castle. We had no passports and had not obtained permission to leave the hospital but I wasn't going to be in Vienna and see nothing of it. The Vienna I saw was not the Vienna of childhood stories. It had taken direct hits and had not yet been restored. The Opera House was a dangling wreck, half of it torn away by bombs. And the Schoenberg Castle was badly damaged as well. Vienna was sad. After a couple of hours I was more than ready to return to the hospital, seek the company of fellow refugees, and get ready to board the train for Munich.

After dark we were led to a train station, where again, cattle cars awaited us. By now, there wasn't one person of any age on whom the significance of climbing onto those cattle cars was lost. Despite our numbers and our eagerness, once we saw the cars we all boarded in silence. It was likely that we all had relatives who'd been taken to Auschwitz in these precise cars – in convoys of death. Traveling in them lowered our heightened spirits back to the level of reality.

We were on our way to Munich, one of the major centers of American occupation. Would we get papers to allow us to enter the United States? The train reached Munich in the middle of the night. We were driven to a school auditorium, again in a polite and civilized manner. In the school auditorium there were already a couple of hundred refugees, but they were all young people. They were sleeping on standard issue army cots with U.S. Army khaki blankets. I assumed that most of them had survived because they were young and fit and moving alone. They were probably all lone survivors of large Jewish families. We were directed to the back of the auditorium and Mechel and I were immediately shown to two empty cots.

There was only one small ceiling lamp so you couldn't see very much. Even in the dim light I saw something I abhorred. I saw rats leaping around on the floor, and jumping from cot to cot. Every few minutes someone screamed they had been bitten or touched by a rat. I did not want anything to do with rats. It was an old Yiddish folktale or what we call a *bubbe maiseh*, a grandmother's tale, that if a pregnant woman saw a mouse or rat during her term the baby would have a birthmark on its face. This nonsense was handed down in my own family as well. A cousin of mine had a small birthmark on his cheek and the family lore was that his mother had seen a mouse and clapped her face in fright, causing this mark on the child's face. I was an intelligent woman, married to a super-rational man, but I was tired, and I was pregnant, and I had been through way too much not to take every precaution. I spent the entire night sitting on a high table – where the rats could not reach me – with my eyes shut.

At daybreak, those of us who were awake asked the people in charge what was going to happen to us next. They explained to us calmly and, I felt, with extreme kindness that we were part of a very large group of survivors. (By May of 1945 literally millions of displaced people were roaming around continental Europe. Of that number, about 100,000 were Jews who had survived in a myriad of ways. Half of that number was "housed" in the DP camps in the Allied occupation zones of Germany and Austria.) We were not going to stay in the auditorium but would visit the Jewish committee that had been put in charge of the welfare of Jews. We were told that we would be given an apartment, probably one from which a German family had been removed or which had been occupied by a German family when its Jewish owners were taken away.

It was clear to me that the tables had been turned completely around. The world was upside down once again, but in a new way. Before the Germans came and took our homes and marched in with boots and guns; now we would displace defeated Germans. The Central Committee of the Liberated Jews in the U.S. Zone of Germany operated from 1945 until 1950. This Jewish agency took over the administrative duties of helping and providing for survivors. We didn't know anything about the Committee at that point and so we thought of it as a new Judenrat.

As the clock struck 7 a.m. Mechel and I made a fast retreat from the rat-infested auditorium and never looked back. Others were lining up for breakfast. I would have starved rather than eat there. We went to the Deutsches Museum where the Committee had its offices. It was ridiculous of us to believe that they would be open at that hour, but I had been so disgusted and distraught by the auditorium that Mechel was eager to get things rolling. He saw a taxi and sprinted to hail it. I tried to keep up with him, and was careless. I slipped on a hidden patch of ice on the dirt-covered road and fell. On my way down I heard a loud crack. Mechel ran back to me. My right ankle was broken.

German women appeared suddenly on the street we thought was deserted and called an ambulance. They waited with us until the ambulance came. It was my first experience with Germans who were not Nazis, or were no longer Nazis. I felt grateful but uneasy. The ambulance driver took our measure quickly and said he would need to take us to the American hospital.

He sped out of town. He was a skilled driver, so in virtually no time we had cleared the city proper and arrived at St. Ottilien, a former nun's cloister located in Landsberg and now serving as both a hospital and a DP Camp. I was embarrassed and felt foolish. Mechel tried to cheer me up but did not succeed.

"Lola, what shall I do with you? You survived the Nazis without a scratch and just hours after we are inside the American zone, you land in the hospital!"

He was trying to be funny and helpful but it wasn't a good tactic to use with me. I was crying. He became tender and told me it was only my ankle, but I was in terrible pain. More than anything else of course, I was concerned that the fall had harmed my baby. I was on a stretcher viewing the hospital from that perspective. What I could see indicated that the former nun's cloister was on beautiful grounds and in a large and stately building. Doctors were abundant, all in white smocks. The nuns were still in residence, acting as nurses and aides, and garbed in their traditional full religious habits. The others, refugees, were in shabbier clothes, some were bedraggled and others were clearly dying and were there for hospice care. I was sent straight to X-ray and then into surgery.

Poor Mechel! How upsetting it must have been for him waiting for me to come out of surgery. I awakened to see his face and just by looking into his eyes I knew all was well with the pregnancy. However, my leg was in a full cast and in traction. It had been a very bad break. By the looks of the contraption to which I was attached, I figured we would not be displacing a German family from their home anytime soon. Nonetheless, we had made it to Munich. "A bump in the road" is how we came to refer to it once I had recovered some of my good humor.

CHAPTER 24

Reunion

I had become an accidental celebrity. I was, it appeared, the first pregnant Jewish woman to be seen anywhere in the liberated zones. Although many of the survivors in Munich were women, most of them were unmarried or were now widows. The other survivors who saw me in the recovery room could not stop staring at me. It was not rudeness. It was disbelief coupled with pride that we were all beginning again. I was that symbol for many of them, particularly the ones who were in the worst condition.

Mechel had been placed in the men's quarters of St. Ottilien. As it was a hospital facility, Mechel really shouldn't have been there at all. However, a couple of nuns had told him to pretend he was unwell when I was having surgery. That was an easy act for Mechel; he was so skinny that his complaint to a doctor that his stomach bothered him made complete sense. It was a much easier performance than the one he had given as a lunatic in prison. The excitement about this obviously pregnant woman in their midst was so intense that he didn't have to pretend being sick after he'd received his bed assignment. Nobody there had any intention of separating us.

My recovery "ward" had a number of patients in it, and all of them with problems of one sort or another. Two beds away was a girl who had her appendix removed in an emergency procedure. She was an exotic-looking girl, handsome, with dark curly hair, vibrant expression, and intense eyes. I did not know Jewish women like this, and I assumed she might be a Yemenite

Jewess, but as I had never to my knowledge seen a Sephardic Jew, it was a wild guess on my part. I found out that she was an active member of the Hashomer Hatza'ir movement, a secular Zionist organization that had tried to resist the Nazis with physical force. After the Nazi defeat, she and a number of her friends and comrades were going to Palestine. She was despondent because her group was going on to sail from Marseilles, but she was not well enough to go with them. Although she seemed lively and robust, the doctors said she could not leave. Understandably, she was most unhappy.

In the evening a group of young men came to say good-bye to her. I did not want to intrude on their farewell because I saw it was an emotional meeting for all of them. They did not want to leave her behind in the hospital, but they could not wait for her release. One of them held a photograph of their group in his hands and presented it to her as a gift. However, a disagreement broke out among the young men, some of whom did not want to part with the picture, probably the only one they had. I could not see their faces to judge their ages because my traction apparatus blocked my view. My roommate finally won the argument, saying that without the photograph she had nothing, but they had each other. She said that she had to have it to keep from forgetting them and to encourage her to come to Palestine and find them. The boys backed down at those remarks and left the photograph with her.

I had a partial view of only one of the boys. He was seated next to her with his back to me. He was wearing a German soldier's coat, and his head was uncovered. He had such gorgeous curly hair that I became nostalgic. My two younger brothers had uncommonly abundant and glorious curls like this young man. I thought to myself that this was the way my life would be from this point forward. I would see a young man or a young woman and I would see in them the outline of my siblings who had been taken away from me.

A few hours later, I struck up a conversation with my roommate. We had different approaches to being Jewish, but I had great empathy for her and for her isolation. I asked her about the handsome young man that had sat the closest to her. She began to cry softly, and so I knew that he was a good friend and that she was feeling agony at the turn of events in her life. "His name is Benjamin," she said to me quietly.

I felt a renewed stab of loss. That was my youngest brother's full name. We called him Beinish, an affectionate diminutive for the name Benjamin. (Now we call him Ben.) My Benjamin had been shoveled into one of those cattle cars to Auschwitz along with the rest of my Munkach family. I wanted to engage her in conversation both because my sorrow would never end and because perhaps I could help her over what I hoped would be only a temporary disappointment.

"Would you show me the photograph?" I asked her. She was happy to share it with me. She handed it to me proudly. I stared at the faces of the young men in the photograph. Then, I burst out crying uncontrollably, pointing to one of them.

"Is this the one you call Benjamin?"

"Yes, why are you sobbing?"

"That is my brother. I thought he was dead. Bring him back here."

I had not seen Ben since Munkach when he was about twelve years old, but his jaw line was distinctive in our family. He had a sharply defined, square jaw. He had changed but it was impossible that it was anyone else but my brother.

The girl said she could not bring him back to the room. I couldn't believe my ears and asked her what she meant. I became incoherent in my frantic appeal to her to bring my brother to me.

"You don't understand. What we do..." She stumbled on her words. She began again. "Please, be quiet. I can't. It's secret. It's very secret."

I became hysterical and called for a nun. "I must have my husband come to me now. I have to talk to him." The nurse-nun asked no questions of me. She and others went to the men's quarters and Mechel rushed to my bedside.

I told him everything and showed him the photograph. Mechel begged the girl to understand that she could not morally do this to me. He was calm but he would not stop admonishing her. She resisted with the ferocity of a wild animal. Mechel took another approach. He asked her to at least tell him where they were. Again, Mechel's requests or demands were met with resistance and refusal to consider releasing a single detail concerning my brother's whereabouts. I continued to wail at the top of my lungs. Finally, she told Mechel they were living in a nearby town.

Mechel whispered to me, "Lola, this is one of the most committed movements in Zionism. Once you join their ranks, you do not leave."

I was unconvinced. They had let the girl leave, hadn't they, and in fact abandoned her in the hospital? I told Mechel that he had to find a way. He had to keep my only surviving sibling from going to Palestine. It was selfish of me to want to prevent my brother from pursuing his dream, but I couldn't bear another separation. I could not let him go. Mechel told me to calm down and said that he would work on a plan, but that I should not be overly optimistic. I resolved to myself that I would be more than overly optimistic. If I had not been in traction, pregnant or not, I suspect I would have gone off by myself to find my "little" brother.

The next morning Mechel came to my bedside with my cousin, Beinish Horowitz, who had been rounded up with my family, survived and ended up in St. Ottilien with the other survivors. The two had worked out a plan. My cousin was willing to seek out my brother. He explained to me that it was not an easy task. The young people were working toward a Jewish state and they had taken an oath of loyalty to each other and to the cause. Our approach had to be carefully orchestrated. My cousin had been in the camps with my brother and they had established a close bond.

My cousin found my beloved brother with his comrades, living in a Zionist kibbutz-like setting. My cousin decided not to take any chances on Ben being recalcitrant.

"Your sister Lola is alive and in the hospital at St. Ottilien and I am sorry to tell you that she is likely to die soon. Please, you must come to see her to say good-bye and then you can return to your comrades. When it gets dark, please slip away and come to the hospital."

Needless to say, my brother was in shock that I was alive and in greater shock that I was dying. He spoke to his leader about the situation with me. Out of more than 200 young people, all orphans from the war, Ben had been chosen to be a leader. Only ten others had been selected. The leader of the group said to him, "You will see your sister in Palestine. She can meet you there. Do you know how many people would give up anything to be in your position?"

The next morning, after a night of agony, but without any question about the personal sacrifice he would make, he reported to his commanding leader. The leader ripped off the pin from Ben's shirt, an emblem that designated his rank within the Zionist group. Ben gave up his dream of helping to create the State of Israel in order to see his only surviving family member before she died.

My cousin met him and brought him to me. The instant he entered my room, he realized that he had been right next to me the day before and did not recognize me. We did not mention the trick my cousin had played on him. It was unnecessary. We were overcome with our love for one another. He was confronted not with the threat of the death of another family member, but with the promise of life in my pregnancy. We told each other our stories of survival.

With Ben on his convoy to Auschwitz were Hershel bacsi, his son Isaac, my aunt, and many others from Munkach. Many Hungarians were still in denial when they were loaded onto the convoys and took with them as much luxury goods and expensive food delicacies as they could carry. They tried to convince themselves they were only being resettled by the Nazis. My family and those in our circle knew the truth and they arrived with nothing. They had heard that anything you brought was left on the train platform at Auschwitz. However, they put diamonds in the soles of their shoes. This was Hershel's idea.

They were also forewarned of the first processing in Auschwitz. Nazi doctors would examine the captive Jews quickly and make their decisions. Some would live and work for a time, and some would die immediately. Still others would be selected for the horrors of medical experimentation, such as those conducted by the infamous Joseph Mengele.

When they got off the train, Ben told us, a German officer made a tempting offer, "You have had a grueling trip. Do you wish to walk or to ride to the camp?" Those who opted to ride were motioned to the line at the right. Ben had the intelligence and quick thinking to say in his good German, "I want to work. I am strong." He stood on tiptoe to look taller and older than he was. He was put in the line to the left.

At the camp, those in the left line took real showers, not the false ones that led people directly into the gas chambers. Ben pretended he did not hear the order to remove his shoes. Somehow, they overlooked his shoes. He was sent to a rock quarry as a slave laborer. Uncle Hershel was too old to endure that sort of work, but with a diamond from my brother's shoe, he was able to bribe someone to let him be a cook in the kitchen. This was a prized place in Auschwitz because it meant access to basic nourishment.

Ben survived the stone quarries but was shipped off to another labor camp. Now, he was not just hauling rocks but had to dynamite them into smaller pieces and load the broken rocks onto wagons. Then the prisoners hauled these heavy wagons up a hill to a construction site. Very few survived this labor. He endured it for the better part of one year. In the spring of 1945, when the Soviets had closed in and liberation had begun, the Nazis rounded up more than 2,000 prisoners in Ben's group and delivered them in convoys to Buchenwald, Bergen-Belsen, and even deeper inside Germany.

During this trip, Ben was injured. Someone cut his throat. He was lucky that he did not bleed to death. The car had been packed with starving and suffering people. After hours without air, water, or food, the guards threw in a few chunks of stale bread. Pandemonium broke out. It was a frenzied scene of survival and insanity. My brother caught a piece of bread but before he could share it with our uncle and our cousin, someone put the knife to his throat. My brother refused to give up the bread. He tore the bread into tiny pieces, no bigger than a walnut. He knew what would happen if they gorged themselves.

My uncle was desperate for more, but Ben held firm to his rule. They would each eat only a tiny piece a day. All around them were those who had eaten their fill and dropped dead. Their digestive systems exploded, unable to handle food in such quantity. Ben shuddered when he told me that he saw some who insanely cut open the stomachs of the dead and took the bloody bread and ate it, only to die.

The train ride to nowhere continued. Without warning, the Allied forces intercepted the train. With the best of intentions and displaying heartfelt generosity and compassion, the Allied soldiers opened tins of meat for the survivors to eat. Hundreds died from gorging themselves. Some of the tins were tainted and our cousin Isaac died from complications of dysentery. Ben became deathly ill from the meat as well and was barely conscious. He only remembered that a priest gathered him up in his arms and brought him to the very hospital of our reunion. It was in St. Ottilien that he saw young people outside in the courtyard singing, and they were all about his age and starting a Zionist group. He joined them when he recovered and they became a family for him.

Then my brother told us the most gruesome fact of all. Of the 2,000 people that had been aboard the train, only about twenty survived. As this small group regained their strength and their mental capacities, they formed small impromptu communes, or kibbutzim, and planned to make a collective escape to Palestine. This is how Ben came to be in the Hashomer Hatza'ir movement. He thought it was optimistic, brave, profoundly Jewish, and daring. For them as ardent Zionists, Eretz Yisrael was the ultimate destination. They vowed they would somehow reach Palestine and work and fight for the Jewish state. As it turned out, because of my brother's love for me, he would not be fighting for the State of Israel or be a part of its beginnings. He would go to Israel but only after statehood had been achieved.

The evening that he had visited the girl in my room in the hospital, he had not noticed me. If my name had been posted on the end of the bed, he might have looked at it, but we cannot know. In any event, because I had been in emergency surgery, they had not yet posted my name. The reunion was one of an indescribable sweetness that embraced us both in the love we had shared as children together. He was a young man now, not a boy, and he was very handsome!

Ben waited for a time before he told me the exact details of Goldie's fate. During the round-up and deportation in Munkach, Goldie somehow got it into her mind to resist. Instead of following orders, she ran away, and was caught almost immediately. She was beaten to a pulp, Ben reported, almost beyond recognition. The rest of the family were waiting to leave on the trains when some men came running carrying a stretcher. On it was my sister, barely alive, and bloodied. They dropped her in front of them. Ben had not imagined she could survive the train ride, but she did. She was put into forced labor as ill and weak as she was. She died in the arms of our aunt, the very woman who might have been her mother-in-law, had she not protested against Goldie's fragility. Tuli, too young for work, had been sent immediately to the gas chambers. I learned from my brother the precise details of the death of Moishe, who had survived the camps and the Death March. When his convoy came under aerial attack, instead of running for shelter he ran into the street, begging the Allies to bomb more of Germany. Either an American or a Soviet bomb had killed him.

Although I had assumed most of these things, and other refugees we had met during our journey had told me some facts, nothing was like the utter agony of hearing the details from my own brother.

We are Jews, however, and for us life must be for the living; we are commanded to live. I mourned but I also took a look around me. I saw the beauty of our surroundings, we had plenty of food to eat, and my husband came to see me every day. I looked to the past with grief and longing, but

I looked forward with hope and joy, and as my tummy expanded and expanded, so did my happiness.

I was moved into a ward with about forty beds, no longer confined to traction, and I started to move around gingerly. People admired my pregnancy and I was a little embarrassed, but I understood that I was a symbol of the future.

We found out that Uncle Yoshe had left Krakow and had come to Munich. Mechel got word to them to come to the hospital and say they were not well. Once inside it would be easier to arrange housing for them. They did that and we were able to help them get into a confiscated German apartment.

There was an active committee of patients distributing some luxuries now available: nylon stockings, clothing of all sorts, chocolate, Ovaltine, and cigarettes. The United Nations Relief and Rehabilitation Administration were distributing all these things. There was also food and medicine sent by Agudath Israel in America. Mechel was happy to have cigarettes again. He had been denied this pleasure and craved the good American brands. Cigarettes became a currency with which to barter. People used them to accumulate cash and necessities and to head for Palestine. Many Germans were nicotine addicts and were willing to barter almost anything to get them.

In the middle of January in 1946, the doctors at St Ottilien said that we needed to go the hospital in Munich to check on the baby's delivery date. It was about an hour away by taxi. The German doctor told me that I was about a week from the birth of my child. He said I should prepare to stay in the hospital for about a week after the baby was born. When we returned to our rooms at St. Ottilien, I needed to get things ready for Mechel and myself before Shabbos, which meant doing some laundry and using the ironing room at the hospital. All our family members gathered together for Kiddush and the meal. Then, as always, Mechel and I said goodnight to each other and he went to the men's quarters. The staff at St. Ottilien had not made arrangements for us to stay together, as we were the only married couple. They really did not know what to do with us, but we were content unto ourselves and were eagerly awaiting the next week and the birth of our child.

CHAPTER 25
Birth and Rebirth

As I started to fall asleep I was aware that this possibly would be the last Shabbos of my life as a woman without a child. Perhaps by the following Shabbos, certainly no longer than two more, I would be a mother. Mechel would be a father. We would be a family. It was a sentiment I had not contemplated before: I would become someone's mother. Of course we had no idea whether we would have a boy or a girl, nor did we care; we prayed only that our child would be healthy. The 10 p.m. curfew was about to begin and I had a sudden urge to go to the bathroom. The lights were just being turned out as I returned to my bed. As I started to get into bed, I had to rush again to the bathroom. Then, a third time, and I didn't make it quite in time. I started to cry. I was ill. The last thing we needed was for me to be ill before childbirth.

I had pains and I couldn't control myself. I didn't understand that I was beginning to go into labor. Without my mother or another female relative to tell me, I was completely bewildered and terrified. A woman told me that I was going to have the baby and pulled the alarm. Immediately, Mechel came to me and also my Uncle Yoshe and my brother Ben. Although it was Shabbos the three of them found a taxi in no time, and we headed for the hospital in Munich. On the way, the real pains of labor began. It was about midnight when we arrived at the hospital and I was in bad shape. Mechel asked for the physician on duty and explained our predicament.

A stern and nasty German doctor came into the foyer of the hospital. It was not the rather pleasant doctor we had seen earlier in the week. "What do you want? How dare you wake me up; what is the matter with you? You are not about to give birth. I know why you came. You just want chocolate and milk. Go away."

There was no point in arguing with him and I told Mechel I wanted to leave. He was beside himself because he couldn't help me and he couldn't confront this hateful doctor. I wondered if he really was a doctor. He had made no attempt to examine me, and although I was dressed nicely, I was quite obviously very pregnant. I went outside and found a bench. I lay down on it, too tired and too embarrassed to make a fuss in front of my own family. I honestly didn't know what was happening to me.

The labor pains came back, and I made faces but didn't cry out. By now, the men were timing them and they were in twenty-minute cycles. Mechel ran to the hospital door again and again, banging on it and begging to be admitted. He was refused. *Six hours* passed and I almost fainted several times. With miraculous timing, a woman passed by just then and said, "Wait a minute. You need help. You are about to deliver. I am a midwife." She picked me up in her arms like a baby and screamed until the door was opened. She carried me into the operating room and the doctor confronted her.

"You may not admit anyone to this hospital without my permission. She will not have that baby for days."

The midwife had a strong Lithuanian Jewish accent. I felt I was in competent and loving hands.

"Really? Well, I'll tell you what, Doctor, I am going to bet you a carton of cigarettes that you are wrong. And she is going to have this baby in less than five minutes."

The doctor accepted her challenge. It was a bizarre scene. However, I knew I was about to have a baby, primarily because the midwife would not have made such an extravagant bet if I were not about to "deliver" for her. Before she turned around from washing her hands, my baby began to come into the world.

It was Shabbos morning, January 19, 1946. A petite woman, I had given birth to a ten-pound baby boy! I was exhausted to say the least. The "doctor" was totally incompetent. Despite the midwife's able intervention

I ended up with a severe infection and ran a high fever. I was too ill to attend my own son's bris. It took place in the home of a Jewish family in Landsberg. We named our baby boy Lazer Zvi (Hershel) Lieber. Lazer had been my father's name and Hershel, the name of my father-in-law. Almost immediately, I told Mechel that I would prefer that we call our son by his second name of Hershel because hearing the name of my father brought too much pain. Mechel understood and was also honored that his son would be known as Hershel. I ended up staying in that hospital for an entire month, struggling with the infection and its aftermath. I grew weak, but the Germans fed me on a diet of beer!

I was released in time for the celebration of my baby's *pidyon haben*. Ordinarily, this is not such a big occasion, as the bris is the ritual event with meaning for most Jews. At a pidyon the guests look on as the father and the *kohen* (descendent of the priestly tribe) perform the *mitzvah* (commandment). But our son's pidyon was a different event. Not only was Hershel, whom we called Heshi, the first Jewish child born in the area after the war, but we were living in a time when most Jews who survived had thought they were the last Jews on earth. Heshi became everybody's baby. At St. Ottilien an enormous number of people came to his pidyon, including representatives from Agudath Israel and all the other DPs in the area. And the Jewish American soldiers who attended all had tears in their eyes.

We now understood what America had contributed to the war effort and that many American soldiers, Jewish and Christian, would never return home. We knew that their sacrifices were enormous. On the other hand, the American soldiers who liberated the camps had seen with their own eyes what had been done to us. So for the Jewish American soldiers, Heshi was their baby too. He stood for those who had not survived and generations that would never be born – our infant boy represented the future. In those moments at Heshi's pidyon haben, when I looked at the Jewish American soldiers and nurses, I grasped the larger vision that American Jews were part of our larger community. My delivery of this baby boy was a message – we would not disappear after all.

As the ceremony started, the most beautiful thing happened. American women, Jewish and Christian, attached to the U.S. Army or other organizations, took off their necklaces and their rings and adorned my baby with these precious ornaments. Music and traditional Jewish circle dancing erupted. Someone put together a guest book and everyone signed it. Heshi

241

was wearing one of the beautiful handmade shirts my aunt had given us, and of course he was lying on the special ceremonial pillow she had ordered before we left Budapest. The birth of my child provided an opportunity for all the Jews there to experience the rebirth of our entire people.

This particular ceremony under those particular conditions at that particular time was extraordinarily moving. The words pidyon haben mean literally "the redemption of the firstborn." In Jewish tradition a firstborn male child belongs to God and so must be "redeemed" by his parents with a symbolic payment. The jewelry placed on the child by all the women present was especially meaningful because it was not only about our family and our first child. We were now a community of hope and of life. And this is the traditional blessing said over Heshi:

> May Hashem bless you and guard you.
> May Hashem illuminate his countenance upon you and endow you
>   with grace.
> May Hashem lift his countenance to you and establish for you peace.

I am certain that everyone there with us at that moment returned home and told his or her own family the story of this day. People we will never see again but whose lives would forever touch ours, reached inside themselves and shared with us the abundant joy of that day. We stood in their midst, Mechel Lieber and Lola Lieber, survivors of the Shoah, with our tiny surviving family surrounding us, welcoming little Hershel Lieber into the Jewish community.

Mechel's words were being carried out; it was truly the beginning of *a world after this*. Mechel's father, Hershel, had been the first to perish in our immediate family. Baby Hershel was a living sign that we would go forward, into the light of many new worlds – and on unto future generations.

* * *

EPILOGUE

Following the pidyon haben, the Liebers sought entry into the United States. They were granted visas under the Czechoslovakian quota and on February 11, 1947, they boarded the S.S. *Ernie Pyle*. They sailed from Bremerhaven and arrived in New York Harbor on February 18, 1947.

Besides Hershel, Mechel and Lola had two more children; Yossi born in 1948 and Mati in 1957. Mechel established himself successfully in the hosiery business from 1947 to 1957. Sadly, he was diagnosed with cancer in 1958. He fought the disease valiantly for more than seven years. He died in 1966 at the age of fifty-one. At the time of his death Lola and Mechel had been married twenty-five years.

Lola subsequently remarried twice and was widowed each time.

Lola continued painting in the United States and is a successful artist. Her work has been exhibited in many art galleries throughout the United States. Her paintings are in a number of private collections and were shown in Yad Vashem in Jerusalem. She still maintains a gallery in the heart of Chassidic Boro Park in Brooklyn, New York. Lola is often commissioned to paint portraits and scenes of Jewish life as well as landscapes and still-lifes.

Well into her 80s today, Lola keeps a remarkably busy schedule between her children and grandchildren, her charitable activities, her friends, and her life as an artist.

Lola often proudly states that the fact that she is the mother of three, grandmother of twelve, including three Mechels, and the great-grandmother of thirty-five and still counting, is her triumph and her final victory over Hitler and his Reich.

Mechel's grandparents, Yechiel Mechel & Miriam Lieber.

Mechel, his mother, two sisters, and cousins vacationing
in Krynica, Poland, in the mid-1930s.

Lola's grandfather, Yosef Segel - Munkach.

Lola's grandfather, Yokel Leser - Krakow.
Oil painting by Lola Lieber, 1963.

Lola's great-grandmother, Chaya Leser, with aunts in Krakow, 1937.

Lola's father, Lazar Leser, during the war.

Lola's mother, Shaindel Leser, during the war in Niepolomice.

Lola, during the war in Budapest, 1943.

Lola's sister, Goldy Leser, 1938.

Lola's brother, Moshe Leser, during the war.

Lola's brother, Ben Leser, after liberation.

Lola's brother, Tuli Leser - Munkach, 1937.

Mechel's father, Hershel Lieber - Krakow.

Mechel's mother, Matel Lieber - Krakow.

Mechel in Krynica.

(All photos from the mid-1930s.)

Mechel's brother, Joel Lieber, in Paris.

Beyla

Sara

Leah

Manya or Yentel

(Four of Mechel's six sisters.)

Rosie Berger and daughter Micheline - Poland, 1941.

Lola's aunt, Hendy Eneman (center), with her daughters, (left to right)
Mimi, Koti, Miri, and Mara - Tel Aviv, 1960s.

Wedding photograph of Mechel and Lola - Niepolomice, 1941.

Family at the wedding of Mechel and Lola - Niepolomice, 1941.
Sitting below Mechel and Lola are their mothers with Ben and Tuli.

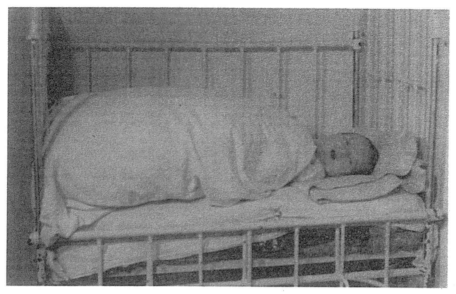

Baby Hershel Lieber, born in January 1946 - Munich, Germany.

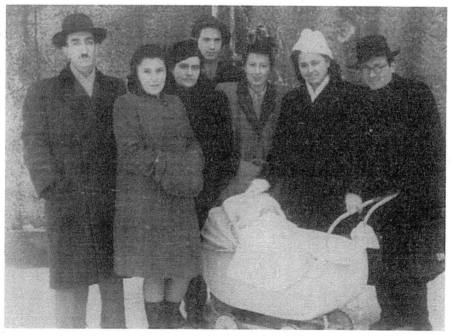

Baby Hershel Lieber, surrounded by members of the family - Munich.
Pictured on the left is Mechel; Lola is in the center with brother Ben behind her.

The S.S. Ernie Pyle, the battle-
ship that brought the Lieber family to America in February 1947.

News-clipping from the World Tele-
graph, of the arrival of Hershel
(Lazar) Lieber to New York.

Postcard written by Mechel notifying of the family's arrival in New York, to Ben in Munich.

Lola and Mechel early 1950s.

Hershel - 1954

Yossi — 1954

Mati - 1965

Lola, Mechel, and Hershel early 1950s.

Lola - 1960

Mechel - 1965

Lieber family after the birth of Mati - 1958.

Rabbi Shloime Halberstam, the Bobover Rebbe. Oil painting by Lola Lieber, 1956.

Bobover Rebbe early 1960s.

FAMILY CHARTS

FAMILY CHARTS

Names in bold are mentioned in the book.

MECHEL'S FAMILY	KILLED IN	SURVIVED	OTHER DETAILS
Hershel Lieber, *father*	Niepolomice		Shot in the forest.
Matel (Berger) Lieber, *mother*	Bochnia		
Mania, *sister*	Unknown		
Yentel, *sister*	Unknown		
Itche, *Yentel's son*	Bochnia		
Baila (Berta), *sister*	Bochnia		
Marilka, *Baila's daughter*	Bochnia		
Chana, *sister*	Unknown		
Sura-Sala Langer, *sister*	Bochnia		
Leah-Lola, *sister*	Bochnia		
Joel Lieber, *brother*		In Italy	After the War moved to Munich, married & died there.
Moshe Lieber, *cousin*		In America	Came to America before the War.

	KILLED IN	SURVIVED	OTHER DETAILS
Rabbi Shloime Halberstam, the Bobover Rebbe		On the run in Hungary & Romania	After the War settled in NY. Opened a yeshiva & rebuilt Bobov Chassidus.

LOLA'S FAMILY	KILLED IN	SURVIVED	OTHER DETAILS
Yosef Segel, *grandfather*	Auschwitz		
Roshe Segel, *grandmother*	Auschwitz		
Lazar Leser, *father*	Bochnia		
Shaindel Segel (Leser), *mother*	Bochnia		
Moshe Leser, *brother*	Death March		Killed by an Allied bomb. Wife Frieda remarried in America.
Goldie Leser, *sister*	Auschwitz		Died within weeks of arrival to Auschwitz.

LOLA'S FAMILY	KILLED IN	SURVIVED	OTHER DETAILS
Benish (Ben) Leser, *brother*		Many camps	Came to America, married Jean in Los Angeles; two daughters Sherry & Gail.
Naftuli (Tuli) Leser, *brother*	Auschwitz		
Beri Segel, *uncle*	Unknown		
Hershel Segel, *uncle*	Auschwitz		Sons: Sruli & wife Esther (Munich); Moshe & wife Seri (Israel).
Issac Segel, *cousin*	Auschwitz		
Shloma Segel, *uncle*	Unknown		
Lezer Segel, *uncle*		Many camps	Started new family in Israel.
Yankel (Jeno) Segel, *uncle*	Terezin		Died after liberation. Daughter Eva (in NY), son Tibi (in Israel).
Baruch (Bela) Segel, *uncle*		Many camps	Started new family in Israel, then moved to America.

LOLA'S FAMILY	KILLED IN	SURVIVED	OTHER DETAILS
Naftali (Nandor) Eneman, *uncle*		In Budapest	With wife Hendi & daughters, Mara, Mimi, Koti, & Alice, went to Israel.
Hendi (Segel) Eneman, *aunt*		In Budapest	With husband Naftali & daughters, Mara, Mimi, Koti, & Alice, went to Israel.
Yokel Leser, *grandfather*	Unknown		
Rivka Leser, *grandmother*	Unknown		
Shaye Asher Leser, *uncle*	Unknown		
Raizel (Leser) Berger, *aunt*	Krakow		Killed in Pogrom in Krakow after the war. (Wife of Yoshe Berger.)
Yosef (Yoshe) Berger, *uncle*		On the run	Came to America, remarried, & moved to Israel.
Moshe Berger, *cousin*	Krakow		Shot to death on street at beginning of war.

LOLA'S FAMILY	KILLED IN	SURVIVED	OTHER DETAILS
Rosie Berger, *cousin*		On the run	Wife of Moshe Berger. Came to America & lived in California.
Micheline Berger, *cousin*		On the run	Rosie & Moshe Berger's daughter. Came to America & lives in California.
Blanka Bruner-Fixler, *niece*			Rosie Berger's niece. Came to America & lives in New York.
Toba (Berger) Pflanzer, *cousin*			Came to America with surviving daughter Helen Muller.
Kraindel (Leser) Blumenfrucht, *aunt*	Unknown		
Menachem M. Leser, *uncle*	Unknown		
Yitzchok Leser, *uncle*		In Belgium	Wife & two daughters survived & lived in Antwerp, Belgium.

LOLA'S FAMILY	KILLED IN	SURVIVED	OTHER DETAILS
Perel (Leser) Horowiz, *aunt*	Auschwitz		Children Beinish Horowitz, Shmiel Horowitz, & Rechel Leser all survived.
Ester Leah (Leser) Miller, *aunt*	Unknown		
Chaim Baruch Leser, *uncle*	Unknown		
Yisroel Meilech Leser, *uncle*	Unknown		
Dovid Noson Leser, *uncle*		In America	Went to New York long before war; four children.
Chaskel Shrage Leser, *uncle*		In Siberia	Came to America with children: Beinish Leser, Shyfra Scharf, & Helen Rubin.

GLOSSARY OF
FOREIGN WORDS AND PHRASES

Aktion [*German*]: Nazi killing spree

Babbiko [*Hungarian*]: grandmother, affectionate diminutive

Bacsi [*Hungarian*]: uncle

Bashert(e) [*Yiddish*]: fated or Heavenly intended (pl.)

Beis medrash [*Hebrew*]: study hall

Belfer [*Yiddish*]: apprentice to a school teacher

Bilkelech [*Yiddish*]: bread rolls

Borei minei besomim [*Hebrew*]: blessing on smelling spices during Havdalah (see below)

Bris [*Hebrew*]: circumcision

Bubbe [*Yiddish*]: grandmother

Bubbe maiseh [*Yiddish*]: nonsense (lit., grandmother's tale)

Challah [*Hebrew*]: twisted Shabbos bread loaf

Chassan [*Hebrew*]: bridegroom (also son-in-law)

Chassid(im) [*Hebrew*]: follower(s) of a Chassidic Rabbi

Chazzan [*Hebrew*]: cantor

Cholov Yisroel [*Yiddish*]: from the Hebrew chalav Yisrael (milk produced under kosher supervision)

Chuppah [*Hebrew*]: canopy traditionally used in Jewish weddings, or the wedding itself

Daven, Davening [*Yiddish*]: pray, praying

Der Eibeshter [*Yiddish*]: the Almighty

Einsatzgruppen [*German*]: Nazi extermination squads

Eretz Yisroel [*Hebrew*]: the Land of Israel

Frumkeit [*Yiddish*]: religious observance

Gabbai [*Hebrew*]: president of a congregation, or Chassidic Rebbe's attendant

Hashem [*Hebrew*]: the Name, refers to God

Hashgachah pratis [*Hebrew*]: Divine providence – the belief that all actions and situations are directed by Hashem

Havdalah [*Hebrew*]: ceremony marking the end of Shabbos – includes the blessings over wine, spices, & fire.

Hora [*Hebrew*]: traditional Jewish circle dance

Ir Va'em beYisroel [*Hebrew*]: a Jewish metropolis/a city significant in Jewish history (lit. a city and a mother in Israel)

Judenrat [*German*]: German-appointed Jewish council to govern Jews

Kaddish [*Hebrew*]: prayer said in praise of God after the death of a close family member

Kapo [*German*]: German-appointed Jewish policeman

Kasher [*Yiddish*]: to make kosher

Kashrus [*Hebrew*]: laws of keeping kosher

Kehillah [*Hebrew*]: congregation or community

Kennkart(e) [*German*]: work pass(es)

Kiddush [*Hebrew*]: blessing said over wine; light repast after praying

Kiddush Hashem [*Hebrew*]: sanctification of God's Name

Kishele [Yiddish]: pillow

Kohen [*Hebrew*]: Priest; descendent of the priestly tribe

Kosher [*Hebrew*]: ritually fit to eat

L' chaim [*Hebrew*]: "To life" – a drinking toast; also an engagement celebration

Maariv [*Hebrew*]: evening prayer service

Mammiko [*Hungarian*]: mother, affectionate diminutive

Matzah/Matzos [*Hebrew*]: unleavened bread eaten during Pesach; singular/plural

Megillah [*Hebrew*]: scroll; Megillas Esther is the Scroll of Esther, story of Purim

Minyan(im) [*Hebrew*]: quorum(s) of ten Jewish men

Mitzvah [*Hebrew*]: biblical or rabbinical commandment

Moiser [*Yiddish*]: informer (based on Hebrew word moser)

Neini [*Hungarian*]: aunt

Noont [*Hungarian*]: a sweet made of honey and nuts, also called Taygelach

Ordungsdienst [*German*]: Jewish police force

Oseh Shalom [*Hebrew*]: the One Who makes peace

Pesach [*Hebrew*]: Passover holiday

Peyos [*Hebrew/Yiddish*]: sidelocks

Pidyon Haben [*Hebrew*]: redemption of the [firstborn] son

Purim [*Hebrew*]: holiday commemorating saving of the Jewish people by Queen Esther

Politischegefangene [*German*]: politial prisoner

Ribboino shel Oilam [*Yiddish/Hebrew*]: Master of the World

Schadenfreude [*German*]: pleasure at another person's suffering

Sedra [*Hebrew*]: weekly Torah reading

Sefer/Sefarim [*Hebrew*]: book/books, term used for books on sacred topics

Seudah [*Hebrew*]: festive or holiday meal

Seudah Shelishis [*Hebrew*]: third Sabbath meal (shalosh-seudos in Yiddish)

Shabbos [*Yiddish/Hebrew*]: Jewish Sabbath, seventh day (Shabbat)

Shechinah [*Hebrew*]: Divine presence

Shema [*Hebrew*]: essential Jewish Prayer beginning, "Hear O Israel, Hashem is our God, Hashem is One"

Shema Yisroel [*Hebrew*]: first two words of the aforementioned prayer

Sheva Brachos [*Hebrew*]: festive meals celebrated for seven days following a Jewish wedding

Shidduch [*Hebrew*]: a match for the purpose of marriage

Shivah [*Hebrew*]: seven-day period of mourning following the death of parents, siblings, children, or spouse

Shoah [*Hebrew*]: exclusive reference here to the Holocaust in Europe during WWII

Shochet [*Hebrew*]: ritual slaughterer

Shul [*Yiddish*]: synagogue

Sukkah [*Hebrew*]: booth used as a temporary home for eating & sleeping during the Holiday of Sukkos (Feast of Tabernacles)

Taanis Esther [*Hebrew*]: Fast of Esther preceding holiday of Purim

Tallis [*Hebrew*]: prayer shawl

Talmud Torah [*Hebrew*]: Jewish religious school, usually for boys

Tanach [*Hebrew*]: Five Books of Moses, Book of Prophets, and the Writings

Tattiko [*Hungarian*]: father, affectionate diminutive

Tefillin [*Hebrew*]: phylacteries

Tikkun Olam [*Hebrew*]: Man's obligation to make the world a better place to live in

Tishah B'Av [*Hebrew*]: Ninth of Av, fast commemorating the destruction of the First & Second Temples

Torah [*Hebrew*]: Hebrew Bible and guide to the Jewish way of life

Treyf [*Yiddish*]: non-kosher

Tzedakah [*Hebrew*]: charity

Yeshiva [*Hebrew*]: Jewish religious school

Yiddishkeit [*Yiddish*]: Judaism

Zeide [*Yiddish*]: grandfather

ABOUT THE AUTHOR

L ola Leser was a privileged sixteen-year-old in 1939 when Germany invaded Poland. The horrors of the Holocaust overtook her almost immediately when she moved to Krakow, Poland, after living for years with her maternal grandparents in Munkach, at that time in Czechoslovakia. It was there, in her grandparents' "enchanted garden," that she discovered her artistic talents.

Before she had a chance to fully mature, Mechel Lieber swept her up into a marriage that was to turn into a loving partnership. That union saw them through years of hiding, of fleeing from shelter to shelter and from city to city, often escaping capture by a hairsbreadth. During those horrid war years, which included weeks of starvation and periods of imprisonment, they lost almost all of their loved ones and witnessed firsthand the unbelievable bestiality and depravities of the Nazis.

Through six harrowing years Lola clung both to her husband and to her staunch faith in the One Above, Who granted them both many miracles. It is that faith and her traditional upbringing that propelled Lola to uphold her Jewish values and rituals under the most adverse conditions. Lola was ever conscious that she was a link in the eternal chain of Jewish survival and continuity against all odds.

On January 19, 1946, now liberated, Lola gave birth to her first child in Munich, and the following year she immigrated to the United States. Her beloved Mechel died of cancer in 1966, leaving her with three children.

Today in her eighties, Lola still paints and is a successful artist. Her work has been exhibited in many art galleries throughout the United States.

Her paintings are in a number of private collections and were shown in Yad Vashem in Jerusalem. She still maintains a gallery in the heart of Chassidic Boro Park in Brooklyn, New York. Lola is often commissioned to paint portraits and scenes of Jewish life as well as landscapes and still-lifes.

Though Lola still keeps busy with social and charitable activities, her family truly comes first. Lola often proudly states that she is the mother of three, grandmother of twelve, and the great-grandmother of thirty-five and still counting. This is her triumph and her final victory over Hitler and his Reich.

Photograph of Lola Lieber with children, grandchildren, and great-grandchildren at her 80th birthday in 2003.

Lola Lieber — Watering the Flowers — 1980

Lola Lieber — Village Path — 1990

Lola Lieber — View from the Terrace in Capri — 1983

Lola Lieber — Tea Party — 1989

Lola Lieber — Woodstock Cottage — 1974

274

Lola Lieber — Pagoda on the River — 1995

Lola Lieber — Manhattan View — 1993

Lola Lieber — The Holy City — 1997

Lola Lieber — Dancing Chassidim — 1986

276

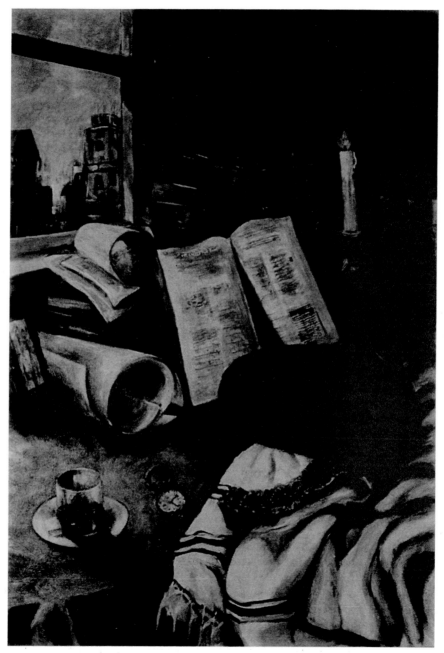

Lola Lieber – Grandfather's Study – 1993

Lola Lieber – Bochnia: On the Way to the Cemetery – 1950

Lola Lieber – Bochnia: Burying the Dead – 1950